NEIL T. ANDERSON
& RICH MILLER

HARVEST HOUSE PUBLISHERS
Eugene, Oregon 97402

Cover design by Terry Dugan Design, Minneapolis, Minnesota.

FREEDOM FROM FEAR

Published by Harvest House Publishers
Eugene, Oregon 97402

Library of Congress Cataloging-in-Publication Data
Anderson, Neil T., 1942-
Freedom from fear / Neil T. Anderson and Rich Miller.
p. cm.
ISBN 0-7369-0072-1
1. Fear—Religious aspects—Christianity. 2. Peace of mind—Religious aspects—Christianity. I. Miller, Rich, 1954- . II. Title.
BV4908.5.A53 1999
241'.3—dc21
99-22506
CIP

Printed in the United States of America.

99 00 01 02 03 04 05 / BC / 10 9 8 7 6 5 4 3

"Life is the pursuit,
not the capture."

—Scott Anderson, *Distant Fires*

We dedicate this book to the loving memory of Scott Anderson. Scott overcame every fear and obstacle in becoming the person God created him to be. Scott, an Air National Guard F-16 pilot, husband, and father, was born to fly. He took off March 23, 1999 and landed safely on the other side in the arms of Jesus.

Acknowledgments

No book is ever written in a vacuum. We are indebted to our parents, former teachers, friends, and fellow workers. They have all contributed to who we are and the contents of this book. We want to thank many who have prayed specifically for this project.

We also want to thank Harvest House for trusting us with the message of this book and for the fine work of editing, designing, and marketing. You have always been a delight to work with.

Thank you to all our brothers and sisters in Christ who courageously told us their stories, some of which are in this book, but all of which touched are hearts.

We want to especially thank our wives, Joanne and Shirley, for their encouragement and contribution. We know you bear the burden of such a project as this. Thank you for putting up with us in such a loving way.

Finally we want to thank our heavenly Father for calling us His children, and Jesus Christ who set us free, and for the Holy Spirit who leads us into all truth. We are indeed blessed with every spiritual blessing in Christ Jesus our Lord.

Contents

Foreword

by Julianne S. Zuehlke, MS, RN, CS
and Terry E. Zuehlke, PhD, LP

But the LORD God called to the man, 'Where are you?' He answered, 'I heard you in the garden, and I was afraid because I was naked; so I hid.'" (Genesis 3:9,10 NIV)

In this familiar passage the Bible clearly identifies the first negative feeling that entered the human experience. God, in His omniscience, knew the many stressful feelings we would encounter once sin had entered the realm of our experience. In the Garden, fear was the original disturbing emotion resulting from Adam's sense of disobedience and rebellion. Anxiety, fear, and panic that originated at the fall have prevailed ever since. Almost everyone has, at one time, felt helpless in the face of these troubling feelings. Today we are living in the "Age of Anxiety."

None of us are beyond the reach of insecurity, self-doubt, and apprehension. In fact, anxiety is among the most prominent emotions treated by psychotropic medications. As Christian professional counselors (Julie is also the director of Care Ministries in a megachurch), the nature and extent of these crippling emotions have been quite apparent in the lives of our clients and church attendees. We know that fear and anxiety, although very common, can be extremely resistant to psychological and/or medical treatment. We frequently work with people caught in issues that seem overwhelming and chaotic to them. They become worried, frightened, and seized with panic. At the root of their issues is a strong sense of disconnection from God and from those in the body of Christ. This sense of isolation and alienation is painful, as is the sense of impatience over how to manage or control the feelings.

Freedom from Fear provides clear answers for those seeking information on how to understand and cope with the feelings of anxiety, fear, and panic. You'll discover how a prevalent lack of understanding of our identity in Christ and our inability to resolve personal and spiritual conflicts are manifest in these specific negative emotions.

It is refreshing to see how Neil Anderson and Rich Miller have focused the general principles of "Freedom in Christ" on the prominent and powerful problem of negative emotions. This book addresses the origin of mental strongholds, the nature of anxiety, mankind's basic fears, and the problem of panic attacks in a balanced, helpful manner. It then provides strong biblical direction for counselors and clients to use in overcoming anxiety disorders. The conclusion provides a powerful presentation of how an understanding of the fear of the Lord is vital for our Christian growth.

Freedom from Fear is valuable because it is biblically sound and practical. It allows us to move beyond the "head knowledge" of traditional counseling approaches and offers healing for the soul by providing perspective on our relationships with God through Jesus Christ. It illustrates how we are to revere Him and, in so doing, find in Him a sanctuary from all other fears. Adam didn't have to be afraid of God and try to hide from Him. He could have gone to God, confessed his sin, and experienced forgiveness and peace of mind. When he didn't, God came to Adam in the midst of his fear. God is the source of our freedom from fear, and He wants to minister His truth to you and me. Read this book and you will appreciate His invitation to bring our anxieties, fears, and panicky feelings to Him. He is our "Wonderful Counselor," the "Great Physician," and "Prince of Peace."

A Note from the Authors

In relating true stories and testimonies throughout the book, we have changed names to protect individual identity and privacy.

For ease of reading we have not distinguished ourselves from each other in authorship or experiences, preferring to use "I" and "we" as opposed to "I (Rich)" or "I (Neil)." The only exceptions are illustrations referring to family.

Introduction

Have you ever been so anxious about the uncertainties of tomorrow that you felt keyed up, fatigued, and irritable? You found it difficult to sleep, and you just couldn't relax because your mind was racing and your muscles were tense. Have you ever been paralyzed by fear to the extent that you couldn't carry out your heart's desire? You knew what was right and you wanted to do the right thing, but some unknown fear kept you from doing it. Have you ever had a sudden episode of acute apprehension or intense fear that came out of the blue? You had shortness of breath and felt like you were being smothered. Your heart pounded causing you to sweat profusely. You began to tremble with feelings of unreality as though you were going crazy. You might have felt chest pains and numbness or tingling in your hands and feet. These are the symptoms of anxiety, fear, and panic, which cripple a large percentage of our population. Perhaps you can relate to the following cry for help:

> *I'm thirty-six years old. For as long as I can remember I have been plagued with fears and anxieties. I was raised in an abusive family and lived under the threat of even worse treatment if I ever told. In the bondage of fear I decided to never tell anyone.*
>
> *I came home one evening and found everyone gone. I was gripped with fear and crawled under my bed. Why weren't they home? Did they think I told someone? What's going to happen when they come back? I could never enjoy the simple little things that accompany childhood.*
>
> *My anxieties and fears followed me wherever I went. I was too afraid to try out for anything where I could possibly fail, and I dreaded every exam. My stomach would tie up in knots from anxiety. I became a perfectionist who had to achieve—whatever the cost.*
>
> *This pattern of fear continued into my teenage years and young-adult life. I tried to accept Jesus twice, but I feared not being good enough. I feared the rejection and ridicule of others, so I tried to keep everyone happy. Even sleep offered no reprieve. The nightmares I suffered as a result of the abuse in my childhood continued into my adult years.*
>
> *I am a parent now, and I fear for my children. Am I an adequate mother? Will my children be hurt or abducted? I know this is robbing me of the life I want to live, but I don't know what to do. I feel like I'm living two lives. On the outside I appear to be a successful teacher, wife, mother, and a contributing member of society. But if people could see the condition of my soul, they would*

see only pain, anxiety, and fear. Can somebody help me? Can I help myself or is this what life is supposed to be?

Anxiety disorders have surpassed depression and alcoholism as the number-one mental-health problem in America. We are experiencing a "blues" epidemic in this age of anxiety, although few people will openly admit to their fears and anxieties. Most suffer through these experiences in lonely isolation. Family, friends, and coworkers are not aware of other people's private nightmares so they can't understand why anxious people don't just "get with it." Perhaps you can relate to one or more of the symptoms we've presented or you are trying to help someone who does.

Are such mental, physical, and emotional reactions to life wrong? Shouldn't we be concerned about things we care about and fear those things that threaten our lives? Wouldn't anybody panic if a lion walked into his room? I probably would! And, yes, a life totally devoid of fear and anxiety would be boring at best and debilitating to our own productivity and self-preservation at worst.

So when does legitimate concern become stifling anxiety, and when does a rational fear become an incapacitating phobia? What are the differences between anxiety, fear, and panic attacks? In order to live a healthy productive life, every child of God needs adequate answers to these critical questions. Let's start by defining terms.

Fear

Fear is the most basic instinct of every living creature. An animal without fear will probably become some predator's dinner. Fear is the natural response when our physical safety and psychological well-being are threatened. Rational fears are learned and vital for our survival. For instance, falling off a chair at an early age develops a healthy respect for heights.

Phobias are irrational fears that compel us to do irresponsible things or inhibit us from doing what we should. Phobias reveal developmental problems and can indicate a lack of faith in God.

Fear is different from anxiety and panic attacks because legitimate fears have an object. In fact, fears or phobias are categorized by their objects as follows:

acrophobia .... fear of high places
agoraphobia .... fear of marketplaces
claustrophobia .... fear of enclosed places
gephydophobia .... fear of crossing bridges
hematophobia........ fear of blood
monophobia .... fear of being alone
pathophobia .... fear of disease
toxophobia .... fear of being poisoned
xenophobia.......... fear of strangers
zoophobia .... fear of animals

In order for a fear object to be legitimate it must possess two attributes: It must be perceived as imminent (present) and potent (powerful). Those who struggle with claustrophobia don't sense any fear until they are actually confronted with the possibility of being in a confined place. Just the thought of such a possibility causes some to shudder. The womb is an enclosed place, so it is safe to assume that a newborn infant doesn't have claustrophobia. Somehow the fear of being confined was learned (as are most fears). Consequently, it can be unlearned.

Fear is based on perception. For instance, a United States customs official saw a colorful, small snake on the Arizona border. He fearlessly picked it up and deposited his trophy in a jar. Later he learned that it was a coral snake—which looks harmless but is one of the most venomous snakes in the western world. He became flushed with fear when so enlightened. Even though the fear object wasn't present, the memory of picking it up made him react as though it were. Most of us have been educated to believe that poisonous snakes are legitimate fear objects. As you read this sentence, you probably sense no fear of snakes because there are none present (potent, but not imminent). What if someone were to throw a rattlesnake into your room, and it landed at your feet (imminent and potent)? You would probably be terror-stricken. Now suppose a dead snake is thrown at your feet (imminent, but not potent). You wouldn't sense any fear—provided you were sure it was dead. The fear object is no longer legitimate when one of its attributes is removed.

The core of most phobias can be traced to the fear of death, man, or Satan. For example, the fear of dying is the likely root of claustrophobia. Scripture clearly teaches that we have no need to fear any of these phobia sources because in each case God has removed one of their attributes. For instance, the reality of physical death is always imminent, but the *power of death has been broken.* Paul teaches that the resurrection of Christ has rendered physical death no longer potent: "Death is swallowed up in victory. 'O death, where is your victory? O death, where is your sting?'" (1 Corinthians 15:54,55). Jesus said, "I am the resurrection and the life; he who believes in Me shall live even if he dies, and everyone who lives and believes in Me shall never die" (John 11:25,26). In other words, those who have been born again spiritually will continue to live spiritually even when they die physically. With such a belief, Paul—and every born-again believer—can say, "For to me, to live is Christ, and to die is gain" (Philippians 1:21). The person who is free from the fear of death is free to live today.

The phobias rooted in the fear of man include rejection, failure, abandonment, and even death. Jesus said, "Do not fear those who kill the body, but are unable to kill the soul; but rather fear

Him who is able to destroy both soul and body in hell" (Matthew 10:28). Peter said, "Do not fear their intimidation, and do not be troubled, but sanctify Christ as Lord in your hearts, always being ready to make a defense to everyone who asks you to give an account for the hope that is in you, yet with gentleness and reverence" (1 Peter 3:14,15). The number one reason Christians don't share their faith is the fear of "man" or, more specifically, the fear of rejection and failure.

Both the Matthew and 1 Peter verses teach that it is God whom we should fear. Two of God's attributes make Him the ultimate fear object in our lives: He is omnipresent (always present) and omnipotent (all powerful). To worship God is to ascribe to Him His divine attributes. We do this for our sake to keep fresh in our minds that our loving heavenly Father is always with us and more powerful than any enemy. The fear of God dispels all other fears because God rules supreme over every other fear object—including Satan. Even though "your adversary, the devil, prowls about like a roaring lion, seeking someone to devour" (1 Peter 5:8), he has been defeated (imminent, but not potent). Jesus came for the very purpose of destroying the works of the devil (1 John 3:8). "When He had disarmed the rulers and authorities, He made a public display of them, having triumphed over them through Him" (Colossians 2:15).

We have been conditioned by our culture to be fearful of people and of things that go bump in the night but not to fear God. The scary movies of our childhoods featured King Kong, Godzilla, and "the Blob," along with the typical parade of psychopathic killers, jealous lovers, criminals, and macho men. Then the cultural tide shifted to the occult and alien abductions. In *The Exorcist*, the poor priest was no match for the demonized girl. (What a tragic contradiction to Scripture!) Satan loves this because he wants to be feared and worshiped.

Persons and objects are worshiped when their perceived power and value are elevated above ourselves. Only God should have that prominence in our lives. We are to worship and fear God. Fear of any object or personality other than God is mutually exclusive to faith in God. The Bible says, "The fear of the LORD is the beginning of wisdom" (Proverbs 9:10). Samuel Johnson said, "Shame rises from the fear of men, conscience rises from the fear of God."[1] Notice the ancient wisdom recorded in Isaiah 8:12,13:

> You are not to say, "It is a conspiracy!" In regard to all that this people call a conspiracy, and you are not to fear what they fear or be in dread of it. It is the LORD of hosts whom you should regard as holy. And He shall be your fear, and He shall be your dread. Then He shall become a sanctuary....

Anxiety

Anxiety is different from fear in that it lacks an object or adequate cause. People are anxious because they are uncertain about a specific outcome or they don't know what is going to happen tomorrow. It is perfectly normal to be concerned about those things which we value, which is why we need to distinguish between temporary anxiety and an anxious trait that persists. A state of anxiety exists when concern is shown *before* a specific event. One can be anxious about an examination that is yet to be taken, or the attendance at a planned function, or the threat of an incoming storm. Such concern is normal and moves a person to responsible action. But we also need to remember that the vast majority of our fears and anxieties are never realized.

In a generalized anxiety disorder an individual exhibits an anxious trait over a long period of time. To be diagnosed as such, the obsessive worrying must occur more days than not for at least a six-month period. Those who struggle with a generalized anxiety disorder experience persistent anxiety and worry. They fret over two or more stressful life circumstances such as finances, relationships, health, or ability to perform. Usually they struggle with a large number of worries and spend a lot of time and energy doing it. The intensity and frequency of the worrying is always *out of proportion* to the actual problem. The worrying is usually more detrimental than the negative consequences the people were initially concerned about.

Someone once said that every decision made is an attempt to reduce further anxiety. People don't like to live in an anxious state and will do almost anything to relieve it. Some adopt driven lifestyles because their minds are never at peace. Sitting silently by themselves is agonizing. Keeping busy may temporarily focus the mind, but it doesn't resolve the problem. It may actually contribute to it and create other problems, including burnout. Others alter their anxious minds with tranquilizers, alcohol, drugs, or food. Marketing temporary cures for anxiety may be the most lucrative business in America. But these cures offer only temporary escapes. Peter admonishes us to cast all our anxieties on Christ—the ultimate cure—because He cares for us (1 Peter 5:7).

Panic Attacks

Unlike fear and anxiety, one has to stretch the imagination to find anything good about panicking other than feed-back information that you may have a physical problem. Some people experience panic attacks when they become physically and emotionally aware of the symptoms of hypothyroidism, hypoglycemia, heart palpitations, or other physical abnormalities. Even though these problems may feel like it at first, they are typically not life threatening. Once the people receive a proper diagnosis, they usually return to a normal life, often without medication.

Panic attacks can also occur spontaneously and unexpectedly without any apparent reason. Such episodes are labeled "attacks" because the panic is not preceded by any abnormal thinking or approaching danger. They may or may not occur with any existing phobias. For example, if someone fears being attacked in public, and he or she start avoiding public places, the original concern or fear can evolve into agoraphobia. Between one and two percent of the American population suffers from panic attacks alone, but five percent suffer from panic attacks complicated by agoraphobia.

Could some of these cases be spiritual? When we speak at conferences, we often ask how many people have been suddenly awakened in a paralyzing grip of fear. They could possibly feel pressure on their chests or experience the sensation of choking or being choked. Or when they tried to respond physically, they would feel like they couldn't move or speak? At least 35 percent of those attending have had such an experience.

A secular doctor or counselor would call these symptoms panic or anxiety attacks. They don't call it a fear attack because they can't identify the object of the fear or establish what is causing the attack externally. We believe these are spiritual attacks. Proper biblical instruction can help a person resolve that kind of spiritual attack in a matter of seconds. However, keep in mind that not all panic attacks are direct spiritual attacks.

Toward a Wholistic Answer

Provided there are no identifiable physical causes, and we are living a balanced life of good nutrition and exercise, it is our contention that a knowledge of God and a right relationship with Him is the only satisfactory answer for these emotional problems. The fear of God overcomes all other fears. Anxiety is overcome by faith in God, and spiritual attacks are overcome by worshiping God in our daily walk.

More than 300 biblical passages tell us not to fear, but little relief will come to someone struggling with phobias if he or she is just told not to fear. That is not a sufficient answer. Such behavioral and legalistic approaches only create more confusion and guilt. Although Christ is the answer, and the truth will set us free, the suffering saint needs to know how to connect with God and how the truth sets us free.

Dr. Edmund Bourne is one of the more credible practitioners seeking to help those struggling with anxiety disorders. He is the author of *The Anxiety and Phobia Workbook*,[2] which won the Benjamin Franklin Book Award for Excellence in Psychology. Dr. Bourne entered this field of study because he personally struggled with anxiety. Five years after the publication of the first edition, his own anxiety disorder took a turn for the worse. This caused him to reevaluate his own life as well as his approach to treatment. In 1998, he published a new book entitled *Healing Fear*. In the foreword he says:[3]

> The guiding metaphor for this book is "healing" as an approach to overcoming anxiety, in contrast to "applied technology." I feel it's important to introduce this perspective into the field of anxiety treatment since the vast majority of self-help books available (including my first book) utilize the applied technology approach.... I don't want to diminish the importance of cognitive behavioral therapy (CBT) and the applied technology approach. Such an approach produces effective results in many cases, and I use it in my professional practice every day. In the past few years, though, I feel that the cognitive behavior strategy has reached its limits. CBT and medication can produce results quickly and are very compatible with the brief therapy, managed-care environment in the mental

> health profession at present. When follow-up is done over one- to three-year intervals, however, some of the gains are lost. Relapses occur rather often, and people seem to get themselves back into the same difficulties that precipitated the original anxiety disorder.

In other words, "They have healed the brokenness of My people superficially, saying, 'Peace, peace,' but there is no peace" (Jeremiah 6:14). Bourne's words read like a modern-day commentary of Colossians 2:8: "See to it that no one takes you captive through philosophy and empty deception, according to the tradition of men, according to the elementary principles of the world, rather than according to Christ." Dr. Bourne believes that "anxiety arises from a state of disconnection."[4] We agree, and the primary disconnection is from God, followed closely with being disconnected from the body of Christ and other meaningful relationships.

From a Christian perspective, cognitive behavior therapy is part of the repentance process when biblically based. Renewing our minds is essential for sanctification, and the truth will set us free. But if that is all we do, then living the Christian life is nothing more than an intellectual exercise. Freedom cannot be fully accomplished without the presence of God and fellowship in the body of Christ. When asked by the Pharisees what the greatest commandment is, Jesus said, "'You shall love the Lord your God with all your heart, and with all your soul, and with all your mind.' This is the great and foremost commandment. The second is like it, 'You shall love your neighbor as yourself'" (Matthew 22:37-39). We absolutely need God, and we also need each other in order to live a free and productive life.

Would you be fearful of a neighborhood bully if you had an armed escort of marines constantly at your side? Would you be anxious for tomorrow if someone with more than adequate resources promised to take care of you? How much more confident would you be if you knew that God would never desert nor forsake you and promised to meet all your needs according to His riches in glory (see Hebrews 13:5; Philippians 4:19)? No mortal can do that for you, and no amount of cognitive (reasoning) restructuring can accomplish what only His presence can. To fully appropriate all we need requires a renewing of our minds. In order to live and walk by faith, we must know the truth. Jesus is the truth (John 14:6). His Word is truth (John 17:17). The Holy Spirit has come to lead us into all truth (John 16:13). That truth will make us free (John 8:32).

We don't know whether Dr. Bourne has a saving knowledge of our Lord Jesus Christ, but in his own search for answers he came to the following conclusion:

> In my own experience, spirituality has been important, and I believe it will come to play an increasingly important role in the psychology of the future. Holistic medicine, with its interest in meditation, prayer, and the role of spiritual healing in recovery from serious illness, has become a mainstream movement in the nineties. I believe there will be a "holistic psychology" in the not too distant future, like holistic medicine, [that] integrates scientifically based treatment approaches with alternative, more spiritually based modalities.[5]

While we laud such movement in the thinking of secular therapists, we are also deeply concerned that the spirituality implied may not be Christ-centered. New Age philosophies of spirituality are more entrenched in secular education than is historical Christianity. Biblical meditation plays an important role in true spirituality, but meditating at the feet of a New Age guru will lead to incredible spiritual bondage. Even the concept of alternative medicine is laced with both good and bad news. The basic intent of alternative medicine is to emphasize that which heals and restores the body to good health, as opposed to focusing on the illness, which has been the dominating focus of medical science. Curing the disease does not ensure good health, but doing those things that ensure good health can potentially cure many diseases.

Alternative medicine is bad news when the underlying beliefs are New Age and eastern philosophies. The rise of New Age teaching on health and wholeness may pose one of the most serious threats to the church in the latter days. This is especially relevant in light of the fact that the Bible teaches a coming apostasy before the Lord returns (see Matthew 24:11,24; 2 Thessalonians 2:1-9). In addition, "the Spirit explicitly says that in later times some will fall away from the faith, paying attention to deceitful spirits and doctrines of demons" (1 Timothy 4:1).

Jesus said, "Peace I leave with you; My peace I give to you; not as the world gives, do I give to you. Let not your heart be troubled, nor let it be fearful" (John 14:27). We have an adequate answer in Christ. As children of God, we don't have just the words of Christ, *we also have the very presence of His life with us and within us.* Things we learned before coming to Christ have to be unlearned through repentance and by the renewing of our minds. Nobody can fix our pasts, but by the grace of God we can be free from them. Only in Christ are we assured victory over our fears. He is the only One we can cast our anxieties upon and find the peace of God that passes all understanding. Only in Christ do we have authority over the god of this world. Jesus, the "Prince of Peace," came to set the captive free.

There is no condemnation for those who are in Christ Jesus (Romans 8:1). We can't solve a problem unless we admit we have one—and we all do. The unconditional love and acceptance of God is what allows us to go to Him in total honesty. We *can* cast our anxiety onto Him because He *does* care for us.

Depression is often the unwanted companion or consequence of anxiety disorders. We recommend that you read Neil's book, *Finding Hope Again*,[6] which explains how to overcome depression. Depression is a natural reaction to losses in life or the sense of being helpless and hopeless. God is our hope and we can turn to Him for help according to the psalmist: "Why are you in despair, O my soul? And why are you disturbed within me? Hope in God, for I shall again praise Him, the help of my countenance, and my God" (Psalm 43:5).

We believe that every child of God can be free from any anxiety disorder and learn to live a liberated life in Christ. We believe there is a peace of God that surpasses all understanding that will guard your hearts and your minds in Christ Jesus (Philippians 4:7). "The LORD your God is in your midst, a victorious warrior. He will exult over you with joy, He will be quiet in His love, He will rejoice over you with shouts of joy" (Zephaniah 3:17). Jesus said, "Come to Me, all who are weary and heavy-laden, and I will give you rest. Take My yoke upon you, and learn from Me, for I am gentle and humble in heart; and you shall find rest for your souls. For My yoke is easy, and My load is light" (Matthew 11:28-30). As you work your way through this book, keep in mind the words of F.B. Meyer:

> God incarnate is the end of fear; and the heart that realizes that He is in the midst, that takes heed to the assurance of His loving presence, will be quiet in the midst of alarm. "No weapon that is formed against thee will prosper, and every tongue that shall rise against thee in judgment Thou shalt condemn." Only be patient and be quiet.[7]

—Neil and Rich

1

A Fortress of Fear

Cabin'd, cribb'd, confined, bound in to saucy
doubts and fears.

—Shakespeare
Macbeth III.iv

Fear is a thief. It erodes our faith, plunders our hope, steals our freedom, and takes away our joy of living the abundant life in Christ. Phobias are like the coils of a snake—the more we give in to them, the tighter they squeeze. Tired of fighting, we succumb to the temptation and surrender to our fears. But what seemed like an easy way out becomes, in reality, a prison of unbelief—a fortress of fear that holds us captive.

National Institute of Mental Health (NIMH) director Steven E. Hyman, M.D., says, "Anxiety disorders are the most common mental illnesses in America, yet many people who have them are suffering in silence and secrecy, inappropriately ashamed or unaware of the availability of excellent treatments."[1]

According to statistics from the Anxiety Disorders Association of America, nearly 20 million Americans (about 1 in 13) suffer from a phobia at some point in their lives. Three to 6 million suffer from panic disorders, while the same number are afflicted with OCD (obsessive-compulsive disorder). Up to 10 million Americans struggle with persistent anxiety (generalized anxiety disorder) every year.[2] Hyman concludes that "people are hungering for information, as shown by the thousands who attend national anxiety and depression screening days and call NIMH and other groups for information."[3]

Not included in the above numbers would be the more subtle fears that keep Christians from stepping out in faith and living a liberated life in Christ. Most Christians struggle with anxieties that wouldn't be classified as a disorder but still impede personal growth. These believers might have a limited understanding of what it means to be a child of God and lack the assurance of God's presence in their lives.

Causes and Cures

What are the root causes of anxiety disorders, and what is the cure or how are they healed? An article from the National Anxiety Foundation reveals their current thinking on panic disorder:

> Twenty years ago Panic Disorder was poorly understood even by most experts. It was called Anxiety Neurosis and was thought by some to stem from "deeply rooted" psychological conflicts and subconscious upsetting impulses of a sexual nature. Now we regard Panic Disorder as more of a physical problem with a metabolic core.
>
> It is not an emotional problem, although after suffering from it, emotionally healthy persons may

> develop depression or other problems....Few experts still cling to the notion that this is not a physical disorder. It is regarded as a physical disorder much like diabetes or pneumonia.[4]

If a panic attack is a physical disorder, then medication along with a balanced regimen of nutrition and exercise is the proper prescription. We acknowledge that it can be. We also acknowledge that medication can be helpful and, in some cases, essential for the treatment of panic disorder and assistance in overcoming fear and anxiety. It is very difficult to process biblical truth in extreme cases of fear and anxiety until the physical symptoms have been reduced through medication. The alleviation of human suffering by legitimate medical means is truly an act of mercy.

Attempting to understand the causes and cures of anxiety disorders on the physical plane alone, however, does not provide an adequate answer. Medical professionals openly acknowledge that many of their clients are sick for psychosomatic reasons. But cognitive and behavioral therapies, along with medication, are not wholistic approaches because they ignore the God of the universe, the god of this world, and the spiritual nature of mankind. Striving for a wholistic answer raises questions regarding our Western, rational worldview.

Four Critical Concerns

First, we are deeply concerned that too many prescriptions for health and wholeness leave out the "Great Physician," the "Wonderful Counselor," and ignore the reality of the spiritual world. To adequately help someone, we must take into account *all* reality that deals with the whole person—body, soul, and spirit. We thank God for the medical professions that have the unique purpose of treating the physical body, but we also delight in God's provision for our souls and spirits. We need both the hospital and the church functioning in proper balance and open to each others' contribution.

Second, we are concerned where faith and hope are essentially placed. God and His Word are the only legitimate objects for our faith. God is the one who comforts us as we place our hope in Him (2 Corinthians 1:4,10). Scripture also teaches His preeminence: "He is before all things, and in Him all things hold together" (Colossians 1:17). That doesn't mean that God doesn't work through a godly pastor, psychiatrist, psychologist, or qualified doctor. He does, and we advise you to pray for His guidance and protection as you seek such help. But to put your faith and hope in any person or medication will prove to be insufficient in the end. The medical model does not treat the whole person nor take into account all reality. And no human can be a valid object for your faith.

Third, we are concerned about priorities. The emphasis in our present culture is to seek every possible natural explanation first, and if that doesn't work then there is nothing left to do but pray. In the Sermon on the Mount, Jesus talked about the problem of anxiety and concluded by saying, "But seek first His kingdom and His righteousness; and all these things shall be added to you" (Matthew 6:33). James said, "Is anyone among you suffering? Let him pray" (James 5:13). The *first* thing a Christian should do about anything is pray, and this is especially true for any mental or emotional problem.

Fourth, we need to avoid the extremes. One end is to believe that taking any medication or seeking any medical help is a lack of faith. Our physical bodies must be fed in order to survive, and they will occasionally need medication because we live in a world filled with germs and viruses. Our bodies are also decaying and often suffer from the abuse of living in a fallen world. The other extreme is to place one's hope solely in medication.

We have seen both errors in our churches. Some will seek medical help but not personal counsel, while others may seek counsel but won't consult a medical doctor. Unfortunately, many people who struggle with anxiety don't seek help at all and, therefore, suffer needlessly.

The Ultimate Cause

In a world of increasing technology, we caution against the subtle erosion of faith in God and the truth of His Word. In one sense, all our problems can ultimately be traced back to the fall of Adam and Eve. God created them to be spiritually and physically alive and intimately related to Him. But when Eve was deceived and Adam sinned, they both died spiritually. They were separated from God. Physical death would also be a consequence, but that didn't happen immediately. God's perfect creation was thrown into chaos.

Because of the fall, the whole creation is groaning and "we ourselves groan within ourselves, waiting eagerly for our adoption as sons, the redemption of our body" (Romans 8:23). Fear was the first emotion recorded in Scripture after the fall. Adam said, "I was afraid because I was naked; so I hid myself" (Genesis 3:10). When the resurrected Christ first appeared to His disciples He found them cowering in fear of the Jews. He simply said to them, "Peace be with you" (John 20:19). God's provision for personal redemption had come.

Anxiety disorders often reveal a disconnection with God and the lack of involvement in a supportive Christian community. However, simply telling people that they must be born-again and find a few Christian friends falls short of comfort, although it is an essential beginning. We all have to go through a growth process that involves the renewing of our minds. What self-confidence we had before Christ must be replaced by confidence in God. Even the self-righteous and overly confident Paul had to be struck down in order to become an apostle. Only then could he say, "Put no confidence in the flesh" (Philippians 3:3).

While recognizing the helpful contributions that medical science and secular psychology have made toward understanding fear and anxiety, we need to remember that freedom and wholeness are only found in Christ. A true knowledge of our heavenly Father and a deep understanding of what it means to be a child of God are essential keys to overcoming the shackles of fear and anxiety. The prophet Isaiah contrasted the worldly ways of overcoming fear with the genuine hope we have in God when he wrote:

> The coastlands have seen and are afraid; the ends of the earth tremble; they have drawn near and have come. Each one helps his neighbor, and says to his brother, "Be strong!" So the craftsman encourages the smelter, and he who smoothes metal with the hammer encourages him who beats the anvil, saying of the soldering, "It is good"; and he fastens it with nails, that it should not totter.
>
> But you, Israel, My servant, Jacob whom I have chosen, descendant of Abraham My friend, you whom I have taken from the ends of the earth, and called from its remotest parts, and said to you, "You are My servant, I have chosen you and not rejected you. Do not fear, for I am with you; do not anxiously look about you, for I am your God. I will strengthen you, surely I will help you, surely I will uphold you with My righteous right hand" (Isaiah 41:5-10).

The Lord tenderly reminds His people of who they are and of His deep and intimate concern for them. And then He provided the antidote for their fears—the experiential knowledge of His powerful presence, provision, and protection. But why is it that one person can read those verses in Isaiah and other similar passages, be encouraged to walk by faith in the Lord, and find the feelings of fear and anxiety fading away while others find little comfort? Assuming these people want to believe and desire to have a right relationship with God and others and live according to Scripture, the reasons they are having trouble connecting are twofold. First, they may lack spiritual understanding and maturity; and, second, they may have many unresolved personal and spiritual conflicts that keep them from having an intimate relationship with God.

A Lack of Understanding

Have you ever wondered why you still feel the same fears and struggle with many of the same anxieties you did before you experienced salvation? To answer that we have to understand what did and did not happen at salvation.

Because of the fall, we were all born physically alive but spiritually dead (Ephesians 2:1). We had neither the presence of God in our lives nor the knowledge of His ways. Consequently, we all learned to live our lives independently of God. This learned independence is a major characteristic of what the Bible calls "the flesh."

The moment we were born-again, we became new creatures in Christ. Old things passed away and new things came (2 Corinthians 5:17). We received the mind of Christ (1 Corinthians 2:16), and the indwelling Holy Spirit that will lead us into all truth. But we still struggle with many of the same fears and anxieties because being saved does not instantly renew our minds. All those old fleshly thoughts and habits programmed into our "computers" are still there. There is no delete button in our memory banks. That is why Scripture says, "Do not be conformed to this world, but be transformed by the renewing of your mind, that you may prove what the will of God is, that which is good and acceptable and perfect" (Romans 12:2). Without the renewing of our minds, we would conclude with Hosea, "My people are destroyed for lack of knowledge" (Hosea 4:6).

Every believer in Christ has a filter through which the Word of God passes in its "journey" from the eye and ear "gates" to the heart. The truth of God's Word is sifted through a grid of previously learned experiences and the emotions associated with them. That grid consists of the individual's belief system about the world—including his or her perception of God, self, and others.

Suppose you were raised by parents who said you would never amount to anything—and you believed it. Throughout childhood, you kept getting the message, "You're a loser!" As a new Christian, you are confronted with an opportunity that would prove your parents wrong if you were successful. Plus, you just recently read in the Bible that you can do all things through Christ who strengthens you (Philippians 4:13). But that nagging little voice that was programmed into your mind for years says, "You will never amount to anything." Your negative identity and fear of failure all but drown out this wonderful truth you just read.

For some people, their thoughts are so clogged with the residue of past trauma, abuse, neglect, disappointments, betrayal, and lies that they remain locked in chains of fear, anxiety, and unbelief. They can't seem to connect with the truth of God's Word. In severe cases, simplistic advice like, "You just need to trust God" or "God says it, you just need to trust and obey" is about as helpful as yelling at a clogged sink, "Why don't you just open up?" The drain will stay plugged until you pour down the clog remover. The clog is their own unbelief or lack of repentance. In reality, they can do it, but they don't believe they can. Years of conditioning have taught them not to. Their fears are more real to them than the presence of God and all His promises. Stepping out in faith takes a lot of courage and the support of the Christian community.

A Lack of Conflict Resolution

Paul said, "I gave you milk to drink, not solid food; for you were not yet able to receive it" (1 Corinthians 3:2). The apostle explains to the Corinthians that their inability to receive solid food was because of their jealousy and strife. Genuine repentance is needed to help them resolve their personal and spiritual conflicts. They may be able to acknowledge the truth in their minds, but when the heat is on, fear and anxiety will overwhelm them once again. James asks the question, "What is the source of quarrels and conflicts among you?" (James 4:1). Essentially he says it is self-centered and worldly living. His answer is to "submit therefore to God. Resist the devil and he will flee from you. Draw near to God and He will draw near to you" (4:7,8). If you try resisting the devil without first submitting to God, you will have a dogfight. If you submit to God but don't resist the devil, you stay in bondage. The following testimony reveals the necessity to have a whole answer:

> *For the past 35 years, I have lived from one surge of adrenaline to the next. My entire life has been gripped by paralyzing fears which seem to come from nowhere and everywhere—fears which made very little sense to me or anyone else. I invested four years of my life obtaining a degree in psychology, hoping it would enable me to understand and conquer those fears. Psychology only perpetuated my questions and insecurity. Six years of professional counseling offered little insight and no change in my level of anxiety.*
>
> *After two hospitalizations, trips to the emergency room, repeated EKGs, a visit to the thoracic surgeon, and*

> *a battery of other tests, my panic attacks only worsened. By the time I came to see you, full-blown panic attacks had become a daily feature.*
>
> *It has been three weeks since I've experienced a panic attack! I have gone to malls [and] church services. [I have] played for an entire worship service, and even made it through Sunday school with peace in my heart. I had no idea what freedom meant until now. When I came to see you, I had hoped that the Truth would set me free, but now I know it has! Friends have told me that even my voice is different and my husband thinks I'm taller!*
>
> *When you live in a constant state of anxiety, most of life passes you by because you are physically/emotionally/mentally unable to focus on anything but the fear which is swallowing you. I could barely read a verse of Scripture at one sitting. It was as though someone snatched it away from my mind as soon as it entered. Scripture was such a fog to me. I could only hear the verses which spoke of death and punishment. I had actually become afraid to open my Bible. These past weeks, I have spent hours a day in the Word, and it makes sense. The fog is gone. I am amazed at what I am able to hear, see, understand, and retain.*
>
> *Before [I read your book]* The Bondage Breaker, *I could not say "Jesus Christ" without my metabolism going berserk. I could refer to "The Lord" with no ill effect, but whenever I said "Jesus Christ" my insides went into orbit. I can now call upon the name of Jesus Christ with peace and confidence...and I do it regularly.*

Her sink was clogged. She got unclogged when her pastor took her through the "Steps to Freedom in Christ," which helped her resolve her personal and spiritual conflicts. (The "Steps to

Freedom" are included in the back of this book. The apostle Paul spoke of these spiritual "clogs" or strongholds in 2 Corinthians 10:3-5 (NIV) when he wrote:

> For though we live in the world, we do not wage war as the world does. The weapons we fight with are not the weapons of the world. On the contrary, they have divine power to demolish strongholds. We demolish arguments and every pretension that sets itself up against the knowledge of God, and we take captive every thought to make it obedient to Christ.

How Strongholds Are Developed

Strongholds are habitual patterns of thinking, feeling, and acting that are deeply ingrained in a person's personality. They are similar in concept to what psychologists call "defense mechanisms," which are unhealthy ways of coping with life. How are they formed? Since we begin our lives without Christ, our minds get programmed from the external world. Even secular theorists say that present-day attitudes and beliefs are primarily assimilated from the environment we were raised in.

There are two primary ways that such attitudes and beliefs are formed. First, they are assimilated from the environment through prevailing experiences, such as the home you were raised in, the schools you attended, the community you played in, and the church you attended (or didn't attend). Second, they are assimilated from the environment through traumatic experiences, such as a death or divorce in the family, frightening experiences, and severe traumas such as rape and other violence.

Strongholds are habit patterns of thought that have been burned into our minds over time or by the intensity of traumatic experiences. They are revealed in our personalities and greatly influence how we live and respond to life. For instance, if you see an adult who is afraid to ride an elevator, you can be sure they have had a negative experience that led to this fear. They weren't born with that fear. Nor is one born with an "inferiority complex." Inferiority complexes are acquired from being raised in a performance-based society and compared to those who appear to be smarter, stronger, or better looking.

The world system we were raised in is totally different from our new citizenship in the kingdom of God. "He delivered us from the domain of darkness, and transferred us to the kingdom of His beloved Son" (Colossians 1:13). Not only has our citizenship changed, but we have personally changed as well. "You were formerly darkness, but now you are light in the Lord; walk as children of light" (Ephesians 5:8). We have to learn how to walk as children of light because we have previously learned to live without Christ.

Anxiety disorders are strongholds or defense mechanisms that were acquired in order to survive, cope, or succeed in life. Though everyone is afraid at one time or another, a person with a stronghold of fear might be described as "fearful," "timid," or even "phobic." Though everyone worries once in a while, a person with a stronghold of anxiety might be described as "a worrier" or "insecure" or perhaps even a "control freak." Rather than live by faith in God, they try to cope with their fears and anxieties with their own natural resources.

Strongholds can form at any time in life, but they are most often formed in early childhood. They can set a pattern for life that, apart from the grace of God, will remain until the grave. Cognitive therapy can help individuals identify false beliefs that are at the root of many anxiety disorders, but they will not be fully resolved without the presence of Christ and the truth of His Word. The following testimony reveals how fear became a stronghold:

> *I have literally lived with crippling, chronic fear all of my life. When I was about seven years old, I had an*

experience in grade school that kicked it off. I was feeling very sick one day at school, and the teacher would not let me go home. I wanted to go very badly but I felt trapped and experienced my first panic.

From there on it became a constant circle. The feelings as a young girl that I felt that day were so scary that I spent the rest of my childhood and teenage years doing everything I could to avoid them. It got so bad that I actually quit school in ninth grade and was tutored at home. Then, at about age 14, I committed myself to a children's home for intense in-house therapy. It was either that or end my life.

It was extremely hard to live there, but it did break the fear cycle because they forced me to push through the fear to attend classes.

But as I returned home, it all gradually came back. I lived in my bedroom, which was my safe place. But eventually I started waking up in the middle of the night with terrible, gut-wrenching panic [attacks]. It was awful, and my parents had no clue as to what was wrong with me.

I spent years visiting doctors and different specialists to no avail. All my fear and panic stayed inside. I could be in a "number 10" panic and most everyone around me would not even know. I think I felt such shame because of it. I didn't want anyone to know that I was sick. It put so much stress on my family, and I hated being the problem.

Psychosocial Development

Most anxiety disorders and even minor struggles with anxiety and fear are a product of our learning experiences and growth process. Let's apply this to Erik Erikson's psychosocial theory of development.[5] Erikson says there are basic stages of human development. Each stage has a particular "crisis" associated with it. If that crisis is not faced successfully, the growth process is impeded, giving way to certain fears and anxieties. The eight stages he developed through the study of various cultural groups around the world are as follows:

Stage	Age	Psychosocial Crisis
1	Infancy (0 to 1 1/2)	Trust v. mistrust
2	Early childhood (1 1/2 to 3)	Autonomy v. shame, doubt
3	Play age (3 to 5)	Initiative v. guilt
4	School age (5 to 12)	Industry v. inferiority
5	Adolescence (12 to 18)	Identity v. confusion
6	Young adult (18 to 25)	Intimacy v. isolation
7	Adulthood (25 to 65)	Generativity v. self-absorption or stagnation
8	Maturity (65+)	Integrity v. despair

In *infancy*, a baby learns trust if parents provide the physical care and emotional nurture he needs. If neglect or abuse takes place, the child may never overcome the fear of abandonment. The stage can be set for a lifestyle of mistrust, fear, and suspicion of others, including (later on) God. Common fears at this age are fear of noise, falling, strange objects, and strange persons. They peak before age two and then generally rapidly decline.[6]

In *early childhood* (the toddler years), the child is learning to explore her world. The fear of being overwhelmed by things bigger than her (like dogs and cats) ought to be allayed by the loving, consistent discipline and limits provided by parents. Again, if that secure foundation of affection and protection is absent, deep-seated insecurities can form in the child. Even in the best of situations, nightmares can begin to show up, evidencing the anxieties of early childhood life.

Play age is a time when a child is free to create. Building things with blocks, coloring, painting, and creating games with animals and dolls is prevalent. If, however, that creativity is squelched by lack of opportunity, confinement, or ridicule, the child can develop a tremendous amount of personal guilt and shame. He can easily become convinced that he is a bad person, and develop a fear of taking risks or expressing himself. Fear of the dark, monsters, and injury can plague a child in this age group. Nightmares are typically even more of a problem at this age than with toddlers.[7]

School age (elementary) children are prime for discovering and developing the talents and abilities God has given them. This is normally when children want to learn to play sports or musical instruments. They enjoy energetic accomplishment and competition. They may develop a keen interest in art and express interest in taking lessons. If a child lacks opportunity or encouragement to explore and enjoy life academically, artistically, or athletically, a strong sense of inferiority can develop. This child may feel like a loser and could struggle with a fear of failure all through life.

It is always appropriate to encourage children to explore and enjoy healthy activities and develop their God-given talents. However, an overemphasis on excelling in these areas can set them up for identity problems in adolescence. If the only time children receive "strokes" is for "performing" in an activity, they get the message loud and clear that their value comes from what they do. But who we are is more important than what we do, and Scripture clearly affirms the value of character over performance.

During *adolescence,* a young person is trying to answer the question, "Who am I?" A considerable amount of identity confusion often takes place before identity achievement.[8] In other words, the young person may vacillate from one role to another (for example, jock to clown to Christian to serious student to party animal and back again) for a number of years before settling the issue. The aggravating thing for parents is that adolescents are adept at playing the chameleon, switching roles to meet the expectations of those they are around. How they act at home or church may be very different from how they behave in school.

The greatest anxiety of adolescence is the fear of rejection by peers. As Christians, it is imperative that we lead our children to the saving knowledge of our Lord Jesus Christ and ground their identities in Christ so they know what it means to be children of God. We want them to mature in the context of a group of Christian friends who can have healthy fun together and who are not ashamed of their faith in Christ.

At this age, it is also extremely helpful for young people to have a close friend, mentor, or youth pastor who is an adult of the same gender. This person can be a God-send to parents, helping children adopt the same values that mom and dad may be struggling to develop in their increasingly independent children.

A strong identity as a child of God with increasing maturity of the fruit of the Spirit paves the way for the *young adult* to develop intimacy in relationships. This is far more than sexual intimacy; it is the ability to relate to another person's deepest hopes, needs, and fears while being vulnerable in return.[9] The freedom to pursue intimacy with another person can be severely hampered by unresolved fears from childhood, whether they be the fear of abandonment, taking risks, expressing self, failure, or rejection.

The pursuit of healthy intimate relationships should occur by the time we are young adults, but for many that freedom does not come until much later. In fact, many people never seem to get there, jumping in and out of relationships with a deep-seated fear of vulnerability and commitment.

Adulthood is a time of productivity and fulfillment. In Christ, the adult believer should be enjoying a sense of fruitfulness and satisfaction from abiding in Jesus and accomplishing His will. Apart from Christ, however, an epidemic of mid-life crises has swept our nation, as ambition, pleasure, power, and possession-driven people question their direction in life. Some people desperately seek to cling to their fast-escaping youth, collectively spending millions of dollars on tanning salons, fitness clubs, and fad diets. Billions of dollars are also being paid for medications to relieve stress, depression, migraines, ulcers, backaches, and panic attacks.

Finally, the years of *maturity* ought to be filled with a deep experience of joy from a life invested for the kingdom of God. This sense of contentment comes from the realization that they have paved the way for the next generation, sharing the wisdom of life lived well.[10]

For too many senior citizens, however, there is a deep bitterness of soul, a disgust of self, and despair over life, according to Erikson. A fear of uselessness accompanied with a meaninglessness of life, as well as the fear of death itself, can turn the twilight years into a nightmare for the individual and those around him or her. Jeremiah spoke of those who "walked after emptiness and became empty" (Jeremiah 2:5).

Though the eight stages of development can overlap and vary in length of time, their sequence is fixed.[11] Any understanding of controlling fears and anxieties we experience in the present can be augmented by an understanding of what has gone on before in the psychosocial and spiritual development of the person. In our opinion the crisis stages of mistrust, shame, doubt, inferiority, confusion, isolation, self-absorption, and despair reveal the lack of a healthy relationship with God. All of those can be overcome when we learn how to trust in God, understand who we are in Christ, and become more like Him.

Although we are most vulnerable to certain fears at certain stages of life, anxiety disorders can develop at almost any age.

For example, the fear of abandonment could have its onset in the life of an adult or senior citizen due to a painful divorce or neglect by grown children. The fear of rejection by others could begin in middle age as the result of humiliation before fellow employees and termination from a job. Traumatic experiences also occur at any age and can send even well-adjusted individuals into a tailspin of fear and anxiety. As human beings we are very fragile and vulnerable. Phobias can arise without warning in very mentally and emotionally healthy individuals.

Defining Phobias

The American Psychiatric Association divides phobias (controlling, irrational fears) into three main categories: specific phobias, social phobias, and agoraphobia.[12] As the name implies *specific* phobias are irrational fears of specific situations or objects. Fear of certain kinds of animals or insects (such as dogs, spiders, snakes) is an example of this kind of phobia. Claustrophobia (fear of closed spaces) and acrophobia (fear of heights) are also examples of specific phobias.

Social phobias involve the fear of being watched, embarrassed, humiliated, rejected, or scorned while doing something in front of other people. The most common example of this type of phobia is the fear of public speaking. This would also apply to the Christian who is afraid to share his or her testimony or witness to an unbeliever. Other examples would include the fear of eating in public, using public rest rooms, and meeting new people.

The typical means of coping with social phobias is called "phobic avoidance," the attempt to eliminate threatening circumstances from one's lifestyle. This obviously poses real problems if the individual is afraid to go to work or school. School phobia is a problem for some children who are unwilling to leave the security of home/parents and take the risk of coping with the perceived threatening environment of school.

Agoraphobia is the third category of fear. The agoraphobic person is afraid to be alone or in a situation in which help or escape would be difficult to find. As mentioned earlier, agoraphobia can be the result of panic attacks.

In one of the testimonies shared earlier in this chapter, the woman who evidenced a serious case of phobic avoidance by eventually quitting school and being tutored at home was suffering from social phobia. She had been so frightened and humiliated by her teacher that she established a pattern of doing everything she could to avoid that kind of pain again. It became so severe that she "lived in her bedroom." Although her testimony doesn't say this, it would not be surprising to find that she became agoraphobic after the onset of her panic attacks. At any rate, fear was the controlling mechanism in her life.

Our minds are a clean slate when we are born, but we are not neutrally predisposed. We were born spiritually dead in our trespasses and sins with an Adamic nature (see Ephesians 2:1-3). God will forgive "iniquity, transgression and sin; yet He will by no means leave the guilty unpunished, visiting the iniquity of fathers on the children and on the grandchildren to the third and fourth generations" (Exodus 34:7). We were born equally in the sight of God, but we were not born with equal opportunity. Some parents are better than others in helping their children develop. Each person also has a God-given temperament that affects how he or she relates to the world. Additionally, God has not equally distributed gifts, talents, or intelligence.

That means that some people are more predisposed to anxiety disorders than others. In the woman's testimony given earlier, not every child would have reacted to her insensitive teacher in the way she did. Some kids feeling sick and being forbidden to go home would have reacted in anger. Others probably would have accepted their fate and withdrawn. Still others would have thrown a temper tantrum. Some of those differences in reactions have to do with our God-given temperaments and personal choice.

Now for the good news. Long before we came to know Him, God knew us (see Ephesians 1:4). "For whom He foreknew, He also predestined to become conformed to the image of His Son" (Romans 8:29). He redeemed us from our futile way of life inherited from our forefathers (see 1 Peter 1:18). Every one of us emerges from the womb vulnerable and needy. We need spiritual life, forgiveness, acceptance, security, significance, and an identity that stands the test of time and pain. The apostle Paul painted a clear picture of our spiritual condition and God's gracious remedy in Romans 5:6-8:

> While we were still helpless, at the right time Christ died for the ungodly. For one will hardly die for a righteous man; though perhaps for the good man someone would dare even to die. *But God demonstrates His own love toward us,* in that while we were yet sinners, Christ died for us (emphasis added).

The woman who struggled with social phobia has an encouraging "part two." It is a testimony of finding freedom and lasting change in Christ.

> *I was not raised to know God. I searched for Him when I was 14, when I felt that I could not take it another minute. But I had no one to whom I could go. I tried praying to Him to help me, but felt that He was so far away. If He created me, I couldn't understand how He could allow me to live in such misery.*
>
> *From then on I felt anger and bitterness toward Him. I chose not to seek Him.*

I eventually got married and, of course, my crippling fear did not get any better. It changed a lot as I got older, probably because I had to learn how to fake it even better. I hated when friends would want to camp out for an evening because I still couldn't do it. But I would pretend. I would tell them, "Sure, what time and where?" But then the panic would set in and I would scramble for excuses to get out of it.

My sister was a Christian and was committed to praying for me. She prayed for 12 long years, never giving up. Praise God! I finally called her in the middle of the night after an evening of misery, feeling again that I could not take living inside this jail anymore. There was a world outside of me that I could never really touch or feel, and it killed me.

I wanted life so badly. And I wanted to be free, so I called her in tears and asked her how to find this Jesus she kept telling me about. She prayed with me on the phone, and I spent the rest of the night reading Scriptures she had given me. They all referred to freedom in one way or another.

Freedom! I felt such hope. That started my journey of renewal. I spent all those years in such crippling fear, fear of fear. It was not knowing that scared me so bad. I learned about what physically happens when we fear something. I continued learning about anxiety and fear and what it can do. Understanding these things was what really set me on the road to peace.

I live today with chronic irritable bowel syndrome because of all the years of hiding in panic. My nerves are pretty shot inside. But my head and my spirit are at peace. I still struggle with going on long vacations. The old tapes still try to run in my head, but I override them with the truth. The truth being that Jesus is with me all the time, and I have nothing to fear.

Indeed "I can do all things through Christ who strengthens me." I found that verse when I first became a Christian, and I still rely on it today. Praise God!

2

Anxious Thinking

> If thou hast a fearful thought, share it not with a weakling, whisper it to thy saddle-bow, and ride forth singing.
>
> —Alfred the Great

While ministering overseas, an attractive single missionary approached me for the purpose of scheduling a counseling appointment. She appeared to have it all together and seemed confident and personable. I was surprised to hear that her presenting problem was agoraphobia. First impressions don't always tell the whole story. She seemed to have a heart for God and truly wanted to serve Him, but her various fears and anxieties were keeping her from being effective. She found it very difficult to be with crowds, and she had a fear of flying, which makes modern day missionary service all but impossible. We scheduled an appointment. This woman was raised in a Christian home and, according to her, had led a morally pure life. Nothing in her testimony revealed why she should be agoraphobic. I asked if she would be willing to go through the "Steps to Freedom in Christ." (The "Steps" are a comprehensive repentance process of submitting to God and resisting the devil. The purpose is to get radically right with God by resolving any personal or spiritual conflicts. See pp. 289-344.) The process revealed several sexual affairs she had never confessed with anyone before. For the first time she faced these sexual sins and found freedom from her past. I didn't see her again until the end of the conference. She approached me privately and said that the symptoms of agoraphobia were gone.

It is hard to imagine that Adam and Eve ever felt anxious or fearful when they were spiritually alive and lived in the presence of God. Sin, however, disconnected them from their loving heavenly Father, and their fallen descendants have struggled with fear and anxiety ever since. In Psalm 38, a depressed David wrote, "For I confess my iniquity; I am full of anxiety because of my sin" (verse 18). David's answer in Psalm 38 was to confess his sins, place his hope in God, and pray for salvation and help from the Lord (see verses 15, 22).

We don't want to give the impression that every anxiety disorder can be cured by prayer and confession, but we do want to say from the beginning that salvation, genuine repentance, and faith in God are essential to live a liberated life in Christ. As Dr. Bourne's statement in the introduction said, "Anxiety arises fundamentally from a state of disconnection." Salvation brings forgiveness of sins and spiritual/eternal life to the believer. The moment we are born-again, the Spirit of God takes up residence in our lives, and we are again connected to God "in Christ." His Spirit bears witness with our spirits that we are children of God (Romans 8:16).

Connected to God

We have found one common denominator with the Christian people that we have counseled regardless of what the problem was. They didn't know who they were "in Christ," and they didn't understand what it means to be children of God. Where was the inner sense of "Abba, Father" (Galatians 4:6)? If the Holy Spirit is bearing witness with our spirits that we are children of God, then why weren't those people sensing that? To be spiritually alive means that our inner self is united with God. We have become a temple of God because His Spirit dwells within us (Romans 8:10,11).

Spiritual life, our union with God, is most commonly portrayed in the New Testament as being "in Christ." For every verse that says Christ is in us, there are ten verses that say we are "in Christ" or "in Him." The truth that every true believer is "in Christ" is one of the fundamental teachings of Paul: "For this reason I have sent to you Timothy, who is my beloved and faithful child in the Lord, and he will remind you of my ways which are *in Christ*, just as I teach everywhere in every church" (1 Corinthians 4:17, emphasis added).

Given that every believer is spiritually alive in Christ and our souls are in union with God, why do we still struggle with anxiety and fear? The answer is twofold. First, in a positive sense a certain amount of fear is essential for our safety and survival, and we should be anxious or concerned for those things we care about. Second, in a negative sense our minds were programmed to live without God. Everything we learned before we came to Christ is still programmed into our memory banks—and there is no delete button. That is why Paul says, "Do not conform any longer to the pattern of this world, but be transformed by the renewing of your mind. Then you will be able to test and approve what God's will is—His good, pleasing and perfect will" (Romans 12:2 NIV).

Double-Minded

The primary word for anxiety, *merimna*, in the New Testament has both positive and negative connotations. Of the 25 uses in the New Testament, 5 of them indicate a sense of caring; the other 20 refer to a distracting and negative sense of worry. The root of *merimna* is the verb *merizo*, which means to draw in different directions or distract. When *merimna* is used as a verb (*merimnao*), it appears to be a conjunction of *merizo*, and *nous*, which means mind. Possibly that is why the translators of the King James Version of the Bible translated "do not be worried" (Matthew 6:25 NIV) as "take no thought" (KJV), and "why are you worried" (Matthew 6:28 NIV) as "why take ye thought" (KJV).

To be anxious in a negative sense is to be double-minded, and James says a double-minded person is unstable in all his or her ways (see James 1:8). This is clearly revealed in Matthew 6:24,25: "No one can serve two masters; for either he will hate the one and love the other, or he will hold to one and despise the other. You cannot serve God and mammon. For this reason I say to you, do not be anxious for your life." The answer to anxiety, according to Jesus, is to seek first the kingdom of God and trust our heavenly Father to take care of us.

Plan A v. Plan B

Since we were all born dead in our trespasses and sins, we had neither the presence of God in our lives nor the knowledge of His ways. Consequently, we all learned to live our lives without God's guidance and influence. Let's call this Plan B: man's way by reason, intuition, and experience (see the diagram on the next page). Before Christ, all we had was plan B. Plan A is God's way that we accept by faith. We learn God's way by choosing to study and believe His Word, which is made possible only by the indwelling presence of God. The apostle Paul says, "A natural man does not accept the things of the Spirit of God; for they are foolishness to him, and he cannot understand them.... But we have the mind of Christ" (1 Corinthians 2:14,16). We also have the Holy Spirit, who will lead us into all truth (John 16:13).

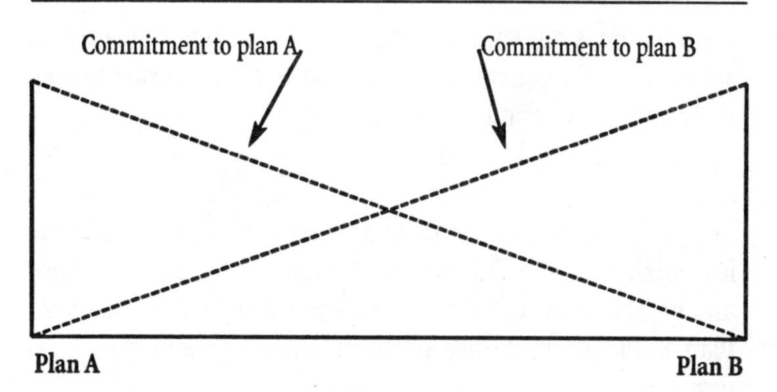

God's plan is not just a better way to live, it always includes His vital relationship with His children. Without the life of Christ we cannot live successfully according to God's plan. We have learned in the past how to cope, succeed, and survive without God and, in the process, developed many phobias, insecurities, and uncertainties. Without eternal life, how could we not fear death? Unless we are secure in Christ, how could we not be anxious for tomorrow? We would have to live in denial or simply not care. Without God we have no choice but to trust in our own limited resources.

False Security

Plan B is always lurking in the back of our minds. These flesh patterns, strongholds, and defense mechanisms will always suggest a way to deal with life's problems on a human level. This is evident when the struggling Christian asks, "Can I totally trust God, or should I just whisper a prayer and then deal with life as though I am solely responsible for making my own way in this world?" Can we say that we trust God if we defend ourselves, meet our own needs, and make our own living using our own resources? Can I cast all my anxieties upon Christ, or do I have to retain some worries in order to make sure everything comes out okay? It is easy to fall back on old ways of coping with life when the pressure is on. Jesus told the Pharisees they were experts at setting aside the commandment of God (Plan A) in order to keep their traditions (Plan B) [see Mark 7:9].

Such waffling between Plan A and Plan B creates its own anxieties for some Christians. They are double-minded, which brings up an interesting possibility. A natural person could have less anxiety than a Christian who wants to straddle the fence and get the "best" of both worlds. The natural person has only Plan B and some do live relatively anxiety free in their own world.

For instance, take the highly educated mathematician who has chosen not to believe in God. He has created his own rationalistic worldview and natural explanation of reality. He doesn't like to be presented with Plan A because that would create a certain amount of anxiety. He has worked hard to ensure that his family's physical needs and safety are provided for. He doesn't like to think about his purpose for being here or consider questions about life after death. He has become his own god. Although that will appear to work for a season, the end result is not attractive: "There is a way which seems right to a man, but its end is the way of death" (Proverbs 14:12).

But for the Christian who is alive in Christ, what power is superior to God and what situation is impossible for Him? Insecurity is depending upon temporal things that we have no right or ability to control. Security is depending on eternal life and values that no one or no thing can take away from us.

Physiological Considerations

Fear and anxiety are the emotional or felt reactions to our perception of life events; they don't occur in a vacuum. Anxiety disorders are a life problem, and to solve them we must consider how the whole person is responding to threatening events or potential disasters.

In the original creation, God formed Adam from the dust of the earth and breathed life into him. This union of divine breath and earthly dust is what constitutes the makeup of every born-again child of God who is both physically and spiritually alive. We have an outer person and an inner person, a material part and an immaterial part. The material or physical part of self relates to the external world through five senses. We can taste, smell, hear, feel, and see. The inner person relates to God through the soul and spirit. Unlike the animal kingdom, which operates out of instinct, we have the capacity to think, feel, and choose. Since we are "fearfully and wonderfully made," it makes sense that God would create the outer person to correlate with the inner person.

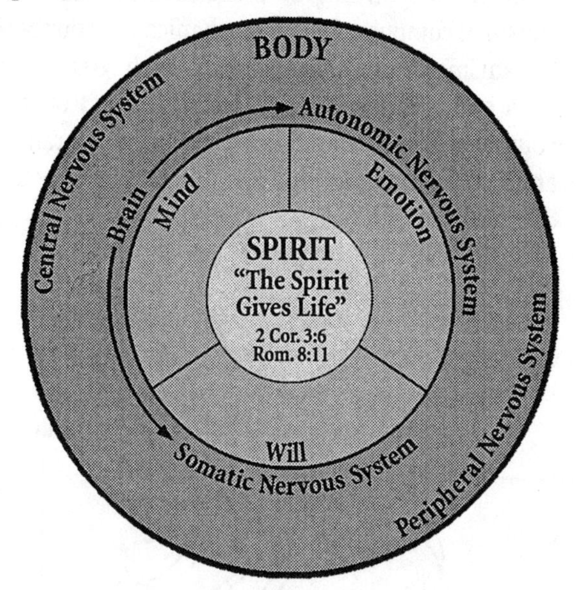

The correlation between the mind and the brain is obvious, but there is a fundamental difference between the two. The brain is physical matter and a part of our natural bodies, but the mind is part of the inner person or soul. The brain and mind together make up a very sophisticated computer operation. Every computer system is comprised of two distinct components, the hardware and the software. The hardware (the computer itself) is obviously the brain in this analogy. The software (the computer program) corresponds to the mind.

The brain functions much like a digital computer that has millions of switching transistors which code all the information in a binary numbering system of 0's and 1's. The miniaturization of circuitry has made it possible to store and compile an incredible amount of information in a computer the size of a notebook. However, mankind has not even come close to making a computer as sophisticated as the one that is now making it possible for you to read and comprehend this book.

A personal computer (PC) is mechanical, but our brains are living organisms composed of approximately 100 billion neurons. Each one is a living organism that in and of itself is a microcomputer. Every neuron is composed of a brain cell, an axon, and many dendrites (inputs to the brain cell) as follows:

Neuron

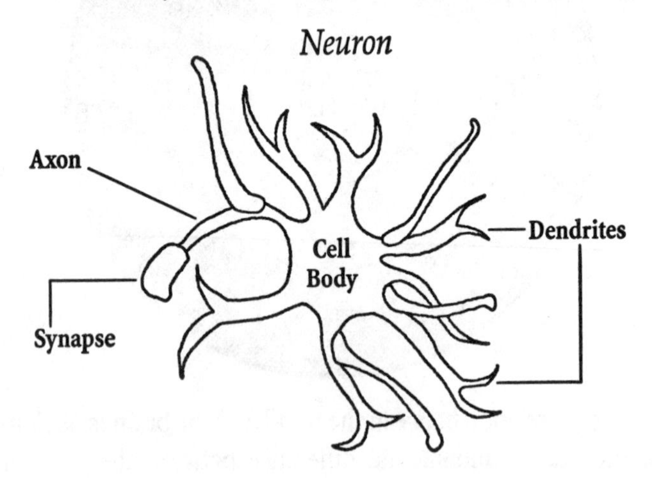

Each brain cell has many inputs (dendrites) and only one output through the axon that channels neurotransmitters to other dendrites. The axon is covered by a myelin sheath for insulation because the cell sends electrochemical messages along the axon. Every neuron is connected to tens of thousands of other neurons. Given that there are 100 billion neurons, the potential number of combinations is mind boggling. There is a junction between the axon of one neuron and the dendrites of another called a *synapse*. Every brain cell receives information through its dendrites, which it processes, integrates, and sends on to other neurons.

In the axon exist many mitochondria, which produce neurotransmitters. When a signal from the cell reaches the axon, it releases neurotransmitters that cross the synapse to other dendrites. There are numerous types of neurotransmitters of which norepinephrine, dopamine, serotonin, and acetylcholine are the most known and possibly the most important for our discussion.

The brain and the spinal cord make up the central nervous system which splits off into a peripheral nervous system. The peripheral nervous system has two channels: the autonomic and the somatic nervous system. The somatic nervous system regulates our muscular and skeletal movements such as speech and gestures; in other words, that which we have volitional control over. It obviously correlates to our will. We don't do anything without first thinking it. The thought-action response is so rapid that one is hardly aware of the sequence, but it is always there. Involuntary muscular movements do occur when the system breaks down, as is the case with Parkinson's disease—a progressive degeneration of nerve cells in one part of the brain that controls muscle movements. Our autonomic nervous system regulates our internal organs. We do not have direct control over our glands. We don't consciously say to our adrenal glands: "adren, adren, adren" or to our thyroid: "thy, thy, thy." They function automatically.

In a general sense, we don't have volitional control over our emotions either. You cannot will yourself to feel good or to like somebody you hate. We do, however, have control of what we think, and we can decide to believe what God says is true. Just as our glands are regulated by our central nervous system, our emotions are primarily a product of our thoughts.

The circumstances of life do not determine how we feel. How we feel is primarily determined by how we interpret the events of life (what we choose to think and believe), and then by how we choose to behave. Between the external stimulus and the emotional response is the brain (receiver) and the mind (interpreter). Threatening external circumstances do not cause us to feel anxious or fearful. The level of anxiety and fear is determined by how we interpret external circumstances.

Suppose you were taking a walk through the Arizona desert and came upon a snake. Your eyes see the snake and send a signal to the brain. The emotional response is completely dependent upon how the mind was previously programmed. If there was no prior knowledge of snakes, the emotional response would be more one of curiosity than fear. Suppose there is some prior knowledge of snakes but not enough to make a distinction between those that are poisonous and those that aren't. The emotional response would likely be instant fear if the person erroneously believed that all snakes were legitimate fear objects. If prior knowledge of snakes was quite extensive and it was easy to immediately see that the snake was not poisonous, the response would again be more curious than fearful. A little knowledge can appear dangerous, but a lot of knowledge liberates.

Two people can look at the same situation and respond totally differently because they don't have the same experience and/or belief system. That is why you will hear one say to another, "I don't know what you have to worry about" or "What are you afraid of?" To those who are knowledgeable, it doesn't make any sense why others are so afraid or anxious. That is why the truth sets us free.

This leads to another important axiom: If what we perceive or choose to believe does not reflect truth, then how we feel does not reflect reality. Let's see how this applies to anxiety. Suppose you have a very intimidating boss and word is circulating around the office that he wants to see you, which makes you very anxious. You don't know why he wants to see you so your mind begins to entertain several possibilities. "Maybe he wants to fire me or chew me out for that simple little mistake I made last week. I think I'll quit and rob him of the satisfaction of lording it over me!" The more you entertain such thoughts the more anxious you become. Finally the hour of your appointment with him arrives, and you are a bundle of nerves. Gingerly you enter his office only to be greeted by all the top brass who are there to congratulate you for the promotion you are about to receive. Had you known the truth before the appointment, your emotional state would have been totally different.

The same axiom holds true for fear. When I was in high school, I delivered the morning paper. One day I physically couldn't because of a back injury I sustained in a wrestling tournament. So I drove the car while my mother carried the papers to the door. I forgot to tell her about this vicious watchdog that came growling and snarling around the corner whenever anyone approached the house. Talk about fear! When that dog came around the corner, my poor mother just about had a coronary. I also forgot to tell her about the chain that stopped the dog from getting near her. There was no fear of that dog in my mind because I knew the truth. My mother, however, didn't have my prior knowledge and experience.

When Stress Becomes Distress

Let's apply this same logic to the problem of stress. When external pressures put demands on our physical system, our adrenal glands respond by secreting cortisonelike hormones into our physical body. Our bodies automatically respond to external pressures. This is the natural "fight or flight" response to the pressures of life. If the pressures persist too long, our adrenal glands can't keep up, and stress becomes distress. The result can be physical illness, or we may become irritated with things that wouldn't bother us physically or emotionally in less stressful times.

Why then, do two people respond differently to the same stressful situation? Why do some actually seize the opportunity and thrive under the pressure while others fall apart? What is the difference between the two? Although we may differ considerably in our physical condition, the major difference lies in the software. It isn't just the external factors that determine the degree of stress. We all face the pressures of deadlines, schedules, trauma, and temptations. The major difference is how we mentally interpret the external world and process the data our brains are receiving.

The mind can choose to respond by trusting God with the assurance of victory (Plan A) or to be the helpless victim of circumstances (Plan B). The Israelites saw Goliath in reference to themselves and were paralyzed by fear. David saw the same giant in reference to God and said, "Let no man's heart fail on account of him; your servant will go and fight with this Philistine.... The LORD who delivered me from the paw of the lion and from the paw of the bear, He will deliver me from the hand of this Philistine" (1 Samuel 17:32,37). Faith in God (what we believe) greatly affects how we interpret and respond to fear objects and impending danger.

David had a lot of faith and, therefore, a lot of confidence in God. He also had a whole heart for Him. Righteous people who walk with God see reality and the complete picture through the eyes of faith in ways that others don't. For instance, the attendant of Elisha saw an army with horses and chariots surrounding the city where they were staying and cried out, "'Alas, my master! What shall we do?' So [Elisha] answered, 'Do not fear, for those who are with us are more than those who are with them.' Then Elisha prayed and said, 'Oh LORD, I pray, open his eyes that he may see.' And the LORD opened the servant's eyes, and he saw; and behold, the mountain was full of horses and chariots of fire all around Elisha" (2 Kings 6:15-17). On the other hand, the unrighteous see things that aren't there: "The wicked flee when no one is pursuing, but the righteous are bold as a lion" (Proverbs 28:1).

Fear is an adrenaline rush. When our minds perceive the presence of a fear object, a signal is sent from our brains to our nervous systems. Our muscles become rigid and tense as the alarm races through our bodies. But it is critically important to understand that the adrenal glands did not initiate the release of adrenaline. They are *responders* not initiators. The hormone was released into the bloodstream after the brain had recorded the external inputs and the mind interpreted the data. And the brain can only function according to how it has been programmed.

God has obviously done some basic preprogramming of our minds from the moment we were conceived in order for us to physically exist. Our autonomic nervous system was functioning in our mothers' wombs. God has also created us with a survival instinct that drives us to seek food, clothing, shelter, and safety. Witness the sucking instinct of a newborn child, for instance. There also seems to be a sixth sense or spiritual discernment that warns of impending doom. Even animals seem to have a God-given instinct that danger is imminent.

The Presence of God Affects Our Bodies

Salvation brings the presence of God into our lives, but there is no immediate change in the physical nature of our bodies. In a similar fashion, what physical changes could you observe in your computer when you slipped in a new program? Even though the same number of hardware components existed in the computer, the screen revealed the presence of the new program. The electronic flow through the computer changed. We should begin to live differently if a new program—Jesus—was loaded into our lives; our eyes have been opened to the truth and the power of the Holy Spirit, enabling us to live by faith. The flow of neurotransmitters would certainly change even though the number of brain cells would remain the same.

There is growing evidence that the programming of our minds, or how we choose to think, affects how the brain operates. If the secretion of adrenaline from our adrenal glands is triggered by how we think or perceive reality, could serotonin or other neurotransmitters be affected by how we think and what we choose to believe? Studies have shown that creating a sense of hopelessness and helplessness results in depression and a change in brain chemistry. Demitri and Janice Papolos, in *Overcoming Depression*, describe an experiment where rats were "taught" helplessness by the use of shock. They were able to measure neurological changes indicating depression at various beta receptor sites. They comment on these secular studies as follows:

> Dr. Henn and his colleagues induced depression in another group of rats, but treated them without medication. They made a behavioral intervention and "taught" the rats how to escape the shock. Actually, a medical student working in the lab knit the rats little sweaters with long sleeves over their front paws. Strings were attached to the sleeves and the researchers could pull the rat's paws up, marionette-like, and train them to push the lever that would stop the shock. With the rats no longer helpless, their

> symptoms of depression abated, and the beta receptor sites returned to their previous state. Dr. Henn and others have concluded from these studies that, just as neurochemistry affects behavior, changes in behavior affect neurochemistry.
>
> Complementary findings have been found in the treatment of human depression. A brief psychotherapeutic treatment called cognitive therapy focuses on the thought processes of a depressed person, in particular the hopeless and helpless thinking, and by changing the negative thought patterns, has proved to be as effective as the antidepressant imipramine in treating the depression.[1]

Your physical body is affected the moment you think anxious thoughts or perceive a fear object. This has tremendous implications for those who are struggling with anxiety disorders and those who are ministering to them. That is why cognitive therapy is the primary method of counseling. Cognitive therapy has its limits, however, if it is not based on the truth of God's Word. God established faith as the means by which we relate to Him and live our lives. Since He doesn't bypass our minds, then neither should we in helping others live whole and productive lives.

The presence of God in our lives will slowly affect our total being, including the physical aspects. According to the words of Paul, "He who raised Christ Jesus from the dead will also give life to your mortal bodies through His Spirit who indwells you" (Romans 8:11). This is evident when we walk by the Spirit since the fruit of the Spirit is "love [the character of God], joy [the antithesis of depression], peace [the antithesis of anxiety], patience [the antithesis of anger], kindness, goodness, faithfulness, gentleness, self-control; against such things there is no law" (Galatians 5:22,23). The connection between the initiating cause (the Spirit of truth working in our lives) and the end result (self-control) is the mind, which directs the brain that, in turn, regulates our glands and muscular movements.

Biblical Faith Leads to Wholeness

Jesus asked the blind men, "'Do you believe that I am able to do this?' They said to Him, 'Yes Lord.' Then He touched their eyes, saying, 'Be it done to you according to your faith'" (Matthew 9:28,29). The external power of Jesus was made effective by their choice to believe. In other words, the Lord chose to bring about a physical healing through the channel of belief. Is this not true in every other aspect of life? We are saved by faith (Ephesians 2:8), sanctified by faith (Galatians 3:3-5), and we walk or live by faith (2 Corinthians 5:7).

God never bypasses our minds; we are transformed by the renewing of our minds. He makes possible the renewing of our minds by His very presence in our lives. We respond in faith by choosing to believe the truth and living by the power of the Holy Spirit, not carrying out the desires of the flesh (Galatians 5:16). Jesus is "the way [how we ought to live], and the truth [what we ought to believe], and the life [our spiritual union with God]" (John 14:6). Even the operation of spiritual gifts incorporates the use of our minds. Paul concludes, "I shall pray with the spirit and I shall pray with the mind also; I shall sing with the spirit and I shall sing with the mind also" (1 Corinthians 14:15).

What About Medication?

Scripture instructs us to live in peace and warns us not to be anxious or fearful. In other words, the focus of Scripture is primarily on the software, not the hardware. Can we have a hardware problem? Of course! Organic brain syndrome, Down's syndrome, and Alzheimer's disease are all hardware problems, and there is little that can be done to cure them. The best software in the world won't work if you pull the plug on your computer or damage it beyond repair. So the brain must be chemically in balance with a normal production and flow of neurotransmitters in order for the mind to function.

Medication can potentially cure endogenous (physiological) depression by stimulating the production of neurotransmitters or bringing the brain back into a chemical balance. Treating depression with medication is usually reserved for those who are severely depressed or have been diagnosed with bipolar depression. We estimate that about 10 percent of those struggling with depression can truly be helped by antidepressants.[2]

It is very difficult to establish causation when treating any kind of mental illness. Which came first—external negative circumstances, poor mental evaluation, lack of faith in God, or a chemical imbalance? Anxiety disorders and depressed moods will likely accompany biochemical changes in the body, but to say that changed biochemistry caused depression or anxiety is as incomplete as saying a dead battery caused the car not to start. We need to ask what caused the battery to fail and find out if there is another reason the car won't start. Is the car out of gas? Is there a faulty alternator or a broken belt? Were the lights left on? Is the battery old and worn out? You can jump start the car using booster cables, which would be enough if the lights had been left on. But a good mechanic would consider many other causes to ensure the car would continue to run in the future.

With the exception of some forms of panic attack, fear and anxiety are rarely cured by medication. The purpose of tranquilizers and some antipsychotic medications is to subdue the nervous system and bring about a state of calmness. Is that wrong? No, and in severe cases it may be necessary to help stabilize a person who has lost control. In less severe cases it calms people down, allowing them to better assess their situation. Too much of this kind of medication, however, can make processing the truth extremely difficult. Also, it is possible to become addicted to prescription drugs, and some medications have serious side effects.

When considering the use of medication, we caution against two extremes. One extreme is to believe that taking medication is a lack of faith or trust in God. We have physical bodies that require physical assistance. We need both the hospital (to take care of our bodies) and the church (to take care of our souls) in proper balance. Taking a pill to cure our bodies is commendable, but taking a pill to cure our souls is deplorable. The other extreme is to place all our hope on medication or to counter every emotional problem with drugs (legal or illegal) or alcohol.

Should a Christian take prescribed drugs for emotional problems? Suppose you are suffering from acid indigestion. Should you take medication to relieve the heartburn? Most people would, and there is nothing wrong with getting temporary relief—but it is not a long-term answer. Your body is saying, "Stop feeding me this junk!" You probably need to consider changing your eating habits, and there is also the possibility that you have a more serious stomach illness such as an ulcer or cancer.

Garbage In, Garbage Out

Computer programmers use the term *GIGO*, which means garbage in, garbage out. If we put garbage into our minds, we will live a polluted life. Jesus said, "The good man out of the good treasure of his heart brings forth what is good; and the evil man out of the evil treasure brings forth what is evil; for his mouth speaks from that which fills his heart" (Luke 6:45). Paul says we have to take every thought captive to the obedience of Christ (2 Corinthians 10:5). It doesn't make any difference whether our thoughts originated from the television set, the radio, a book, a speaker, from our own memory banks, from the pit, or from our own original thinking. We take *every* thought captive to the obedience of Christ.

If what we are thinking is not true according to God's Word, then don't pay attention to it. Instead, do what the apostle Paul says we are to do: "Finally, brethren, whatever is true, whatever is honorable, whatever is right, whatever is pure, whatever is lovely, whatever is of good repute, if there is any excellence and if anything worthy of praise, let your mind dwell on these things" (Philippians 4:8). You don't get rid of negative thoughts by trying not to think of them. You overcome them by choosing the truth—and keep choosing it until the negative thoughts are drowned out or are completely replaced by the truth. If you want to experience the freedom that Christ purchased for you and the peace of mind that passes all understanding, then choose to think only those thoughts that align with the Word of God.

Discerning Viruses

Computer owners have been warned about the potential for their computers contracting a virus, which can cause severe damage to existing programs. Computer viruses are often not accidental; they are intentional. They may come from store-wrapped software that gets contaminated by disgruntled employees. And some devious people have purposefully created programs that are designed to introduce a destructive virus into any system that accesses them. Therefore, most computer systems have programs that scan for viruses—and so should we.

It is not always easy to detect a virus in our own belief system because the major strategy of the enemy is deception. Every Christian is subject to tempting, accusing, and deceiving thoughts. The most devious of Satan's schemes is deception because if you are tempted you would know it, if you are accused you would know it, but if you are deceived you wouldn't know it.

That is why we are to put on the armor of God. We're to stand against Satan's fiery darts aimed at our minds by taking up the shield of faith.

The father of lies was at work from the very inception of creation. Eve was deceived, and she believed a lie. Paul writes, "But I am afraid, lest as the serpent deceived Eve by his craftiness, your minds should be led astray from the simplicity and purity of devotion to Christ" (2 Corinthians 11:3). That is why Jesus prays for those who would follow Him: "I do not ask Thee to take them out of the world, but to keep them from the evil one.... Sanctify them in the truth; Thy word is truth" (John 17:15,17). Commenting about the latter days of the Church Age, Paul wrote, "But the Spirit explicitly says that in later times some will fall away from the faith, paying attention to deceitful spirits and doctrines of demons" (1 Timothy 4:1).

We have seen evidence of this all over the world. People struggle with their thoughts, have difficulty concentrating, and some actually hear "voices." These "voices," or negative thoughts, are usually self-condemning, suicidal, delusional, and phobic—which result in feelings of guilt, shame, fear, and anxiety. How could people not feel fearful and anxious if they were thinking those kinds of thoughts? A secular therapist or doctor would likely see the cause as a chemical imbalance and prescribe an antipsychotic or tranquilizer to treat the anxiety disorder.

We don't want to rule out that possibility altogether, but serious questions need to be asked. How can a chemical produce a personality or a thought? How can our neurotransmitters randomly fire in such a way as to produce a thought that one is opposed to thinking? We believe that those negative thoughts are patterns of the flesh learned from living in a fallen world or they are the fiery darts from Satan that Scripture clearly warns us about. A therapist with a secular worldview would not even consider such possibilities.

In our experience, those symptoms often reveal a battle for the mind. Instead of suggesting new or additional medication, we help people resolve their personal and spiritual conflicts by submitting to God and resisting the devil (James 4:7). You cannot experience the fruit of the Spirit if you are believing a lie, dabbling in the occult, holding on to bitterness, boasting in pride, living in rebellion, or sinning. Those issues must be resolved in order to experience the peace of God.

The minds of those struggling with anxiety disorders are riddled with contaminated thinking and erroneous thoughts about themselves, God, and their circumstances of life. Connecting with God through genuine repentance and renewing our minds to the truth of His Word will result in every born-again Christian experiencing the truth that the "peace of God, which surpasses all comprehension, shall guard your hearts and your minds in Christ Jesus" (Philippians 4:7).

3

Casting All Your Anxiety on Christ

> Said the Robin to the Sparrow, "I should really like to know why these anxious human beings rush about and worry so?"
>
> Said the Sparrow to the Robin, "Friend, I think that it must be that they have no heavenly Father such as cares for you and me."
>
> —Elizabeth Cheney

A husband paces the floor nervously while his wife's surgery drags on...

A single mom stares at the TV, unable to go to bed until her teenage daughter returns from a date...

A little boy cries himself to sleep, worrying if his arguing parents will divorce...

A businessman agrees to keep working overtime to help put his son through college...

An elderly woman calls her daughter...again...just to make sure she's okay.

Christians should be concerned about the welfare of their families, but their own insecurities could lead to excessive control. At one end of the spectrum are those who don't care so they don't worry about others: "Go ahead and jump, I don't care." "So what if people are going to hell; that's their problem." Nobody worries about the things they don't care about. At the other end of the spectrum are those who seem to worry about anything and everyone, but the motivating factor is their own insecurity. They are needy people as we all are. At the center of the spectrum is God who cares so much that He would give His only begotten Son, but He doesn't worry. Why? Because He is omnipotent, and with God all things are possible (Luke 18:27). God is not insecure and neither is the child of God who is alive and free in Christ. Jesus said, "All things are possible to him who believes" (Mark 9:23).

Security in Christ

We can only live at the center of this spectrum when we are secure in Christ. We will be secure in Christ when we know and choose to believe that He will never leave or forsake us (Hebrews 13:5), and when we are confident that He will meet all our needs according to His riches in glory (Philippians 4:19). The most critical needs are the "being needs," and they are the ones that can only be and are most wonderfully met in Christ. The most basic need is spiritual life, and Jesus "came that we may have life, and have it abundantly" (John 10:10). Having a spiritual identity and eternal heritage is also a critical being need. John writes, "But as many as received Him, to them He gave the right to become children of God" (John 1:12) and "see how great a love the Father has bestowed upon us, that we should be called children of God; and such we are" (1 John 3:1). Acceptance, security, and significance are other crucial needs that are met in Christ as follows:

In Christ

I Am Accepted

I am God's child (John 1:12)
I am Christ's friend (John 15:15)

I have been justified (Romans 5:1)
I am united with the Lord and one with Him in spirit (1 Corinthians 6:17)
I have been bought with a price; I belong to God (1 Corinthians 6:20)
I am a member of Christ's body (1 Corinthians 12:27)
I am a saint (Ephesians 1:1)
I have been adopted as God's child (Ephesians 1:5)
I have direct access to God through the Holy Spirit (Ephesians 2:18)
I have been redeemed and forgiven of all my sins (Colossians 1:14)
I am complete in Christ (Colossians 2:10)

I Am Secure

I am free from condemnation (Romans 8:1,2)
I am assured that all things work together for good (Romans 8:28)
I am free from any condemning charges against me (Romans 8:31ff.)
I cannot be separated from the love of God (Romans 8:35ff.)
I have been established, anointed, and sealed by God (2 Corinthians 1:21)
I am hidden with Christ in God (Colossians 3:3)
I am confident that the good work that God has begun in me will be perfected (Philippians 1:6)
I am a citizen of heaven (Philippians 3:20)
I have not been given a spirit of fear, but of power, love, and a sound mind (2 Timothy 1:7)
I can find grace and mercy in time of need (Hebrews 4:16)
I am born of God, and the evil one cannot touch me (1 John 5:18)

I Am Significant

I am the salt and light of the earth (Matthew 5:13)
I am a branch of the true vine, a channel of His life (John 15:1,5)
I have been chosen and appointed to bear fruit (John 15:16)
I am a personal witness for Christ (Acts 1:8)
I am God's temple (1 Corinthians 3:16)
I am a minister of reconciliation (2 Corinthians 5:17ff.)
I am God's coworker (2 Corinthians 6:1)
I am seated with Christ in the heavenly realm (Ephesians 2:6)
I am God's workmanship (Ephesians 2:10)
I may approach God with freedom and confidence (Ephesians 3:12)
I can do all things through Christ who strengthens me (Philippians 4:13)[1]

Jesus fed the hungry, healed the sick, and dined with sinners. When asked why He did that, He responded with an instruction: "Go and learn what this means, 'I desire compassion, and not sacrifice,' for I did not come to call the righteous, but sinners" (Matthew 9:13). Jesus cared because it was His nature to care—and that should be our nature as well. We are motivated by the Spirit of God to love because He first loved us, to be merciful because He has been merciful to us, and to forgive because He has forgiven us. We care because we have been and are being cared for by our heavenly Father.

Peace is the antithesis of anxiety. If you desire peace, you have to pursue the Prince of Peace and learn to live a responsible life dependent upon Him. You can't just do away with anxiety; you *overcome* when you abide in Christ. Everybody desires a peaceful life and to be relatively free from anxiety, but there are limits to what a person can hope for in this world. According to Paul, every believer has eternal peace the moment he or she is born-again: "Therefore having been justified by faith, we have peace with God through our Lord Jesus Christ" (Romans 5:1). What we need is internal peace, and we can have it if we learn to "be anxious for nothing, but in everything by prayer and supplication with thanksgiving let your requests be made known to God. And the peace of God, which surpasses all comprehension, shall guard your hearts and your minds in Christ Jesus" (Philippians 4:6,7). God's peace is present even when we don't fully understand how things will work out. An awareness of an anxious spirit should drive us to find the peace of God by turning to Him and assuming our responsibility to think: "Finally, brethren, whatever is true, whatever is honorable, whatever is right, whatever is pure, whatever is lovely, whatever is of good repute, if there is any excellence and if anything worthy of praise, let your mind dwell on these things" (Philippians 4:8).

Externally we want peace on earth, but we may not always have that. Some things are beyond our right or ability to control. "If possible, so far as it depends on you, be at peace with all men" (Romans 12:18). Let's face it, external peace doesn't always depend upon us. If someone doesn't want to be reconciled with others, it can't be done. But we should always be peacemakers because "blessed are the peacemakers, for they shall be called sons of God" (Matthew 5:9). Keep in mind that our internal peace and sense of worth cannot be based on the external world, which is under *God's* control.

Some insecure people try to resolve their anxieties by attempting to order their external world. They wrongly believe that controlling people and circumstances will accomplish this. They are basing their lives on a false belief. The fruit of the Spirit is "self-control," not spouse-control or child-control or employee-control. The peace of God orders our internal world not our external world. In summary:

Eternal	Peace *with* God	This we have
Internal	Peace *of* God	This we need
External	Peace *on* earth	This we want

The Right Goal

We can't always control the circumstances of life or other people, and, in many cases, we shouldn't even try. The right goal is to become the people God has called us to be. Nothing can grow if there is no life present. Christ is the sanctifying agent who enables us to be like our heavenly Father, and nothing can keep that from happening except ourselves.

Suppose a mother has adopted the goal of having a loving, harmonious, happy Christian family. Who in that family can block that goal? Every member of the family can, and all of them will at some time. But who could block her goal of becoming the mother and wife that God has called her to be? Nobody! She is the only one. It is a legitimate desire to have a happy and harmonious family, but if her identity and sense of worth is dependent upon that, she is going to struggle with a lot of anxiety and become a controller.

This is illustrated by a suit salesman who attended one of our conferences. Afterward, he shared the following delightful story.

> *This has been the most liberating week of my life. I have been a Christian for several years, but I have been a terrible witness to my Jewish boss. I have continuously struggled with anger and anxiety because of the job. My goal was to sell suits, and whenever I didn't make a sale I got mad. I started approaching every day with anxiety. Will I sell my quota or will this be another frustrating day? My boss had to talk to me about my anger and attitude.*

This week I realized that I had the wrong goal. I learned that I was just supposed to be the suit salesman that God called me to be. My previous goal was to sell suits and make money. To accomplish that goal I had learned how to manipulate customers. And to do that, I frequently sold them suits which weren't right for them. This week I started considering the needs of the customer for the first time. I even talked one gentleman out of a sale because it just wasn't right for him.

Last night my boss asked me if I was all right. I was so free from anxiety that he thought I was sick or something. This was the first week I actually enjoyed going to work. Would you believe it, I sold more suits this week than I ever have before.

Where Is Your Treasure?

In the Sermon on the Mount, Jesus teaches that anxious people have two treasures and two visions because they are trying to serve two masters. He goes on to teach that "double-minded" people also worry about tomorrow. Most, if not all, our anxieties can be traced to what we treasure in our hearts and to our lack of faith in God's provision for tomorrow. Jesus said in Matthew 6:19-21 NIV:

> Do not store up for yourselves treasures on earth, where moth and rust destroy, and where thieves break in and steal. But store up for yourselves treasures in heaven, where moth and rust do not destroy, and where thieves do not break in and steal. For where your treasure is, there your heart will be also.

Treasures on earth have two characteristics. First, there is the decay of all things physical, which is the law of entropy. This second law of thermodynamics says that all systems become increasingly disorderly and will eventually decay. If rust doesn't destroy it, then moths or termites will. The American dream for some is to have a cabin in the hills and a boat in the marina. It would take a fair amount of energy to keep both in repair. They would probably experience a lot more peace if they rented a cabin or a boat and let somebody else take care of the repairs. Second, because of the value of earthly treasures, there is always the concern for security. It is hard to be anxiety free if we are worried about our possessions. The more we possess, the more we cause others to covet. This opens the door for fear about thieves breaking in to steal.

Personal security comes from relationships not possessions. It is amazing what we can live without if we have deep meaningful relationships. Even then we can't guarantee human relationships, but we can rely on the promises of God that He will always be there for His children who trust in Him. Mary must have realized this when she and her sister, Martha, entertained Jesus for dinner. Mary chose to sit at the feet of Jesus and hang on His every word. "Martha was distracted with all her preparations; and she came up to Him, and said, 'Lord, do You not care that my sister has left me to do all the serving alone? Then tell her to help me.' But the Lord answered and said to her, 'Martha, Martha, you are worried and bothered about so many things; but only a few things are necessary, really only one, for Mary has chosen the good part, which shall not be taken away from her'" (Luke 10:40-42).

The critical question is, "What do you treasure in your heart?" Be honest. Do you spend much time thinking about earthly treasures? Do you worry about your possessions and compare them with what others have? Do you feel prideful when you have more than others? Do you feel jealous when you have less?

Now ask yourself another question: Which of the present material possessions that you have or long for would you take in exchange for love, joy, peace, patience, kindness, goodness, faithfulness, gentleness, and self-control? A new car? A cabin in the hills? Status at the top of the corporate ladder? A sexy spouse? The tragedy is that many believe these things will give them true happiness. But no material possession or social position can produce the fruit of the Spirit. "Beware, and be on your guard against every form of greed; for not even when one has an abundance does his life consist of his possessions" (Luke 12:15).

There is nothing inherently wrong with owning possessions. It is the *love* of money, not money itself, that is the root of all sorts of evil (1 Timothy 6:10). (There is an exercise at the end of this chapter to help you understand or deal with too much emphasis on materialism. See page 87.) Paul's words in 1 Timothy 6:17-19 give the right orientation and balance:

> Instruct those who are rich in this present world not to be conceited or to fix their hope on the uncertainty of riches, but on God, who richly supplies us with all things to enjoy. Instruct them to do good, to be rich in good works, to be generous and ready to share, storing up for themselves the treasure of a good foundation for the future, so that they may take hold of that which is life indeed.

Single Vision

Jesus said, "The lamp of the body is the eye; if therefore your eye is clear, your whole body will be full of light. But if your eye is bad, your whole body will be full of darkness. If therefore the light that is in you is darkness, how great is the darkness!" (Matthew 6:22,23). Ancient tradition viewed the eyes as the windows through which light entered the body. If the eyes were in good condition, the whole body would receive the benefits that light bestows. But if bad, the whole body would be plunged into the darkness, which breeds disease. An "evil eye" was a Jewish metaphor for a grudging or jealous spirit.

Jesus said, "No one can serve two masters; for either he will hate the one and love the other, or he will hold to one and despise the other. You cannot serve God and mammon. For this reason I say to you, do not be anxious for your life" (Matthew 6:24,25). There will be no peace serving two masters. Our only choice is to decide which master we will serve. Whichever master we choose to serve, by that master we shall be controlled.

Denying Self-Rule

Jesus said, "If anyone wishes to come after Me, let him deny himself, and take up his cross daily, and follow Me" (Luke 9:23). Denying ourselves is not the same as self-denial. Great athletes, politicans, and cult leaders have learned how to deny themselves certain pleasures in order to win or promote themselves and their causes. Self is still the dominate force, the one in charge. Denying self is denying self-rule. God never designed our souls to function as masters. We are either serving God or mammon at any one given time (see Matthew 6:24). We are deceived if we think we are really serving ourselves. Self-seeking, self-serving, self-justifying, self-glorifying, self-centered, and self-confident living are in actuality serving the world, the flesh, and the devil.

We have to die to ourselves in order to live in Christ. We are forgiven because He died in our place. We are delivered because we have died with Him. Paul says, "I have been crucified with Christ; and it is no longer I who live, but Christ lives in me; and the life which I now live in the flesh I live by faith in the Son of God, who loved me, and delivered Himself up for me" (Galatians 2:20). If we hang on to our natural identity and heritage, we rob ourselves of an infinitely better spiritual identity and heritage.

When we pick up our cross daily, we are actually picking up the cross of Christ. There is only one cross. It provides forgiveness for what we have done and deliverance from what we once were—both justification and sanctification.[2] We are new creations in Christ and identified with Him:

in His death (Romans 6:3,6; Colossians 3:1-3)
in His burial (Romans 6:4)
in His resurrection (Romans 6:5,8,11)
in His ascension (Ephesians 2:6)
in His life (Romans 5:10,11)
in His power (Ephesians 1:19,20)
in His inheritance (Romans 8:16,17;
Ephesians 1:11,12)

F.B. Meyer said, "Earthly thrones are generally built with steps up to them; the remarkable thing about the thrones of the eternal kingdom is that the steps are all down to them. We must descend if we would reign, stoop if we would rise, gird ourselves to wash the feet of the disciples as a common slave, in order to share the royalty of our Divine Master."[3] Jesus said, "Follow Me." Self will never cast out self; we have to be led into it by the Holy Spirit. "For we who live are constantly being delivered over to death for Jesus' sake, that the life of Jesus also may be manifested in our mortal flesh" (2 Corinthians 4:11). Here is where we dare not harden our hearts.

The voices from the world, the flesh, and the devil will scream in our minds, "But it seems so austere. God only wants to control me, and I have to give up everything!" Don't believe the lie because nothing could be further from the truth. "For whoever wishes to save his life shall lose it, but whoever loses his life for My sake, he is the one who will save it" (Luke 9:24). The statement is a play on words. Those who seek to find their identity and purpose for living in the natural order of things will some day lose it. No matter how much we accumulate in this lifetime, it will all be burned up in the final judgment. It is nothing but wood, hay, and stubble. We cannot take it with us.

The Call to Sacrifice

It seems to be the great ambition of mankind to be happy as animals instead of being blessed as children of God. The cross calls us to sacrifice the pleasure of things to gain the pleasures of life. If you shoot for this world, you will miss the next. But if you shoot for the next world, God will provide the good things of this world as well as make provision for the next. Paul puts it this way: "Discipline yourself for the purpose of godliness; for bodily discipline is only of little profit, but godliness is profitable for all things, since it holds promise for the present life and also for the life to come. It is a trustworthy statement deserving full acceptance" (1 Timothy 4:7-9).

Gaining the Higher Life

We sacrifice the lower life to gain the higher life. Jesus told the disciples that "the Son of Man must suffer many things, and be rejected by the elders and chief priests and scribes, and be killed, and be raised up the third day" (Luke 9:22). Matthew recorded that, "Peter took Him aside and began to rebuke Him, saying, 'God forbid it, Lord! This shall never happen to You.' But He turned and said to Peter, 'Get behind Me, Satan! You are a stumbling block to Me; for you are not setting your mind on God's interest, but man's'" (Matthew 16:22,23).

This memorable rebuke seems mercilessly severe, yet even the crediting of Satan as the source describes exactly and appropriately the character of the advice given by Peter. "Save yourself at any rate; sacrifice duty to self interest, the cause of Christ to personal convenience." This advice is truly satanic in principle, for the whole aim of Satan is to get self-interest recognized as the chief end of man. Satan is called the "prince of this world" because self-interest rules this fallen world.

Man unwittingly serves Satan because he is deceived into thinking he is serving self. Jesus counters by sharing the way of the cross, the foundational principle for life in Christ, which is the repudiation of our natural lives.

The cross also calls us to sacrifice the temporal in order to gain the eternal. Martyred missionary Jim Elliot said it well: "He is no fool who gives up what he cannot keep in order to gain what he cannot lose." We don't have a lack of money in our western world; we have a lack of contentment. Paul says, "Godliness actually is a means of great gain when accompanied by contentment. For we have brought nothing into the world, so we cannot take anything out of it either. And if we have food and covering, with these we shall be content" (1 Timothy 6:6-8).

Don't Worry About Tomorrow

To help us live anxiety free, Jesus first dealt with our possessions. Now He deals with our provisions. The materialist struggles with the first, the doubter with the second. The real question is whether we trust God. Jesus said:

> For this reason I say to you, do not be anxious for your life, as to what you shall eat, or what you shall drink; nor for your body, as to what you shall put on. Is not life more than food, and the body than clothing? Look at the birds of the air, that they do not sow, neither do they reap, nor gather into barns, and yet your heavenly Father feeds them. Are you not worth much more than they? (Matthew 6:26).

Trusting God for tomorrow is a question of our worth. Birds are not created in the image of God, but we are! Birds will not inherit the kingdom of God, but we will. If God takes care of the birds, so much more will He take care of us. Observe the lilies of the field: "If God so arrays the grass of the field, which is alive today and tomorrow is thrown into the furnace, will He not much more do so for you, O men of little faith? Do not be anxious then" (Matthew 6:30,31).

God lays His own reputation on the line. If we will trust and obey Him, He will provide. This is a question of God's integrity. Does He care for us, and will He provide for our needs? "Your heavenly Father knows that you need all these things.... Therefore do not be anxious for tomorrow; for tomorrow will care for itself. Each day has enough trouble of its own" (Matthew 6:32,34). He is asking us to trust Him and take one day at a time.

The essential will of God is that we live responsibly today by faith and trust God for tomorrow. Are we people of little faith or do we believe the fruit of the Spirit will satisfy us more than earthly possessions? Do we really believe that if we hunger and thirst after righteousness, we shall be satisfied? If we seek to establish God's kingdom, will God supply all our needs according to His riches in glory? If we believe these things, then we will "seek first His kingdom and His righteousness; and all these things shall be added to you" (Matthew 6:33).

The following poem provides a nice summary and also encourages us to take one day at a time.

Today

There are two days in every week about which we should not worry, two days which should be kept free from fear and apprehension.

One of these days is Yesterday with its mistakes and cares, its faults and blunders, its aches and pains. Yesterday has passed forever beyond our control.

All the money in the world cannot bring back Yesterday. We cannot undo a single act we performed; we cannot erase a single word we said. Yesterday is gone.

> The other day we should not worry about is Tomorrow with its possible adversaries, its burdens, its large promise and poor performance. Tomorrow is also beyond our immediate control.
>
> Tomorrow's sun will rise, either in splendor or behind a mask of clouds...but it will rise. Until it does, we have no stake in Tomorrow, for it is yet unborn.
>
> This leaves only one day...Today. Any man can fight the battles of just one day, it is only when you and I add the burdens of those two awful eternities...Yesterday and Tomorrow that we break down.
>
> It is not the experience of Today that drives men mad...it is remorse or bitterness for something which happened Yesterday and the dread of what Tomorrow may bring.
>
> —Author unknown

Casting All Your Cares Upon Christ

People consume alcohol, take street drugs, turn to food, have illicit sex, mindlessly repeat mantras, and escape to cabins, boats, and motor homes to reduce their anxiety. One lady said, "Whenever I feel anxious, I go on a shopping spree!" More prescription drugs are dispensed for the temporary "cure" of anxiety than for any other reason. But when the temporary "cure" wears off, we have to return to the same world with the added problem of the negative consequences of the escape mechanisms.

The *real* Healer has invited us to cast all our anxieties on Him because He cares for us:

> Humble yourselves, therefore, under the mighty hand of God, that He may exalt you at the proper time, casting all your anxiety on Him, because He

> cares for you. Be of sober spirit, be on the alert. Your adversary, the devil, prowls about like a roaring lion, seeking someone to devour. But resist him, firm in your faith, knowing that the same experiences of suffering are being accomplished by your brethren who are in the world (1 Peter 5:6-9).

Prayer is the first step in casting all your anxiety on Christ. Remember Paul's word: "Be anxious for nothing, but in everything by prayer and supplication with thanksgiving let your requests be made known to God" (Philippians 4:6). Turning to God in prayer demonstrates your reliance on Him. We suggest a prayer similar to the following:

> *Dear heavenly Father, I come to You as Your child, purchased by the blood of the Lord Jesus Christ. I declare my dependence upon You, and I acknowledge my need of You. I know that apart from Christ I can do nothing. You know the thoughts and intentions of my heart, and You know the situation I am in from the beginning to the end. Sometimes I am double-minded, and I need Your peace to guard my heart and my mind.*
>
> *I humble myself before You and choose to trust You to exalt me at the proper time in any way You choose. I place my trust in You to supply all my needs according to Your riches in glory and to guide me into all truth. I ask for Your divine guidance so that I may fulfill my calling to live a responsible life by faith in the power of Your Holy Spirit. Search me, Lord, and know my heart and my thoughts. I want to please You and serve You. In Jesus' precious name I pray, amen.*

The *second step* is to resolve any personal and spiritual conflicts you may have. The 1 Peter passage instructed us to humble ourselves before God and resist the devil. In other words, make sure that our hearts are right with God. This is the same instruction James gives: "Submit therefore to God. Resist the devil and he will flee from you" (James 4:7). The purpose is to get radically right with God and eliminate any possible influences of the devil on your mind. Remember, "the Spirit clearly says that in later times some will abandon the faith and follow deceiving spirits and things taught by demons" (1 Timothy 4:1 NIV). You will be a double-minded person if you pay attention to a deceiving spirit. (The "Steps to Freedom in Christ" in the back of this book will help you submit to God and resist the devil, "and the peace of God, which surpasses all comprehension, shall guard your hearts and your minds in Christ Jesus" [Philippians 4:7].)

In our experience, most major anxieties are resolved by these first two steps, but you may still have some anxious thoughts about life events. This is common because a little anxiety motivates us to responsible behavior. If you have successfully completed the first two steps, then work through the following sequence, which is summarized in the anxiety worksheet at the end of the chapter.

The *third step* is to state the problem; a problem well-stated is half solved. In anxious states of mind, people can't see the forest for the trees, so put the problem in perspective. Generally speaking, the process of worrying takes a greater toll on a person than the negative consequences of what they worried about. Many anxious people find tremendous relief by simply having their problems clarified and put into perspective. "Will it matter for eternity?" is the important question.

The danger at this juncture is to seek ungodly counsel. The world is glutted with magicians and sorcerers who promise incredible results. Their appearances may be striking. Their credentials may be impressive. Their personalities may be charming, but their characters are bankrupt. "Do not judge according to appearance, but judge with righteous judgment," Jesus said in John 7:24. "How blessed is the man who does not walk in the counsel of the wicked, nor stand in the path of sinners, nor sit in the seat of scoffers!" (Psalms 1:1).

Fourth, separate the facts from assumptions. People may be fearful of the facts but not anxious. Sometimes we're anxious because we don't know what is going to happen tomorrow. Since we don't know, we make assumptions. A peculiar trait of the mind is its tendency to assume the worst. If the assumption is accepted as truth, it will drive the mind to its anxiety limits: "Through presumption comes nothing but strife" (Proverbs 13:10). Therefore, as best as possible, verify all assumptions.

Fifth, determine what you have the right or ability to control. Your sense of worth is tied only to that for which you are responsible. If you aren't living a responsible life, you should feel anxious. Don't try to cast your responsibility onto Christ; He will throw it back. But do cast your anxiety onto Him because His integrity is at stake in meeting your needs—if you are living a responsible and righteous life.

Sixth, list everything you can do that is related to the situation that is under your responsibility. When people don't assume their responsibilities, they turn to temporary cures for their anxiety. Remember, "the work of righteousness will be peace" (Isaiah 32:17). Turning to an unrighteous solution will only increase your anxiety in the future.

Seventh, follow through and accomplish everything on your list from six. Then commit yourself to be a responsible person and fulfill your calling and obligations in life.

Eighth, once you are sure you have fulfilled your responsibility and you're praying and focusing on the truth, the rest is God's responsibility. Any residual anxiety is probably due to assuming responsibilities that God never intended you to have.

A Prayer to Overcome Materialism

Dear heavenly Father, Your Word says that the love of money is the root of all sorts of evil and that some people, by longing for it, have wandered away from the faith and pierced themselves with many griefs.

I confess that I have longed for money and the things it can buy. I now realize that such longings have hurt my relationship with You and others. I confess that I have treasured earthly possessions in my heart instead of storing up treasures in heaven. I also confess the pride that comes from money and possessions. I have sought temporal security in possessions instead of eternal security in You.

I choose to humble myself before You and trust You to supply all my needs according to Your riches in glory. I am thankful for the way You have supplied my temporal and eternal needs. Teach me to be a good steward of the social position and material possessions You have blessed me with. I now ask You to reveal to my mind any of the ways I have been materialistic, misguided, deceived, unfaithful, controlling, abusive, or falsely driven, including:

1. purchasing material possessions and making them a source of pride and social status instead of storing up treasures in heaven
2. robbing God of His tithes and offerings by selfishly hoarding the money for myself
3. neglecting my family and their spiritual and emotional needs because I believed that striving for material success was more important
4. abusing my family, friends, or coworkers in order to achieve financial or social success

5. succumbing to the stress and anxiety of materialistic pursuits and turning to alcohol, drugs, sex, food, or tobacco to find temporary relief
6. being more concerned about "keeping up with the Joneses" and what people say than about seeking God and discerning His will
7. closing my eyes to the needs of the poor and hardening my heart with a judgmental attitude or critical spirit
8. becoming lukewarm in my love toward God; thinking I am rich and in need of nothing when in reality I am wretched, miserable, spiritually poor, and blind

Lord, I have sinned by (name the sin). *I repent of my sinful ways. I praise You and thank You that I am forgiven of all my sins. Teach me to be content with the food and clothing You provide. I commit myself to seeking You first and to storing up treasures in heaven. I believe that godliness is profitable for this age and the one to come. In Jesus' precious name I pray, amen.*

Overcoming Anxiety Worksheet

1. Go to God in prayer.

2. Resolve all known personal and spiritual conflicts.

3. State the problem.

4. Separate the facts from the assumptions.

   a. Facts relating to the situation.

   b. Assumptions relating to the situation.

   c. Verify the above assumptions.

5. Determine your active response.

   a. What you can control as a matter of personal responsibility.

   b. What you have no right or ability to control.

6. List everything related to the situation that is your responsibility.

7. Follow through on your list of responsibilities. Become accountable to someone for fulfilling your goals.

8. If you have fulfilled your responsibility and continue to walk with God in prayer, according to Philippians 4:6-8, the rest is God's responsibility.

4

The Fear of Man

He that fears you present, will hate you absent.

—Thomas Fuller (1654–17340
Gnomologia

In Hannah Hurnard's classic book *Hinds' Feet on High Places,* the main character, a woman named Much-Afraid, encounters the Shepherd, a picture of Christ. He tenderly places the sharp thorn of Love into her heart and invites her to join Him on a journey into the mountains.

Much-Afraid is thrilled to know that at the end of her journey she will be healed of her lameness and ugliness and will receive love in return. She eagerly accepts the Shepherd's invitation and sets off for her cottage to make preparations for her departure from the Valley of Humiliation.

She is especially excited to go because her relatives, the Fearings, have been pressuring her to stay and marry her cousin Craven Fear, whom she despises. The following excerpt from the book illustrates graphically the terror that can control someone who is in bondage to the fear of man:

> She walked singing across the first field and was halfway over the next when suddenly she saw Craven Fear himself coming toward her. Poor Much-Afraid; for a little while she had completely forgotten the existence of her dreadful relatives, and now here was the most dreaded and detested of them all slouching toward her. Her heart filled with a terrible panic. She looked right and left, but there was no hiding place anywhere, and besides it was all too obvious that he was actually coming to meet her, for as soon as he saw her he quickened his pace and in a moment or two was right beside her.
>
> With a horror that sickened her very heart she heard him say, "Well, here you are at last, little Cousin Much-Afraid. So we are to be married, eh, what do you think of that?" and he pinched her, presumably in a playful manner, but viciously enough to make her gasp and bite her lips to keep back a cry of pain.
>
> She shrank away from him and shook with terror and loathing. Unfortunately this was the worst thing she could have done, for it was always her obvious fear which encouraged him to continue tormenting her. If only she could have ignored him, he soon would have tired of teasing and of her company and would have wandered off to look for other prey. In all her life, however, Much-Afraid had never been able to ignore Fear. Now it was absolutely beyond her power to conceal the dread which she felt.
>
> Her white face and terrified eyes immediately had the effect of stimulating Craven's desire to bait her. Here she was, alone and completely in his power.[1]

Many of us can relate to Much-Afraid's plight. As we read this story we are painfully reminded of times we were bullied (or bullied others) as children. Separated from the protection of parents or friends, we were intimidated into submission by somebody who was bigger, stronger, smarter, or more aggressive.

Maybe the bully was your brother or sister. Sadly, for many it was a parent. Maybe for you it still is. Maybe the one you fear is your boss. Or, more tragically, your spouse. It could even be your own child who has manipulated the reins of household control away from you.

Although we will be confronted by people and situations that frighten us, it is clear from Scripture that we are not to be controlled by the fear of man. Jesus addressed this issue with His disciples:

> A disciple is not above his teacher, nor a slave above his master. It is enough for the disciple that he become as his teacher, and the slave as his master. If they have called the head of the house Beelzebul, how much more the members of his household! Therefore do not fear them, for there is nothing covered that will not be revealed, and hidden that will not be known. What I tell you in the darkness, speak in the light; and what you hear whispered in your ear, proclaim upon the housetops. And do not fear those who kill the body, but are unable to kill the soul; but rather fear Him who is able to destroy both soul and body in hell (Matthew 10:24-28).

Jesus lived in the real world, and He understood the reality of our situation and what people can do to each other. Others can ridicule us, reject us, and ruin our reputations. They can physically harm us and even take our lives (if God allows them to). Jesus experienced all of those things, and yet He was never controlled by the fear of man. He was truly free.

Strongholds of Fear

The fear of God is the one fear that dispels all other (unhealthy) fears. "The fear of man brings a snare, but he who trusts in the LORD will be exalted" (Proverbs 29:25). We are living in bondage if we fear man more than God. What is actually holding us in bondage, though, is our own lack of knowledge and belief in God. The fear of man is a stronghold that must be broken in order for us to experience the freedom to live as Jesus did. Notice how a stronghold of fear was developed in the following testimony.

> *When I was 11, my family moved to an upscale town in New York that was predominantly white. The folks there weren't used to living next to blacks. I remember standing at a water fountain in the sixth grade and having a classmate ask me if I had a tail. I remember walking past a school bus and having a boy hold up a drawing of a man with a noose around his neck and scream that it was me.*
>
> *I recall being so starved for acceptance that I thought it was a compliment when someone told me, "We don't consider you to be a nigger. You're different."*
>
> *Against this backdrop was a dysfunctional home, where my mother filled my head with lies. She told me I was gay because I didn't date. She said I was stupid because my grades stunk. She guaranteed that I would die by the time I turned 16 because my life was so futile.*
>
> *This hostility shaped my view of myself. By the time I was 18, I was so stripped of confidence that I couldn't look a person in the eye. I was filled with doubt, fear and struggled with a poor self-image.*

A deep-seated insecurity and fear of man can form in our lives when negative labels are slapped on to our souls at a young age. Like scarlet letters, these labels broadcast to the world around us our inadequacies (or someone's perception of our faults). A sense of personal shame and inferiority breaks our spirit.

In the testimony above, it is obvious how a young man such as this would fear rejection from people. He experienced the sting of racial slurs. His mother, instead of affirming him, called him gay and stupid and told him his life was futile and that he was doomed to die young. Like a puppy brutally whipped, he learned at an early age that it is easier to steer clear of people and not make waves than it is to risk being ridiculed and rejected.

When I hit puberty, I thought I had contracted a terminal illness. Almost overnight my body declared Civil War against me. My face broke out, my teeth stuck out (so I had to endure the private prison of braces), and my body height and weight in one year went from five feet, six inches and 120 pounds, to six feet and 120 pounds! I wasn't skinny; I was *skeletal.* I became a convenient target for other insecure kids at school who were glad to find someone in worse shape than they were!

At first I tried to fight back against the sneers and rude comments of my peers, but after a while I gave up. Feeling ganged-up on by the world, I withdrew in fear and shame. Tired of walking out of the lunch line and finding no one to eat with in the cafeteria, I chose to bring my lunch to school and eat in a vacant classroom by myself. It was a very sad and lonely time of life. I retreated into my own little world, writing anti-war and anti-injustice poetry. I felt increasingly angry against "the establishment" that had created such an unfair system of acceptance and rejection based on physical appearance.

My fear of rejection by people drove me deeper and deeper into myself. Without Christ, there is only darkness inside. My room became my womb and might have become my tomb if not for Jesus.

Controlled by Human Expectations

My story, and the one preceding it, is an example of how the fear of man can put a stranglehold on the life of a person without Christ. But children of God also reel under the effects of this stronghold as well, especially when we confuse our expectations and what others expect of us with what God expects from us. The following testimony is from a woman in full-time ministry:

> *I was working for a Christian missionary organization in the area of communications, which was my expertise. I, however, was wanting more responsibilities when my leader asked me to assist the director in her assorted duties. I gladly accepted.*
>
> *Within the next six months I personally had taken on the added job of helping local people minister in a nearby country that was spiritually oppressed. It was a needed ministry and one I personally owned in my heart.*
>
> *A few months later I was approached again with the opportunity to add the title of office manager to my plate. I accepted, knowing that I was probably the best person for the job and that there was no one else to take the position since our staff was small at the time.*
>
> *Within another six months my leader approached me again with the idea of being personnel coordinator as well. I accepted, however this time I felt trapped—like I had to take on this added responsibility or let the leadership and the organization down.*
>
> *After working five different jobs for a few months, I conferred with my leader and told him I needed to get rid of some responsibilities because I felt I could not handle them all. I was not doing any of them well.*
>
> *He said I needed to get a handle on time management and left it at that. I felt like, yes, it was my fault that*

I could not handle the jobs given to me. So I cried out to God to help me and went back to all my jobs feeling trapped by the leadership as well as by my own feelings of needing acceptance. If I could do these jobs well, then I would know that I am really accepted by the people over me and also by God. I could not let anybody down. I had taken on a perfectionist outlook. I had to do everything right.

I had to make it work. I worked long, stressful hours every day. I left work feeling inadequate, like I just was not good enough. I never could measure up to my own expectations, much less those of others, and I felt like a failure.

The Courage to Say No

This woman's struggle with saying no is symptomatic of a people-pleaser. People-pleasers are looking for affirmation from others and fear rejection and disapproval. When do we say no to the responsibilities offered to (or dumped on) us by those in authority over us? And when do we submit and simply accept those tasks as from the hand of God? What criteria do we use to gauge our decision to remain with a company or seek employment elsewhere? When are feelings of entrapment the result of our own wrong attitudes or a warning that we are being victimized? Can we trust God to supply all our needs if we lose employment for living righteously?

These are tough questions for those fearing rejection and needing the approval of others. Such Christians are double-minded, "driven and tossed" by the winds of self-doubt. Unless they turn to God or He mercifully intervenes, they will eventually be unable to continue in their positions because of anxiety disorders, physical maladies, or job incompetence. Fortunately, God's merciful intervention was the case for this woman whose testimony concludes:

Finally I was transferred to another part of the world but with the same organization. God had heard my prayer and rescued me. He took me out of a situation I could not handle. It was His grace and mercy.

At this new location, the leadership was very wise and discerning. That first week they saw how burned out and hurt I was. They did not give me any added responsibilities, but gave me love and acceptance. God used this time to bring healing to my heart and soul. He taught me what it meant to be accepted for who I was. I learned to just be.

He loved me in my disappointments and fears and showed me that I didn't have to strive anymore for acceptance from Him or others—that I was wonderful in who He made me to be. I did not have to try and be anything else but me. I came to realize that God loved me for who I was, His daughter, and not because of what I could do for Him.

Only One Legitimate Fear Object

We become subject to the fear of man when we are not secure in the unconditional love and acceptance of God. It is also easy to forget the omnipresence and omnipotence of our invisible God when confronted by various fear objects we can see. That is why we need to worship God. When we ascribe to Him His divine attributes in worship, we are keeping our minds filled with the knowledge of His presence. God drove this point home when He reproved His people through the prophet Isaiah for their faint-heartedness in the face of human enemies:

> I, even I, am He who comforts you. Who are you that you are afraid of man who dies, and of the son of man who is made like grass; that you have forgotten

> the LORD your Maker, who stretched out the heavens, and laid the foundations of the earth; that you fear continually all day long because of the fury of the oppressor, as he makes ready to destroy? But where is the fury of the oppressor? (Isaiah 51:12,13).

In these verses, God presents a stark contrast between man and Himself. The bottom line is that people live and die like grass, and God is the Creator of heaven and earth (including the grass!). Why be afraid of man who may oppress temporarily, when God is the eternal, all-powerful comforter? A fear object has to be potent and present. As long as we live on planet Earth, people will be present. What power do they have over us that cannot be overcome in Christ? None. We may be rejected by people, but we will always be "choice and precious in the sight of God" (1 Peter 2:4).

In our opening story from *Hinds' Feet on High Places*, Much-Afraid took her eyes off the Shepherd and was overwhelmed with Fear. She found help from the All-Powerful One when she cried out in fear and pain:

> [Craven Fear] caught hold of her, and poor Much-Afraid uttered one frenzied cry of terror and pain. At that moment Craven Fear loosed his grip and cringed away.
>
> The Shepherd had approached them unperceived and was standing beside them. One look at his stern face and flashing eyes and the stout Shepherd's cudgel grasped in his strong, uplifted hand was more than enough for the bully. Craven Fear slunk away like a whipped cur, actually running from the village instead of toward it, not knowing where he was going, urged by one instinct alone, to find a place of safety.[2]

Feel the Fear, but Trust in God

Fear of man and faith in God cannot be operative at the same time. We will always struggle with tempting thoughts and fearful feelings, but they do not have to keep us from making the volitional choice to walk by faith in God. That is courage—making the choice to walk by faith and do what's right even in the face of fear. Being alive and free in Christ doesn't mean that we will never feel fear. It means that such fears no longer have any power over us if we exercise our faith in God.

There will be times when you will be afraid or hesitant to speak the truth in love, and the fear of man will motivate you to lie to others. Giving in to those fears will only compound the bondage. Paul admonishes us to "lay aside the old self, which is being corrupted in accordance with the lusts of deceit, and that you be renewed in the spirit of your mind, and put on the new self, which in the likeness of God has been created in righteousness and holiness of the truth. Therefore, laying aside falsehood, speak truth, each one of you, with his neighbor, for we are members of one another" (Ephesians 4:22-25).

If you are afraid to say no, when God has said no, you are a bond-servant of man. The apostle Paul said of himself, "Am I now seeking the favor of men, or of God? Or am I striving to please men? If I were still trying to please men, I would not be a bond-servant of Christ" (Galatians 1:10). You cannot serve two masters. Trying to keep from ruffling the feathers of those around you will cause you to eventually compromise your stand for Christ.

The Courage to Share

Paul preached the gospel of grace knowing that it ran cross-current with the preaching of the Judaizers who wanted to bring new Gentile converts under the yoke of the law. Paul ferociously attacked their false teaching and took some painful shots while protecting the church from heresy. How many believers are scared into silence when they ought to be proclaiming from the rooftops what God has done for them in Christ? How many times do we sense the inner urging of the Spirit of God to witness for Christ, but we keep quiet with the excuse that we don't want to appear pushy, preachy, or insensitive?

Do we value our own safety and security more than the soul of another person? Most of us would emphatically say no, but when an opportunity arises to share our faith we are paralyzed by fear. Where does that fear come from? "God has not given us a spirit of fear, but of power and of love and of a sound mind" (2 Timothy 1:7 NKJV).

Phobias drain our power and make physically strong people feel weak and paralyzed. It takes away love for others and drives us into a whirlpool of self-centeredness. Fear of mankind is mutually exclusive from the love of mankind. Love is self-giving, but fear is self-protecting. Love moves toward others; fear causes us to shrink from others. Fear steals our wisdom and clear thinking and replaces it with confusion and error.

Dr. Bill Bright's personal life and ministry as founder and president of Campus Crusade for Christ is a testimony of the power of the Holy Spirit in witnessing. In his bestselling book *Witnessing Without Fear*, he wrote:

> Witnessing for our Lord is something we all know we should do....Yet witnessing is an activity we frequently shrink from. To intrude in someone else's life seems not only threatening but blatantly presumptuous. We fear offending the other person, fear being rejected, fear doing an inadequate job of representing our Lord and even being branded a "fanatic."[3]

In the chapter "Why More Christians Don't Witness," Dr. Bright suggests three main reasons for believers' timidity in evangelism: spiritual lethargy (not being filled with the Spirit due to sin), lack of proper training, and listening to the devil's lies.[4]

It stands to reason that if the gospel is the power of God for salvation, then the enemy will do all he can to keep God's people from being the ambassadors He has called them to be. Satan is the father of lies, and if we believe him we will keep silent. The truth will set us free, but lies will keep us in bondage.

Some of the specific lying "lines" the enemy tries to feed us, according to Dr. Bright, are:

- Mind your own business—you don't have any right to force your views on someone else.
- You're going to offend this person. Don't say anything.
- That person will think you're a fanatic.
- This person will say no, and you'll be embarrassed.[5]

Notice that each one of the devil's lies is targeted at our own insecurities. We naturally want other people to like and respect us. We feel more comfortable when things are peaceful, free of conflict or controversy. And so far too often we keep quiet...or we talk about everything under the sun except Jesus and our faith in Him.

Peaceful Obedience

I was flying from Miami back to my home in Atlanta. I was exhausted from back-to-back trips (including a trip to China). I had settled down in my window seat, pleased that no one was in the center next to me. I had exchanged some polite conversation with the gentleman in the aisle seat, even mentioning my work in the ministry. He had responded positively, so I concluded that the man was probably a Christian.

I had assumed that the Lord would expect no further conversation out of me. After all, I was tired, the man was reading, and I'd already talked to him. As I thanked God for the snack the flight attendant handed me, I sensed this still, small voice inside saying, "Tell this man about Me."

I wasn't happy at all about God's plan for "disturbing my peace," but I knew I had to follow His leading. I muttered some question like, "So, Bill, is going to church an important part of your family life?" Not exactly an Academy Award-winning opening line, but it was fine with God!

"No, not at all. We haven't really gone to church in a long time. I guess you could call me a kind of modern-day Deist" [one who believes in a God who is distant and uninvolved with humanity since creation].

Silently confessing my hesitancy to obey and my inaccurate discernment of my traveling companion's spiritual condition, I jumped right in. Thirty minutes later I had shared my testimony and presented the gospel. I sensed God wanted me to encourage him to read the Gospel of John to see who Jesus is for himself, something he was willing to do.

I concluded our conversation with a challenge that maybe the God he thought was not involved in his life had in actuality supernaturally put us on the same flight. I had missed the flight I was supposed to be on, while his flight was delayed five hours—just long enough for me to sit two seats away!

As I walked off the plane, I found myself energized, not drained by the conversation. I was filled with peace and joy, knowing that someone living life on an expressway to hell had been shown the exit ramp.

As I look back at that experience, I really had very little to lose by sharing the gospel with the man on the plane. He could have told me that he wasn't interested in talking about God, and I would have felt some disappointment or sadness at his hardness of heart. At worst he may have been a little rude, and I would have felt some embarrassment. But that's about it.

Even though I knew there was much to gain and little to lose, I still had to fight the battle within me to overcome the fear of witnessing. His need to hear the gospel (salvation) was far more important than what I could lose by telling him the truth (temporary deprivation of comfort). Knowing that helped me get over the fear, but Peter shares an even greater means to overcome the fear of witnessing:

> But even if you should suffer for the sake of righteousness, you are blessed. And do not fear their intimidation, and do not be troubled, but sanctify Christ as Lord in your hearts, always being ready to make a defense to everyone who asks you to give an account for the hope that is in you, yet with gentleness and reverence (1 Peter 3:14,15).

What Do We Have to Lose?

How do you find the courage to face fear and do what's right when the stakes are much higher? It is one thing to be embarrassed for a moment by a stranger; it is something much more risky when a job (and its salary or opportunity for advancement) is involved. Even more tenuous is a situation where a close relationship with a loved one is in jeopardy. Or when one's personal health, safety, or life is at stake.

As long as we perceive that somebody or something has the power to destroy anything we value, we will be in bondage to that fear object. And that fear will paralyze us into a life of compromise or withdrawal. The coward always asks, "What do I stand to lose?" The courageous person always asks, "What do I stand to gain?" One sees the risks, the other sees the opportunities. Consider again the courageous example of David in 1 Samuel 17.

King Saul and his warriors were drawn up for battle against the Philistines in the valley of Elah. Each side was stationed on a mountain with the valley in between.

The Philistine warrior, Goliath, all nine feet, nine inches of him, issued a challenge to the Israelites. He would fight a Hebrew soldier one-on-one, and whoever killed his opponent would bring victory for the whole army. And the losing side would serve the winners. Goliath issued his blasphemous challenge to the Israelite army for 40 days. Scripture records the response of God's people: "When all the men of Israel saw the man, they fled from him and were greatly afraid" (1 Samuel 17:24).

The young shepherd boy, David, however, had enough courage to take on the challenge. Armed only with his slingshot and five smooth stones, he prepared for battle. Saul offered his own armor to David, believing the boy needed man's help to win God's battle.

David knew better. In his young life he had already killed a lion and a bear. The giant would be no more trouble than they were, because he knew God was his rescuer. "And David said, 'The LORD who delivered me from the paw of the lion and from the paw of the bear, He will deliver me from the hand of this Philistine'" (1 Samuel 17:37). So David confidently went out to meet Goliath and prevailed over him with a sling and a stone, cutting off the giant's head with his giant sword.

Why was David willing and able to take on Goliath when no one else was? King Saul and his men saw themselves in relation to the giant and trembled. David saw Goliath in relation to God and triumphed. There was no question in the young shepherd's mind that God would deliver this Philistine warrior into his hands.

Could David have been killed? Of course. But that did not seem to even be an issue for David. He knew that his life was ultimately in God's hands, not Goliath's. He valued his relationship with God more than his own life, and, in David's eyes, God's glory was at stake. For him, life was nothing compared to the glory of God, and so there was no other alternative than to fight for the honor and name of his King.

A Higher Calling

To overcome the fear of man we must live for something higher than what Dr. Francis Schaeffer called our "personal peace and affluence." The apostle Paul said, "For to me, to live is Christ, and to die is gain" (Philippians 1:21). Put anything else in the formula and it doesn't work. For to me, to live is my family, to die would be total loss. For to me, to live is my career, to die would be total loss. Being free from the fear of death is not a license to commit suicide; it is a means to live responsibly today. Someone once said, "There is only one life [and] it will soon be past, only what has been done for Christ will last." This way of thinking and living enabled Paul to bear up under horrendous suffering. Consider his litany of afflictions in 2 Corinthians 11:23-26:

> Are they servants of Christ? (I speak as if insane) I more so; in far more labors, in far more imprisonments, beaten times without number, often in danger of death. Five times I received from the Jews thirty-nine lashes. Three times I was beaten with rods, once I was stoned...[in] dangers from robbers, dangers from my countrymen, dangers from the Gentiles, dangers in the city, dangers in the wilderness, dangers on the sea, dangers among false brethren....

Paul explained why he was such an unstoppable force for the gospel, and why he was willing to leave the temporal security of pleasing man to find the eternal security of Christ:

> If anyone else has a mind to put confidence in the flesh, I far more: circumcised the eighth day, of the nation of Israel, of the tribe of Benjamin, a Hebrew of Hebrews; as to the Law, a Pharisee; as to zeal, a persecutor of the church; as to the righteousness which is in the Law, found blameless. But whatever things were gain to me, those things I have counted as loss for the sake of Christ. More than that, I count all things to be loss in view of the surpassing value of knowing Christ Jesus my Lord, for whom I have suffered the loss of all things, and count them but rubbish in order that I may gain Christ... (Philippians 3:4-8).

Using financial terminology, Paul placed everything he humanly was, and worked for, or dreamed of becoming, in the debit column. He wrote it off as pure loss. In the credit column was one thing—to know Christ and become like Him. Paul wanted to become like Jesus in His death. He wanted to be like Him in His resurrection. He was so in love with Jesus that he wanted to experience Christ's sufferings just so he could be more like Him!

Such a man is untouchable, immovable, unshakable, unstoppable. The devil could not deter him from preaching the gospel, and neither could godless people. He was a living, breathing example of what John wrote about in Revelation 12:11: "And they overcame him [the devil] because of the blood of the Lamb and because of the word of their testimony, and they did not love their life even to death."

Freedom from Control and Abuse

As long as we believe that people have something we need for our own physical or psychological well being, we will be dependent upon them and fear the possibility they will withhold it. For example, if you believe you need the love, approval, and acceptance of another person, you will be in some way subject to him or her. I knew a 40-year-old wife and mother of three children who was so afraid of her mother that she would do anything she said. Everything she did was motivated by what her mother would say. She was still trying to win her approval and was afraid that she would be disinherited. She was in bondage because of what she believed.

This kind of dependency makes one a person-servant not a servant of God. Nobody has that right to control our lives; only God has that right. That doesn't mean a husband, a wife, a child, or an employee shouldn't be submissive, but it does mean that nobody can keep you from being the person God has created you to be. It takes a lot of faith and courage to be submissive yet not controlled in abusive situations. Submission is trusting God to work through someone less than perfect—husbands, wives, parents, and employees—and by so doing find favor with God (1 Peter 2:13-17; 3:1-7).

If you are being harassed or abused in the workplace, you need to appeal appropriately to your chain of command for redress. If that is not possible, seeking other employment may become necessary. In any event, trust God to provide and appeal to Him in prayer for guidance. In the case of ongoing abuse in the home, the Lord has provided protection for victims through police and other governmental agencies. (To acquiesce to that abuse, even in the name of submission, is potentially very dangerous for you. You will never help an abuser by allowing him or her to continue in sickness and sin.) Turn the abuser in to responsible authorities. Getting help for yourself and the abuser is the most loving thing you can do.

At times like these, the church ought to provide sanctuary for victims of abuse, even to the point of offering a safe place to go until the danger has passed or the abuse has ceased. Christ wants to manifest His caring presence and protection for the oppressed through His people, the church.

David and Paul had one belief in common—they knew that God was the source of life and that He was their ultimate provision and protection. God does work through people, such as our parents or the police, as a means of meeting our needs and for our protection. But they are not perfect providers and protectors, and when they abdicate their responsibilities we have no recourse but to appeal to the laws of our land and trust God. Like all of us, Paul had to learn by experience:

> At my first defense no one supported me, but all deserted me; may it not be counted against them. But the Lord stood with me, and strengthened me, in order that through me the proclamation might be fully accomplished, and that all the Gentiles might hear; and I was delivered out of the lion's mouth. The Lord will deliver me from every evil deed, and will bring me safely to His heavenly kingdom; to Him be the glory forever and ever. Amen (2 Timothy 4:16-18).

You might be saying, "But I'm not David or the apostle Paul." True enough. Neither are we. But we are alive "in Christ," and empowered by the Spirit of God to live by faith:

> For you have been called for this purpose, since Christ also suffered for you, leaving you an example for you to follow in His steps, who committed no sin, nor was any deceit found in His mouth; and while being reviled, He did not revile in return; while suffering, He uttered no threats, but kept entrusting Himself to Him who judges righteously (1 Peter 2:21-23).

Jesus was able to endure harsh treatment at the hands of evil men because "He kept entrusting Himself to Him who judges righteously." That is the primary means by which we overcome the fear of man. Remember, in order for fear to be legitimate an object must be present and potent (able to harm us). We overcome the fear of man by removing just one of those two attributes.

We cannot avoid the presence of people and fulfill our calling to be the salt of the earth and light of the world. We are ambassadors for Christ. But we can overcome the power that we are inclined to think they have over us. We do that by placing ourselves completely and unreservedly in the hands of the One who has promised to provide for us and protect us. The psalmist cried out to God, "From my distress I called upon the LORD; the LORD answered me and set me in a large place. The LORD is for me; I will not fear; what can man do to me?" (Psalm 118:5,6).

Despite the power that Pharaoh had to cruelly afflict the Israelites, Moses was not afraid of him. Hebrews 11:27 says, "By faith he left Egypt, not fearing the wrath of the king; for he endured, as seeing Him who is unseen." That is bottom line faith: confidence that the God we cannot see is far greater than the people we can.

Overcoming the Fear

As we conclude this chapter, we encourage you to do some prayerful soul-searching. Ask the Lord to show you any fears that you have of man and why. Pray that He would reveal the nature of the hold people have over you. In what way(s) are you finding it hard to entrust yourself to Him who judges righteously? Let Psalm 56:1-9 provide a framework for freedom from the fear of man:

> Be gracious to me, O God, for man has trampled upon me; fighting all day long he oppresses me. My foes have trampled upon me all day long, for they are many who fight proudly against me. When I am afraid, I will put my trust in Thee. In God, whose word I praise, in God I have put my trust; I shall not be afraid. What can mere man do to me? All day long they distort my words; all their thoughts are against me for evil. They attack, they lurk, they watch my steps, as they have waited to take my life. Because of wickedness, cast them forth, in anger put down the peoples, O God! Thou hast taken account of my wanderings; put my tears in Thy bottle; are they not in Thy book? Then my enemies will turn back in the day when I call; this I know, that God is for me.

The *first* thing we do about anything is go to God in prayer. Tell Him openly and honestly who you are afraid of. He already knows, but you need to be in agreement with Him. Ask Him for wisdom to discern why you are afraid.

Second, make sure you are right with your heavenly Father. Have you resolved all your personal and spiritual conflicts? Are you more afraid of the voice of man than you are of the voice of God? What fear objects have you elevated above the fear of God? It is not a sin to feel afraid, but if the fear of man is controlling you then God is not.

Third, worship God for who He is. Ascribe to Him His divine attributes of omnipotence and omnipresence. Acknowledge the truth of His Word. Thank Him for His unconditional love and acceptance and for His promise of provision and protection.

Fourth, make an honest assessment of what harm people can do to you. This is where life is tested. Either God is able to make up for what others have taken away or He isn't. If you believe He is more than able to meet your needs, you can walk by faith even in the face of man's cruelty. If you doubt that He can or will, then fear will rule.

Fifth, remember that none of your pain or suffering has gone unnoticed by your Father in heaven. He knows your needs and hears your prayers.

Finally, stand firm in your faith knowing that God is for you. You are His child. He will not allow you to be tempted [tested] beyond what you are able, but will always provide the way of escape so that you may be able to endure (see 1 Corinthians 10:13). Entrust yourself into His hands, for He truly judges righteously. Nothing can separate you from the love of God:

> What then shall we say to these things? If God is for us, who is against us? He who did not spare His own Son, but delivered Him up for us all, how will He not also with Him freely give us all things?
>
> Who will bring a charge against God's elect? God is the one who justifies; who is the one who condemns? Christ Jesus is He who died, yes, rather who was raised, who is at the right hand of God, who also intercedes for us.
>
> Who shall separate us from the love of Christ? Shall tribulation, or distress, or persecution, or famine, or nakedness, or peril, or sword?
>
> Just as it is written, "For Thy sake we are being put to death all day long; we were considered as sheep to be slaughtered."
>
> But in all these things we overwhelmingly conquer through Him who loved us. For I am convinced that neither death, nor life, nor angels, nor principalities, nor things present, nor things to come, nor powers, nor height, nor depth, nor any other created thing,

> shall be able to separate us from the love of God, which is in Christ Jesus our Lord (Romans 8:31-39).

David won his battle against Goliath. The apostle Paul fought the good fight, but was eventually martyred for his faith. They are both with Jesus in heaven. Church history is filled with the stories of martyrs who overcame the fear of man, but be assured that God will always make it right in the end for those who put their trust in Him. You need to know that victory over fear is ours in Christ. We don't have to give the fear of man control in our lives. Here's a story of victory over the fear of man that probably saved a marriage.

> *Seven years after I became a Christian I was sitting in a church service and the pastor asked a question: "Is there anyone else here that would like to follow Jesus in obedience through baptism?"*
>
> *That was the beginning of my real fear. It meant getting up in front of the congregation, giving a testimony of how I became a believer, and then getting immersed in a tank. Getting immersed wasn't the problem. Speaking in front of the congregation was a minor problem. But losing my wife was a major problem.*
>
> *As it turned out, my wife wouldn't even attend. She was upset that I was becoming a clone like all the other people in that church. At least that was her viewpoint.*
>
> *Well, the day came, and I was very scared to say the least. But I knew courage was needed, and I would have to get through it to get it over with.*
>
> *I was very blessed that God gave me boldness to share my faith from then on. No one could shut me up!*
>
> *And then the real fears began.*
>
> *I had started a business, and we were looking forward as a family to the American Dream—earning a*

million dollars. Then things started to go very badly in the business because I shared my faith with a customer. He became very angry with me for leaving my old church. The next thing I knew he took away the business he was giving us, which was one third of our revenue.

We were doing over a million dollars in business that year.

Again, fear struck. I was afraid I would lose my job, house, and family. Several people prayed for me and though I did lose the business, God gave me a better job with less working hours and more pay.

As I was progressing along in my Christian walk, a friend of mind told me to share something with my wife. You see, our marriage started getting worse because of my walk with Christ. She didn't want any part of it. He said that I needed to confront her with this question the next time she started to criticize me about Jesus.

Well, I told him, "You are crazy! She will just want a divorce this time."

Again, fear developed very strongly.

The question was, "Why do you reject Jesus?" I said that would be all I needed to do. She would ask for a divorce.

Sure enough, that night she started criticizing me about my faith. I asked her the question and as expected she said it was about time for a divorce—the thing I dreaded most to hear.

But she started listening to me that night and started to read her Bible!

To make a long story short, within one month she received the Lord and has been as committed as I am (and sometimes much more!).

As I was reflecting on this two years ago when I was reading your book The Bondage Breaker, *God showed me what the root of my fears was during a prayer time. When I was eight years old I was awakened suddenly in bed with an intense fear. I thought a snake was in bed with me. I was paralyzed for a moment until I had the courage to count to three and bolt out of bed and back into the living room where my parents were.*

Naturally, they came back into the room with a flashlight to show me nothing was there. But do you see the correlation: i.e. snake and Satan? The fears don't come back much anymore, but when they do, because of your ministry, I know now I have the authority in Christ to send them away, using the Word of God as my sword. Thanks for being faithful to help us live free in Christ.

5

The Fear of Death

He lives, he wakes—'tis Death is dead, not he.

—Percy Bysshe Shelley
Adonais XLI

In Ernest Becker's Pulitzer Prize-winning *Denial of Death*, he writes, "The fear of death haunts the human animal like nothing else; it is the mainspring of human activity."[1]

In a recent article in *USA Weekend* magazine, the results of a scientific poll revealed what Americans fear. Over 1000 adults were surveyed. The results are fascinating in that most of the fears are related to the fear of death (most of the rest involved financial fears):

54%	Being in a car crash
53%	Having cancer
50%	Inadequate Social Security
49%	Not enough money for retirement

36% Food poisoning from meat
35% Getting Alzheimer's
34% Pesticides from food
33% Being a victim of individual violence
32% Inability to pay current debts
30% Exposure to foreign viruses
28% Getting AIDS
25% Natural disasters
24% Unsafe or sick building
23% Losing job
22% Being in a plane crash
21% Suffering a work-related injury
20% Stock market crash
18% Being a victim of mass violence[2]

Surveys like these are somewhat reflective of current events. Being a victim of mass violence, for example, would have been much higher on the list if the survey had been taken right after the bombing of the Federal Building in Oklahoma City. Fearing natural disasters would be higher in areas recently struck by tornadoes, earthquakes, or floods.

People are afraid of dying. Nine out of ten Americans believe the world is less safe than when they were growing up. Forty percent feel unsafe taking a walk alone at night within a half mile of home. Seven out of ten have taken some precaution to ensure their safety within the past year (locking their cars while inside them, locking windows at home, avoiding certain foods, avoiding chatting with people on the Internet).[3]

The younger generation seems to be feeling this angst regarding death even more acutely. For example, almost half the adults between ages 18 to 24 think they have been stalked by a stranger in the past year, a much higher percentage than older adults.[4] Forty-nine percent of teenagers in 1997 were worried about dying, as opposed to just 38 percent in 1988.[5]

A telephone survey of 1017 preteens randomly selected nationwide showed that 51 percent of them were "very" or "somewhat" concerned about their own death, and 65 percent were worried about their parents' deaths.[6] A Kaiser Permanente and Children Now poll showed that 42 percent of 11- to 17-year-olds are worried that they may die young as a result of violence.[7]

Such fears are not totally unfounded. Surveys show that 1 in 20 high school students have at some time carried a gun to school because they fear being attacked.[8] The statistics don't reveal how many students who carry weapons are in such a mental and emotional state that they might precipitate such an attack. Recent school shootings and uncovered plots to target other students or teachers have only accentuated fears.

What has contributed to this growing phenomenon of the fear of death in America? Ernest Becker describes "the emergence of man as we know him: a hyperanxious animal who constantly invents reasons for anxiety, even when there are none."[9] How have we become a nation of worriers, especially as it relates to the fear of dying? Gavin de Becker, author of the bestseller *The Gift of Fear*, puts it this way:

> Worry is the fear that we manufacture, and those who choose to do it certainly have a wide range of dangers to dwell upon. Television in most major cities devotes up to 40 hours a day [sic] to telling us about those who have fallen prey to some disaster and to exploring what calamities may be coming next. The local news anchor should begin each evening's broadcast by saying, "Welcome to the news; we're surprised you made it through another day. Here's what happened to those who didn't." Each day, we learn what the new studies reveal: "Cellular phones can kill you"; "The dangers of debit cards";

"Contaminated turkey kills family of three. Could your family be next?"[10]

There is no question that media sensationalism has burdened each new generation in America with an increasingly unbearable load of fearful images: violent crime scenes (and violent crimes in progress!), airplane crash footage, teary-eyed disaster victims picking through wreckage, and so on. Like prophets of doom, each newscast would not be caught dead without its share of wailing sirens and flashing police lights. And that doesn't even include the prime-time TV shows and day-time talk shows!

Not surprisingly, over 90 percent of people have some fear of flying, and more than 35 million Americans avoid airplanes altogether.[11] Every hour on prime-time TV there are three murders, according to studies done by Dr. George Gerbner, director of Philadelphia's Cultural Indicators Research Project.[12] Crime-related news stories more than tripled during the first half of the 90s, even though our nation's crime rates have remained about the same or decreased slightly, according to the Center for Media and Public Affairs in Washington, D.C.[13] During that same period, murder stories on the evening news shows of the three main networks have increased ninefold![14]

The media must own up to some responsibility for fostering a national environment of fear. But they are only responding to the viewers' curiosity who want to see and hear the bad news. People watch car racing with the anticipation of seeing a wreck. Sporting analysts capture all the disasters of the day along with a few highlights in their five-minute segments on the nightly news. They wouldn't show it if people didn't watch. We can't help but develop a greater sense of fear if that is what we continue to subject ourselves to.

Gerbner tracked "heavy viewers" of TV (more than three hours daily) and "light viewers" (two hours or less). He found that the "heavy viewers" were 5 to 15 percent more likely to view the world as hostile.[15] The fear of death, though exacerbated by a market-driven media, is by no means a recent phenomenon. The writer of Hebrews spoke to that issue nearly 2000 years ago:

> Since then the children share in flesh and blood, [Christ] likewise also partook of the same, that through death He might render powerless him who had the power of death, that is, the devil; and might deliver those who through fear of death were subject to slavery all their lives (Hebrews 2:14,15).

What is true today in the twentieth century was also true in the first century—and every century since the fall of man. People are in bondage to the fear of death unless they have eternal life in Christ Jesus, who holds the keys of death and Hades (Revelation 1:18). The following story illustrates how the fear of death can shackle a believer in Christ, and how the truth and power of Christ delivers from that fear:

> *I am 30 years old. When I was five my mother and father took me to a witch doctor to help cure my nosebleeds. My parents were to say a few prayers and then place a silver coin on my forehead. Shortly after the nosebleeds ended I became obsessed with dying. A tremendous fear came over me that would not subside.*
>
> *I accepted the Lord when I was 25. Two years ago the fear of dying came back full force after giving my testimony at a women's Bible study sharing day. The fear was oppressive.*
>
> *Every day I chose clothes to wear that I thought would be my death clothes. How was I going to die? The thoughts in my mind were petrifying. I would die and my*

three-year-old would grow up without a mom. I would die and my husband would marry a beautiful blonde.

Where were these thoughts coming from? I asked God to remove this fear.... I became familiar with all the "fear" Bible verses. It was so overwhelming...I thought I was going crazy.

I came across The Bondage Breaker...*I was in bondage. I remember crying out to God to show me what was holding me back. I prayed the prayers...and when I came to the part of renouncing my sexual sins I tried to envision every man I had ever had sex with...what they looked like or what their name was.... I prayed for these men.... I prayed that their names were written in the Lamb's book of life.... I felt the fear leaving me...the fear of being unworthy to stand before God...the fear of getting AIDS...the fear of dying.*

This may sound funny but with every prayer I almost felt a poof coming out of my mind. Then I slowly asked the Lord why this fear had plagued me for so long...and I remembered long ago going to the witch doctor...that, to this day, my mom claims was a man of God.

I truly believe that a curse was placed on my life when I was five. I lived 28 years infested with fear. I didn't care how I lived and became a loose woman because I was sure I would never live to see the consequences.

Thanks be to God from whom all blessings flow and that there truly is freedom in Christ.

There are many origins for the fear of death. The woman in the testimony above was vulnerable due to the aftereffects of an occult "healing" in childhood. The enemy had gained a foothold in her life through the witch doctor's activity. The devil often operates that way. When you turn to him for help, you may get temporary relief in one area but a worse bondage in another. The demonic presence was obviously infuriated by this woman's public witness for Christ and sought to shut it down by intimidation.

Other people struggle with the fear of death because of close calls with dying. John, a missionary bush pilot in Africa, had two close calls while flying his plane. He became agoraphobic. By the end of his first term on the mission field, he was barely able to leave the house for any reason. The seeds of fear were planted early in life, as his testimony reveals.

> *After so many years of deception that held me in bondage and fear, I am set free in Christ. Praise His name.*
>
> *At age 14, my hobby was amateur radio. I enjoyed tuning across the bands and finding faraway stations. When the lights out time came, I would turn the amateur radio off, get in bed, plug in an earphone to my AM radio and continue listening for faraway broadcast stations.*
>
> *In time I located a station in New York state. At 10 P.M. I heard their news, station ID, and the introduction to the next program, the CBS Radio Mystery Theater. From that night on for the next four years I was hooked to that program, falling asleep with images of suspense and fear flooding my mind. If only I had known what I was setting myself up for.*
>
> *Sometime thereafter a voice began to tell me just when the phone would ring and who was on the other end without fail.*
>
> *I was also able to tell my parents secret habits about people that I knew to be true, even when meeting an individual for the first time. Sometime in the future, often years later, my folks would remark to each other and ask me, "How did you know?"*

> *After I received my driver's license the same voice would tell me where the speed traps were on the interstate. My mom once told me that during my years at Bible school I was blessed with tremendous spiritual insight because of all the things I knew and could do. Spiritual insight is right; however, [it was] the wrong kind.*
>
> *Not always did the voice tell me truth. The voice would actually become rough and tell me to burn my arms with my soldering iron or poke out my eye with a screwdriver. When I would climb my radio tower to repair antennas at 100 feet, the voice would often tell me to jump off.*
>
> *The battle for my mind at those moments while on the tower was so intense that just trying to keep safety and good practice in the front of my mind would cause great debilitating fear.*
>
> *This same fear began motivating my daily activities. Although the voice in my head would often tell me that I was stupid, ugly, dumb, fat and would never amount to anything, 90 percent of the time it told the truth. So I just kept listening to it.*

John found his freedom in Christ when he finally realized that the "voice" was not God at all (as he sometimes thought), but the voice of the enemy. The devil, who once held the power of death, is obsessed with death and dying. And he delights in overwhelming people, even God's people, with the fear of death. He was tormenting John until he renounced two spirit guides. One was passed down from his paternal grandmother, and the other had gained entrance during his addiction to scary radio stories.

I had the opportunity to see John six months after he went through the "Steps to Freedom in Christ," and he was a changed man. Controlling fear was ancient history for him. When he went back to Africa to collect his possessions (for transition back to America), he told me he had more ministry in the lives of people in those two weeks than he'd had in the three years prior to his furlough! People were so amazed by the changes in his life that he would stay up till two or three o'clock in the morning sharing what God had done for him!

The fear of death seems to center on four main issues. We will address each of these areas of fear from a biblical standpoint. These fears involve the following:

1. The fear of dying and going to hell. People who fear they have committed the unpardonable sin would also fall into this category.
2. The fear of dying and leaving loved ones behind.
3. The fear of loved ones dying.
4. The fear and horror about the actual dying process (the fear of being brutally murdered, experiencing terrible pain).

Salvation Conquerors Death

All those who have never repented of their sins and received the Lord Jesus Christ as Savior by faith should be afraid of death! We were all born dead in our trespasses and sins (Ephesians 2:1). Salvation is a free gift from God's grace, but, like any gift, it must be received (John 1:12; Romans 5:17). God's forgiveness is received by faith, not by good works (Ephesians 2:8,9). No amount of spiritual devotion or pious practices will earn us a place in heaven. We cannot save ourselves. Jesus paid the penalty for our sins when He died on the cross. His resurrection made possible our new spiritual and eternal life in Him. Our responsibility is to humbly admit our helpless state as sinners in need of a rescuing Savior, and trust in Jesus to forgive our sins and give us life.

The moment we receive the Lord Jesus as Our Savior, we become children of God. We are chosen and adopted into His family. We become new creations in Christ. The old has passed away and new things have come! All this He does to the praise of the glory of His grace.

Therefore, we dare not neglect so great a salvation. The Word of God brings good news but also a stern warning: "He who believes in the Son has eternal life; but he who does not obey the Son shall not see life, but the wrath of God abides on him" (John 3:36). There is a heaven to be gained and a hell to be shunned. Have you made the decision to trust only in Jesus Christ as your Lord and Savior?

It is not enough to believe in who Jesus was or is. Nor is it enough to feel a sentimental attraction to Him or go to church or even perform some religious practice. The Bible is clear: You must make a definite decision to receive Him into your life and trust only in Him for your salvation. If you have never made that decision, we urge you to do so right now. Today is the day of salvation (see Hebrews 3:15, 2 Corinthians 6:2).

"Whoever will call upon the name of the Lord will be saved" (Romans 10:13). "But as many as received Him, to them He gave the right to become children of God, even to those who believe in His name" (John 1:12). You can make that decision right now by expressing the following prayer in faith, choosing to turn from your sin and receive Jesus Christ as Lord and Savior. We encourage you to pray out loud:

> *Dear Lord Jesus, I thank You that You loved me so much that You gave Your life on the cross for my sins. You shed Your precious blood to forgive and cleanse me. I confess that I have sinned, and I am in need of Your saving grace. I acknowledge my need for You because I cannot save myself. I renounce all attempts to work my way to heaven or earn Your approval through religious devotion or rituals.*

I now open my heart to You, Jesus, and receive You as my Savior and Lord. I believe that You defeated death by rising from the dead on the third day. I thank You that You have given me eternal life. Give me a new heart and spirit within me. Lead me into all truth so that I will have no fear of death.

Thank You, Lord, for Your forgiveness and my new life in You as Your child. In Jesus' name I pray, amen.

If you were sincere in making your decision through prayer, you can be sure that the Lord God heard and answered. You can also be assured of your salvation: "These things I have written to you who believe in the name of the Son of God, in order that you may know that you have eternal life. And this is the confidence which we have before Him, that, if we ask anything according to His will, He hears us" (1 John 5:13,14).

There is simply no other way to escape the fear of dying and going to hell than through Jesus. He physically died and was temporarily separated from God so that we would not have to be. And now He is seated at the right hand of our heavenly Father, and He has prepared a place for us in eternity. One day He will come back for us (John 14:1-3).

The moment you chose to receive Christ, He took up residence in your life. Salvation is "Christ in you, the hope of glory" (Colossians 1:27). His Spirit will bear witness with your spirit that you are a child of God (Romans 8:16). Spiritual life means that your soul is in union with God. You are "in Christ" and Christ is in you. Being spiritually alive in Christ is the one definitive issue that constitutes salvation according to 1 John 5:11,12: "And the witness is this, that God has given us eternal life, and this life is in His Son. He who has the Son has the life; he who does not have the Son of God does not have the life."

Did you just ask the Son of God to come into your life? Then you have eternal life right now! God wants you to have the assurance of eternal life. Make the basis of your faith the unshakable truth of God's Word, and not the shaky ground of feelings or personal opinions. Here are two more encouraging Scripture passages that proclaim the believer's victory over death and hell!

> O death, where is your victory? O death, where is your sting? The sting of death is sin, and the power of sin is the law; but thanks be to God, who gives us the victory through our Lord Jesus Christ (1 Corinthians 15:55-57).
>
> Jesus said to her, "I am the resurrection and the life; he who believes in Me shall live [spiritually] even if he dies [physically], and everyone who lives and believes in Me shall never die" (John 11:25,26).

Unless Christ comes back first, all of us will die physically. But in Christ, none of us will die, spiritually. Eternal life is not something you get when you die. In fact, if you don't have spiritual life before you physically die, you will face nothing but hell. We will separate from our physical bodies when we die and be instantly in the presence of God. Paul says, "We walk by faith, not by sight—we are of good courage, I say, and prefer rather to be absent from the body and to be at home with the Lord" (2 Corinthians 5:7,8).

Remember our formula for conquering fear? To eliminate a fear object, only one of its attributes must be eliminated. Physical death is still imminent, "inasmuch as it is appointed for men to die once and after this comes judgment" (Hebrews 9:27). But God has overcome the power of death. It is no longer potent "in Christ."

The Unpardonable Sin

Despite all the biblical assurances to the contrary, many believers struggle with the fear that they have committed an unforgivable sin. This is a critical matter to resolve since one of the pieces of the armor of God is the helmet of salvation (see Ephesians 6:17). Those who are tormented by this fear usually suffer in silence. They think they have committed the unpardonable sin by blaspheming the Holy Spirit. Usually this fear is born out of ignorance or it is an attack of the enemy. The passage under consideration is Mark 3:22-30:

> And the scribes who came down from Jerusalem were saying, "He is possessed by Beelzebul," and "He casts out the demons by the ruler of the demons." And He called them to Himself and began speaking to them in parables. "How can Satan cast out Satan? And if a kingdom is divided against itself, that kingdom cannot stand. And if a house is divided against itself, that house will not be able to stand. And if Satan has risen up against himself and is divided, he cannot stand, but he is finished!
>
> But no one can enter the strong man's house and plunder his property unless he first binds the strong man, and then he will plunder his house. Truly I say to you, all sins shall be forgiven the sons of men, and whatever blasphemies they utter; but whoever blasphemes against the Holy Spirit never has forgiveness, but is guilty of an eternal sin"—because they were saying, "He has an unclean spirit."

It is the unique work of the Holy Spirit to draw people to Christ. Those who come to Christ are the children of God, and their sins and blasphemies are forgiven because they are in Christ. That is why no Christian can commit the unpardonable sin. If you reject the witness of God's Spirit, then you never come to Christ in the first place. Standing in front of the scribes and

Pharisees was the Messiah—Jesus, the Son of God—and they attributed His ministry of delivering people from demonic bondage to the devil. They even accused Jesus of being possessed by Satan! They totally rejected the witness of the Spirit.

We have talked with many believers who question their salvation and are under heavy conviction. The very fact that they are feeling convicted for their sins is the best evidence that they are Christians or the Holy Spirit is convicting them of their sinful nature and leading them to salvation. This is further evidence that they have not committed the unpardonable sin. If the Holy Spirit was not at work in them, their sins wouldn't even be bothering them.

The devil is an accuser. He is like a prosecuting attorney deceptively seeking to discredit and discourage a witness on the stand. He points his slimy finger and says, "Aha! You've done it now! There's no hope for you. You've blasphemed the Holy Spirit!" Perhaps you have questioned some spiritual gift, anointed preacher, or apparent supernatural manifestation. Is that blaspheming the Holy Spirit? Of course not. In fact, it could be necessary discernment. Listen to John's instruction: "Beloved, do not believe every spirit, but test the spirits to see whether they are from God; because many false prophets have gone out into the world" (1 John 4:1). A Christian can grieve the Holy Spirit and even quench the Holy Spirit, but that is not unpardonable (see Ephesians 4:30; 1 Thessalonians 5:19).

The Bible says "there is therefore now no condemnation for those who are in Christ Jesus" (Romans 8:1). There is a heaven and hell difference between the Holy Spirit's conviction and the devil's accusations. If you come under the conviction of the Holy Spirit and repent, it is over with. But if the devil accuses you and you believe his lies, it never ends—no matter how many times you confess or try to repent. Satan accuses the brethren day and night (Revelation 12:10). Such accusing and condemning thoughts are not from the Lord.

To resolve this, *first* you need to know the truth. *Second*, if those accusing thoughts continue, it may be due to some unresolved personal or spiritual conflicts. (In that case, go through the "Steps to Freedom in Christ" at the end of his book.) *Third*, you must learn to take every thought captive to the obedience of Christ (2 Corinthians 10:5). *Fourth*, express the following personalization of Colossians 2:13-15 in prayer:

> When I was dead in my transgressions and the uncircumcision of my flesh, He made me alive together with Him, having forgiven me all my transgressions, having canceled out the certificate of debt consisting of decrees against me, which was hostile to me. And He has taken it out of the way, having nailed it to the cross. When He disarmed the rulers and authorities, He made a public display of them, having triumphed over them through Him.

Leaving Loved Ones Behind

Probably every parent at one time or another has been confronted by this fear. The reality that our own lives are like "a vapor that appears for a little while and then vanishes away" means we must adequately prepare for the possibility that our deaths may precede our loved ones.'

Ultimately, freedom from this fear comes from realizing that all things, even our loved ones, belong to God. Life is an entrustment, and He requires us to be good stewards of what He has given to us (1 Corinthians 3:23–4:2). That should motivate us to be responsible people, but it shouldn't create a paranoia about things we cannot control. Our heavenly Father knows our needs and He watches over those He loves.

Jesus clearly warned His disciples that He was not going to be physically on earth for long (Matthew 16:21)—and neither are we. We need to develop an eternal perspective of life, not a temporal one. The psalmist said, "Precious in the sight of the LORD is the death of His godly ones" (Psalm 116:15). That verse does not make sense from a temporal perspective, but it makes all the sense in the world from an eternal perspective. Those who have physically died in Christ are with Him, and they are far better off than when they were here.

But what about those we leave behind? To be a good steward, we should make plans for our own impermanence. It is wise to have a will drawn up that clearly indicates how your money and possessions will be distributed when you die. Clear plans should be laid out regarding who becomes the caregivers for minor children or dependent adults in the case of death. Life insurance policies should be kept accurate so that beneficiaries are up-to-date. Above all else, talk about it. Physical death is a reality of life. The person who is free from the fear of death is free to live a responsible life today.

Finally, you must entrust your loved ones to the care of Your heavenly Father, and do it now. Our children and loved ones do not belong to us. It is only while we are living that we can help connect our loved ones to the Lord. By so doing, we invest wisely for the future, maximizing the days that are ordained for us. And then, by God's grace, we will be ready to go when He calls us home. The apostle Paul preferred to be with the Lord, but he decided to be a good steward of the time allotted to him until God called him home. His example encourages us to do the same:

> For to me, to live is Christ, and to die is gain. But if I am to live on in the flesh, this will mean fruitful labor for me; and I do not know which to choose. But I am hard-pressed from both directions, having the desire to depart and be with Christ, for that is very much better; yet to remain on in the flesh is more necessary for

> your sake. And convinced of this, I know that I shall remain and continue with you all for your progress and joy in the faith... (Philippians 1:21-25).

The Fear of Loved Ones Dying

The loss of a child may be one of the most devastating experiences that anyone could go through. It must be, since the number one social response is the divorce of the parents. The following testimony reveals the fear and pain of parenting:

> *My greatest fear is no different than any other parent...the fear of losing a child. I was always afraid that something may happen to them and I would not know it...I could not help them.*
>
> *In November of 1975, I became a mother, never to be the same.... How I loved that child...a beautiful little boy, Michael Jon. I knew if I held on too tight he would not be able to grow...that I would smother him.*
>
> *How hard it is to let go, to let them fall, scrape their knees, to take those first steps. If you think about it, fear is very much a part of motherhood.*
>
> *It reached a point when he was 20 years old, with a smile that would melt your heart...a zest for life...I had to say, "Lord, if You can move mountains, You can take care of this boy."*

This mother's faith was strong and her trust in the Lord complete. But ultimately the decision to follow Christ lies with each one of us. Unfortunately, this young man chose not to lean on the Lord for strength and understanding during a hard time in his life. He took his own life October 20, 1996.

It was two years after her son's suicide that this dear woman bravely shared her testimony of pain with us. She has endured more anguish in those 24 months than most people suffer in a lifetime. Her ability to go on with life and even write so openly about her grief is testimony to the healing grace of God.

Life is a gift, a responsibility, a stewardship over which God has given us a measure of oversight, but not ultimate control. If we choose to follow Christ and accept Him as our Lord and Savior, He watches over us. We aren't guaranteed physical immortality—all of us will eventually die. But we are guaranteed eternal life if we accept Jesus' sacrifice for us and follow Him. He appoints the time of our birth and the time of our death.

It was not fatalism but bottom-line faith that moved Job to say, after the death of his children and the loss of his health, "Naked I came from my mother's womb, and naked I shall return there. The LORD gave and the LORD has taken away. Blessed be the name of the LORD" (Job 1:21). Scripture commended Job for his faith, declaring that Job "did not sin nor did he blame God" (Job 1:22).

The fear of losing a loved one can easily cause one to cross the line from being a responsible and protective parent to being an overprotective and irresponsible parent. When that happens, mothering becomes smothering. Vanessa Ochs, in her book *Safe and Sound: Protecting Your Child in an Unpredictable World* comments: "When protection turns to overprotection, regardless of how we rationalize, regardless of how and why it was motivated...it has serious, long-term consequences for a child's self-esteem and sense of well-being."[16] Ochs goes on to describe overprotection as "an insidious form of child abuse. You are locking a child's horizons in the closet. The difference is, this abuse is caused by an enormous amount of love."[17]

This kind of "protection" can masquerade as genuine love, but in reality it is motivated by fear. Because we cannot bear the thought of how much it will hurt us to see our loved ones harmed or killed, we do everything we can to control people and circumstances to avoid experiencing that pain. In the process, we end up perpetuating a stronghold of fear in our families, producing children who are as phobic as we are.

Finding the balance is increasingly difficult for parents in a world filled with danger. We must trust in God and believe in our children. We are called to encourage—not discourage—one another. Fear would never allow children to cross the street, but responsible parents know the risk must be taken and so they teach their kids how to do it safely. Greater risks will be required as children get older. We will develop emotional cripples if we don't communicate trust and instill confidence in the next generation. We will end up alienating the very loved ones we are seeking to hold on to if we don't.

We should always exercise godly wisdom and caution in the face of real danger, but we can't always be with them. So we need to teach our loved ones how to live courageously and commit them to the care of the only One who can be with them every moment of the day. It is not enough to prepare them for the physical dangers that exist, you also need to consider the spiritual battle. We recommend that you read *Spiritual Protection for Your Children.*[18] For the protection of your children, use the following prayer, based on Psalm 139, as a guide:

> *Dear Lord, You have searched and known (names of loved ones). You know when they sit down and stand up. You understand all the things that are going on in their minds. You know where they are going and how they will get there. There is nothing hidden from You at all. You even know what they say before they say it.*
>
> *Lord, You put an invisible shield behind them and in front of them and lay Your hand gently upon their heads. This is so wonderful to me and far beyond my ability to understand. But I thank You for Your protection.*

I thank You that there is no place they can go where You are not already there. No matter how far they go to the north, south, east, or west, You will lead them. And if they are in danger, You can grab them and rescue them at any time. Even in the middle of the night, when I am most afraid of where they might be and what they might be doing, You see what is going on as if it were the middle of the day. Thank You, Lord, that You watch over them while they sleep, warding off unseen dangers that would attack them when they are most vulnerable.

You created them, Lord, so You know what they need far better than I do. So I commit them into Your care as their Creator and Father.

Take a good look inside me, O Lord, and see what is in my heart. Show me if I am in any way being controlled by fear and anxiety. I know that those things will result in harmful behavior toward my loved ones. Take me by the hand, dear Lord, and lead me in Your everlasting way of life. In Jesus' name I pray, amen.

Fear of the Dying Process

It is one thing to overcome the fear of death, it is another thing to overcome the fear of dying. We can all look forward to seeing our Lord face to face. It is our hope. But nobody looks forward to the process of dying, especially if it is long and painful. Such prospects develop a lot of phobias toward diseases, medications, medical tests, and even doctors. Some don't want to know the truth about their physical condition because they are afraid they couldn't handle it. Many people try to manage their fears by living in denial. And then there's the possibility of a violent death, such as being victimized in a crime.

Bonnie Crandall, in her book *Panic Buster*, lists 28 things that she was afraid of, including: "weather, passing out, driving, clouds, food, bees, dogs, heights, crossing the street, strong wind, someone in the house, the dark, bathtub water, being alone, gas fumes, buses and taxis, tornadoes and blizzards."[19] She was also afraid to be in places where she might lose control and be embarrassed.

Her comments about this aspect of the fear of death show how irrational fear can be, as well as the power of God to change a life:

> *That [being afraid of those 28 things] was long ago. As I look over my list now much of it seems ridiculous. But it certainly wasn't at the time. Also, I must confess, I'd still be afraid if a tornado actually came and I was in or near one. But, at that time I was afraid we'd have a tornado even if it got only a little stormy outside. There didn't even have to be a watch or warning posted!*
>
> *I was afraid of the bathtub water because I was weak and shaky so much of the time. I felt as though I'd pass out and slip under the water and drown. Actually most of these worries do boil down to the fear of death, and the good news is that God conquered death when Jesus rose from the grave.*[20]

People who struggle with the fear of death are caught in the "what if" syndrome. They tend to imagine the worst, even though over 99 percent of the time the worst doesn't happen or isn't even threatened. They are afraid to drive across bridges because they are thinking, "What if the bridge collapses?" They are afraid to eat at a restaurant because they are thinking, "What if I get food poisoning?" There is usually no logical basis for their fear, so it is very hard to reason them out of their mindset. Telling someone who has a fear of flying that an airplane is the safest way to travel will probably not eliminate the fear.

People who are afraid of dying in a violent or painful way often suffer from hypochondria. Hypochondria is the overly anxious preoccupation with one's health, often resulting in the irrational fear of being seriously or terminally ill. They often read medical journals to learn about various illnesses and their symptoms. A normal person may be annoyed by a headache and take an aspirin, but to the hypochondriac a headache is far more ominous. They start thinking, "Maybe I have meningitis or a brain tumor." Almost any symptom, no matter how innocuous, can launch a hypochondriac into an emotional spiral of fear and morbidity. Their primary battle is in their minds. They see themselves as being vulnerable targets for every marauding malady that stalks the planet.

Even though there are diseases and germs in this world, our focus must be on the healthy balance of nutrition, exercise, and diet. Supplementing our diets with minerals and vitamins, strengthening our bodies with aerobic exercises, and getting enough rest will strengthen our immune systems. We should be health-oriented, not illness-oriented.

The fear of dying painfully or violently has some basis in reality. There really are dangers out there, and some of us will die painfully slow or suddenly and tragically. But those who are obsessed with these fears seem to lack the assurance of God's presence and His sustaining grace. Plus, they have allowed their minds to ruminate on every negative possibility instead of thinking about "whatever is true, whatever is honorable, whatever is right, whatever is pure, whatever is lovely, whatever is of good repute..." (Philippians 4:8).

Some fears have no basis in the reality of the physical world. Fear has an object, but in this case it is imaginary. The fear originates in the mind, which is the basic characteristic of neurosis. Extremely fearful people see and hear things that nobody else does. Typically that would be called mental illness, which is defined as being out of touch with reality and abnormally anxious. (But anybody caught in a spiritual battle for his or her mind would fail on both counts and there would be nothing organically wrong with that person. We will explore this possibility in a later chapter.)

Grace to Help in Time of Need

The truth is that many people fear what has not yet happened, and those fears are not helping them live a responsible life today. Their focus for living has been taken off God. Consider the words of Psalm 63:1-5, written by David who faced the real prospect of being killed almost daily:

> O God, you are my God, earnestly I seek you; my soul thirsts for you, my body longs for you, in a dry and weary land where there is no water. I have seen you in the sanctuary and beheld your power and your glory. Because your love is better than life, my lips will glorify you. I will praise you as long as I live, and in your name I will lift up my hands. My soul will be satisfied as with the richest of foods; with singing lips my mouth will praise you (Psalm 63:1-5 NIV).

God's people throughout the ages have suffered the most awful atrocities at the hands of cruel and evil people. In fact, being an outspoken Christian in some countries of the world today is tantamount to signing your own death warrant. The prophets and saints of old "experienced mockings and scourgings, yes, also chains and imprisonment. They were stoned, they were sawn in two, they were tempted, they were put to death with the sword" (Hebrews 11:36,37).

Stephen was the first martyr in the early church. His death, recorded in Acts 7:54-60, is a testimony of the sufficiency of God's grace, even at the moment of death:

> Now when they [the Sanhedrin] heard this, they were cut to the quick, and they began gnashing their teeth at him. But being full of the Holy Spirit, he

> gazed intently into heaven and saw the glory of God, and Jesus standing at the right hand of God; and he said, "Behold, I see the heavens opened up and the Son of Man standing at the right hand of God." But they cried out with a loud voice, and covered their ears, and they rushed upon him with one impulse.
>
> And when they had driven him out of the city, they began stoning him, and the witnesses laid aside their robes at the feet of a young man named Saul. And they went on stoning Stephen as he called upon the Lord and said, "Lord Jesus, receive my spirit!" And falling on his knees, he cried out with a loud voice, "Lord, do not hold this sin against them!" And having said this, he fell asleep.

How was he able to endure such agony while maintaining such dignity? By the grace of God! That same dynamic enabling is available to every child of God. "For we do not have a high priest who cannot sympathize with our weaknesses, but One who has been tempted in all things as we are, yet without sin. Let us therefore draw near with confidence to the throne of grace, that we may receive mercy and find grace to help in time of need" (Hebrews 4:15,16).

But remember that God's grace is always given to help at the time of need, not in advance. We an count on His grace today to meet today's needs. We must wait for tomorrow to receive the strength to endure tomorrow's trials.

Only the grace of God can sustain us during such times of need. We close this chapter with a spiritual version of 911. When faced with a crisis dial up Psalm 91:1. This verse and the ones that follow constitute one of most powerful chapters in the Bible regarding the protective hand of God:

He who dwells in the shelter of the Most High will abide in the shadow of the Almighty. I will say to the LORD, "My refuge and my fortress, my God, in whom I trust!"

For it is He who delivers you from the snare of the trapper, and from the deadly pestilence. He will cover you with His pinions, and under His wings you may seek refuge; His faithfulness is a shield and bulwark.

You will not be afraid of the terror by night, or of the arrow that flies by day; of the pestilence that stalks in darkness, or of the destruction that lays waste at noon. A thousand may fall at your side, and ten thousand at your right hand; but it shall not approach you. You will only look on with your eyes, and see the recompense of the wicked. For you have made the LORD, my refuge, even the Most High, your dwelling place. No evil will befall you, nor will any plague come near your tent.

For He will give His angels charge concerning you, to guard you in all your ways. They will bear you up in their hands, lest you strike your foot against a stone. You will tread upon the lion and cobra, the young lion and the serpent you will trample down.

Because he has loved Me, therefore I will deliver him; I will set him securely on high, because he has known My name. He will call upon Me, and I will answer him; I will be with him in trouble; I will rescue him, and honor him. With a long life I will satisfy him, and let him behold My salvation (Psalm 91).

6

The Fear of Failure

> The danger is not that we should fall...but that we should remain on the ground.
>
> —John Chrysostom

His sons and his brothers are Mel Farr's best friends, but worry is his most constant companion. It's what made him go to the University of Detroit at night back in the 1960s after practicing all day with the Detroit Lions. It's what made him spend his off-season in training to become one of the first black auto dealers in the United States. It's what wakes him up at 3 o'clock some mornings.

"Guess what I do then? I get up and go to work. It's not work that kills the man. It's worry that kills the man. I'd much rather work than worry."

Farr, 52, is the most successful black auto dealer in America and owner of the nation's second-largest

African-American-owned private business. His 14 franchises in five states gross more than a half-billion dollars in sales annually. In the not-too-distant future, he envisions that his dealership will take in more than a billion dollars each year.

Everything about him spells success. Yet, while he is clearly proud of all that he's accomplished since leaving high school in Beaumont, Texas, 34 years ago, it is the prospect of failure that keeps Farr driving as well as flying.

"The minute you think you're there is when you stop trying. It's very difficult to stop something once it starts going down. My motivation is the fear of failure."[1]

Mel Farr is the epitome of what many would call a successful man and yet his driving force is the fear of failure. He is not alone. I once heard a denominational leader say, "As I travel and talk to our pastors I have come to the conclusion that their number-one motivation in ministry is the fear of failure."

Irrational fears either compel us to do that which is irresponsible or prevent us from doing that which is responsible. The fear of failure motivates some to be successful and others not to risk trying anything at all, thereby avoiding any possibility of failure. Fear has an object, but in this case what is it? Everybody has their own criteria for judging success and failure. One person's success is another person's failure. One student could fear the possibility of getting a "B" on an exam, and another student would consider that the ultimate success. You could be a complete success in the eyes of God and a total failure in the eyes of the world.

A Biblical Definition of Success

Who is more successful, a 40-year-old pastor of a 200-member church, or a 40-year-old pastor of a 2000-member church? Which parent is more successful, the father of a corporate president or the mother of a retarded child? Who is the more successful student, the one who gets a perfect report card or the one who needs a tutor after school? You can't answer these questions because no two people have the same opportunity or potential.

God has not equally distributed gifts, talents, or intelligence to His children. Suppose two people were created exactly the same. One was born in Connecticut to wealthy parents. The other was born in a remote jungle to parents who couldn't read or write, nor have they even seen modern civilization. Both children have a certain potential for life, but how would you define success for either one? They certainly don't have the same opportunities or desires to accomplish the same educational or material objectives.

Paul said, "We are not bold to class or compare ourselves with some of those who commend themselves; but when they measure themselves by themselves, and compare themselves with themselves, they are without understanding" (2 Corinthians 10:12). You lack understanding if you determine your success or failure by comparing yourself with others. There must be some other standard of evaluation for success by which we can motivate our lives. The first instruction in the Bible on success is given in Joshua 1:7,8 just before they were about to go into the promised land:

> Only be strong and very courageous; be careful to do according to all the law which Moses My servant commanded you; do not turn from it to the right or to the left, so that you may have success wherever you go. This book of the law shall not depart from your mouth, but you shall meditate on it day and night, so that you may be careful to do according to all that is written in it; for then you will make your way prosperous, and then you will have success.

First Principle of Success

The Israelites' success did not depend on favorable circumstances in the promised land, nor on the cooperation of the Philistines. They would be successful and prosperous if they understood God's Word and faithfully lived it. To be successful in life, you have to first know God and His ways. That is the first biblical principle of success. "Thus says the LORD, 'Let not a wise man boast of his wisdom, and let not the mighty man boast of his might, let not a rich man boast of his riches; but let him who boasts boast of this, that he understands and knows Me, that I am the LORD who exercises lovingkindness, justice, and righteousness on earth; for I delight in these things,' declares the LORD" (Jeremiah 9:23,24; see also 1 Corinthians 1:31).

Nobody set the standard for success higher than the apostle Paul. He had intelligence, social status, favorable circumstances, and drive. He was the ultimate achiever and leading candidate for theologian of the year when Christ struck him down. Listen to how he describes his before and after drive for success:

> If anyone else has a mind to put confidence in the flesh, I far more: circumcised the eighth day, of the nation of Israel, of the tribe of Benjamin, a Hebrew of Hebrews; as to the Law, a Pharisee; as to zeal, a persecutor of the church; as to the righteousness which is in the Law, found blameless. But whatever things were gain to me, those things I have counted as loss for the sake of Christ. More than that, I count all things to be loss in view of the surpassing value of knowing Christ Jesus my Lord, for whom I have suffered the loss of all things, and count them but rubbish in order that I may gain Christ (Philippians 3:4-8).

Paul is not the only person to climb the corporate ladder only to find out it was leaning against the wrong wall. The feeling of success that comes from winning the race, getting the promotion, graduating at the top of the class is very fleeting. What happens when you get there? Does it satisfy? Do you need to climb one rung higher? "For what does it profit a man to gain the whole world, and forfeit his soul? For what shall a man give in exchange for his soul?" (Mark 8:36,37). What does satisfy? Take your highest standard of success in terms of appearance, performance, status, and possessions and then ask yourself: "If I were able to accomplish or possess it, would I be forever satisfied?"

I accomplished my educational goal when I got my second doctorate. Talk about anticlimactic! I was just happy it was over with. By that time in my life I knew I was a child of God the day before, and I was a child of God the day after. I'm sure nobody put a "Dr." in front of my name in the Lamb's book of life, and I don't believe that achievement caught the attention of any angels in heaven. But what happens in heaven when one sinner repents? "I tell you, there is joy in the presence of the angels of God over one sinner who repents" (Luke 15:10).

There is only one thing that completely and continuously satisfies. Jesus said, "Blessed are those who hunger and thirst for righteousness, for they shall be satisfied" (Matthew 5:6). Nothing else can satisfy like living a righteous life and being intimately related to our heavenly Father. Loving relationships satisfy, but the satisfaction that comes from titles, degrees, possessions, and accomplishments is fleeting at best.

Second Principle of Success

It took three years in the desert for Paul to move his ladder over to the right wall. He couldn't stay on the top rung and just push it over to the right wall. He had to start on the bottom rung as we all do. But with new focus he set out in the right direction and, with a determination to succeed, proceeded to climb:

> Not that I have already obtained it, or have already become perfect, but I press on in order that I may lay hold of that for which also I was laid hold of by Christ Jesus. Brethren, I do not regard myself as having laid hold of it yet; but one thing I do: forgetting what lies behind and reaching forward to what lies ahead, I press on toward the goal for the prize of the upward call of God in Christ Jesus (Philippians 3:12-14).

Paul was again motivated to succeed, but with a new goal. He pressed on to lay hold of whatever Christ wanted for him. Christ had chosen Paul for a purpose, as He has chosen all of us. To be successful we have to become the people God created us to be. This is the second principle of success. It is also God's will for our lives. The fact that nobody and nothing can keep us from being the person God has created us to be is the good news. Only we can keep that from happening.

We may not have enough time to accomplish what we want in life, but we have precisely enough time to do God's will. We may not be able to reach the position we hoped for, but what position is higher than being seated with Christ in the heavenlies? We can try to make a name for ourselves in the world, but what name could we make for ourselves that is better than being called children of God?

Scripture doesn't provide any instruction on career choices. I don't think God cares whether you become an engineer, carpenter, or plumber, although He will provide guidance for such career choices. Career choices are dependent upon our God-given capabilities and reasonable opportunities. God does care what kind of engineer, carpenter, and plumber you are. It is part of our calling to serve in certain roles, but the roles do not determine who we are. It isn't what you do that determines who you are, it is who you are that determines what you do. So who are you? "Beloved, now we are children of God, and it has not appeared as yet what we shall be. We know that, when He appears, we shall be like Him, because we shall see Him just as He is. And everyone who has this hope fixed on Him purifies himself, just as He is pure" (1 John 3:2,3).

Neither does Scripture provide any instruction on setting career goals. Biblical objectives for personal performance are all related to character and righteous living. Suppose your goal to become successful was to have your own small business, be a good witness in the community, live in a comfortable home in the right part of town, and have a nest egg set aside for retirement. Sounds like the American dream. With a lot of hard work, your business is showing a good profit and you are well on your way to achieving your goals.

Then one day you discover that your trusted bookkeeper has been stealing money from the business. Instead of prosperity, you find yourself facing the possibility of bankruptcy. To save the business, you mortgage your home and borrow money from your retirement savings. About the time your creditors have been paid off, the market goes bad and you have to lay off employees. Finally you sell the business and seek employment elsewhere. Your house is mortgaged, your retirement is gone, and your business has failed. Despite your best efforts, what you feared the most has happened. Are you a failure?

Did those trials and tribulations keep you from being the person God created you to be? Did those circumstances, which you had no ability to control, take away your hope for the future? The apostle Paul wouldn't think so. He wrote, "We also exult in our tribulations, knowing that tribulation brings about perseverance; and perseverance, proven character; and proven character, hope; and hope does not disappoint, because the love of God has been poured out within our hearts through the Holy Spirit who was given to us" (Romans 5:3-5). It is hard for us to envision that God may actually thwart our career goals in order to make us the people we are called to be. The worldly idea of success can ruin a good person.

The trials and tribulations of this world can add to our fear of failure if we have the wrong definition of success. But they actually contribute to the right goal of proven character, and that is where our hope lies. Trials or tribulations cannot destroy us, but they do reveal who we are and they help us become who God created us to be. There is no crisis we can't come through as better people if that is our definition of success.

Fred was a realtor who had the goal of selling two houses per week. His average last year was one-and-a-half homes per week, so he thought he would give himself an additional incentive. He wanted to be the salesperson of the year, and the added income would enable him to buy the house he dreamed of. After one month he sold only three houses. Fear of failure motivated him to try harder, but his efforts didn't bear fruit. The pressure he put on himself started to show up in very negative ways. He became irritable and controlling because he needed to get others to cooperate with him so he could accomplish his goal.

Then the unthinkable happened. He was fired for being a disruption at the office. How could he tell his wife? All their dreams went up in smoke. He became so depressed that all he could do was sit around the house. All he could think was, "I'm a failure!" Finally he called his pastor for an appointment.

After hearing his story, his pastor said, "Fred you're a good person, but I think you had the wrong goal. All God asks of us is to be the people He created us to be. There is nothing wrong with being the salesperson of the year and winning a trip to Hawaii, or buying a better house to live in, but that alone wouldn't satisfy you nor would it mean you were successful. To be successful, all you had to do was be the salesperson, husband, and father God wanted you to be. During this time did you put the needs of your customers, wife, and children ahead of yours?" Paul said, "Do not merely look out for your own personal interests, but also for the interests of others. Have this attitude in yourselves which was also in Christ Jesus."

The western-world definition of prosperity—materialism—led to the "prosperity gospel": "If you believe, you can achieve, and the evidence of that is prosperity." There is some truth to that because God does want us to prosper. He certainly has not called us to fail. But what is our definition of doing well? John wrote, "Beloved, I pray that in all respects you may prosper and be in good health, just as your soul prospers" (3 John 2). *God wants our souls to prosper.* We ask again, What would you exchange for love, joy, peace, patience, kindness, goodness, faithfulness, gentleness, and self-control, which is the fruit of the Spirit?

Third Principle of Success

Under the inspiration of God, the apostle Peter wrote, "As obedient children, do not be conformed to the former lusts which were yours in your ignorance, but like the Holy One who called you, be holy yourselves also in all your behavior; because it is written, 'You shall be Holy, for I am Holy'" (1 Peter 1:14-16). Who we are is far more important than what we do, because what we do flows from who we are. The scriptural order is character before career and maturity before ministry. Eventually this should lead to accomplishing something "for we are His workmanship, created in Christ Jesus for good works, which God prepared beforehand that we should walk in them" (Ephesians 2:10).

We can't just sit around in holy piety. Jesus said, "Let your light shine before men in such a way that they may see your good works, and glorify your Father who is in heaven" (Matthew 5:16). We have all been given by God a certain life endowment that He expects us to use to His glory. Paul wrote, "Let a man regard us in this manner, as servants of Christ, and stewards of the mysteries of God. In this case, moreover, it is required of stewards that one be found trustworthy" (1 Corinthians 4:1,2).

To be successful, we must be good stewards of that which God has entrusted to us. This is the third principle of success. In the parable of the talents, we learn that God has given some five talents, others two, and still others only one. In the parable, the one given five talents gained five more and the one given two talents gained two more. The one given one talent dug a hole in the ground and buried it. On the day of accountability, God ordered the worthless slave, who did nothing, to be cast from His presence and what he had was to be given to those who were faithful with what had been entrusted to them.

God has not equally distributed gifts, talents, or intelligence, and He knows that we don't all have the same opportunities. Therefore, we will not be required to produce the same fruit. But He does require us to use what we have been given. Our potential for success does not lie in opportunity but in faithfulness. What we want to hear is, "Well done, good and faithful slave; you were faithful with a few things, I will put you in charge of many things; enter into the joy of your master" (Matthew 25:21).

A Biblical Definition of Failure

In addition to being the authoritative Word of God, the Bible is a book of failures. Moses struck the rock in anger and failed to reach the promised land. Elijah slew 450 prophets of Baal, but ran from Jezebel. David slew Goliath but also slept with Bathsheba and brought great pain on his family. Peter told the Lord to His face that he would go to prison and even be willing to die for Him, then he turned around and denied Him three times.

Even Jesus failed to accomplish what His disciples had hoped for, but He perfectly fulfilled His calling. Failure by our standards is not sin, but faithlessness is. Many of the heroes mentioned in Hebrews 11 would be considered flops by modern-day standards. But they weren't mentioned because of their accomplishments; they were commended for their faithfulness. "And all these, having gained approval through their faith, did not receive what was promised, because God had provided something better for us, so that apart from us they should not be made perfect" (Hebrews 11:39,40).

The book of Proverbs says, "For a righteous man falls seven times, and rises again" (24:16). To stumble and fall is not failure. To stumble and fall again is not failure. Failure comes when you say, "I was pushed," and then fail to get up again. We have failed ourselves if we blame others for our lack of progress or rationalize why we can't get back up. We have failed others when we don't assume our responsibility in the body of Christ.

There are two kinds of failures: moral failure and failure to meet certain objectives. Moral failure cannot be blamed on anyone but ourselves. Such failure needs to be acknowledged only to the extent of the exposure and to those potentially affected by the sin. If only God knows, then confess only to Him unless others have been or could be affected by the sin. "If we confess our sins, He is faithful and righteous to forgive us our sins and to cleanse us from all unrighteousness. If we say that we have not sinned, we make Him a liar, and His word is not in us" (1 John 1:9,10). So you have sinned. Confess it, get back up again, and keep moving forward. It is a moral failure to blame someone else or never acknowledge your sin to God. If your sin has been evident to others, then your confession should be only to the scope of those who know. The opposite of confession is not only silence, but also rationalization.

A mistake is never a failure unless you fail to learn from it. Everybody has failed to accomplish his or her objectives at times. We have failed in the past, and we will fail tomorrow.

Many who are afraid to fail never try—or they give up when they feel the slightest resistance. Failure is the line of least persistence. People don't fail; they give up trying. Theodore Roosevelt had great insight regarding success:

> It is not the critic who counts, nor the man who points out how the strong man stumbled or where the doer of deeds could have done better. The credit belongs to the man who is actually in the arena, whose face is marred by the dust and sweat and blood; who strives valiantly; who errs and comes short again and again; who knows the great enthusiasms, the great devotions, and spends himself in a worthy cause; who, at the best, knows in the end the triumph of high achievement; and who, at the worst, if he fails, at least fails while daring greatly, so that his place shall never be with those cold and timid souls who know neither victory or defeat.

Success is 90 percent attitude and 10 percent aptitude. Those who accomplish something in their lives will look back and say it was persistence that got them there. Success is 10 percent inspiration and 90 percent perspiration.

Taking the Risk

Stepping out in faith is a risk, but life is a risk. We all like the security of the trunk, but the fruit is always out on the end of the limb. An anonymous author wrote:

> To *laugh* is to risk appearing the fool.
> To *weep* is to risk appearing sentimental.
> To *reach out* for another is to risk involvement.

> To *expose feelings* to another is to risk exposing your true self.
> To *place your ideas, your dreams* before a crowd is to risk their loss.
> To *love* is to risk not being loved in return.
> To *live* is to risk dying.
> To *hope* is to risk despair.
> To *try* is to risk failure.
>
> But risks must be taken because the greatest hazard in life is to risk nothing. The person who risks nothing does nothing, has nothing, is nothing. He may avoid suffering and sorrow, but he simply cannot learn, feel, change, grow, love...live. Chained by his certitudes, he is a slave; he has forfeited freedom. Only a person who risks is free.

If you were to make a list of a rogues gallery of the most offensive people in the world, who would be on the top of your list? Now compare it with the Lord's in Revelation 21:7,8:

> He who overcomes shall inherit these things, and I will be his God and he will be My son. But for the cowardly and unbelieving and abominable and murderers and immoral persons and sorcerers and idolaters and all liars, their part will be in the lake that burns with fire and brimstone, which is the second death.

We would expect murderers, sorcerers, and idolaters to be on the list, but how many would guess that the list would be headed by cowardly and unbelieving? God does not look with favor on those who limp along in unbelief and never take the risk of living by faith because of fear of failure. It is the mark of a Spirit-filled Christian to be strong in the Lord and courageous.

When the early church was threatened, they turned to God in prayer: "And when they had prayed, the place where they had gathered together was shaken, and they were all filled with the Holy Spirit, and began to speak the word of God with boldness" (Acts 4:31). "For God has not given us a spirit of timidity, but of power and love and discipline" (2 Timothy 1:7).

Susan Jeffers was raised to believe that she couldn't. Then one day this timid soul decided she wouldn't, no, she couldn't live that way any longer. She writes:

> *Part of my problem was the nonstop little voices inside my head that kept telling me,* "You'd better not change your situation. There's nothing else out there for you. You'll never make it on your own." *You know the one I'm talking about—the one that keeps reminding you,* "Don't take a chance. You might make a mistake. Boy, will you be sorry!"
>
> *My fear never seemed to abate, and I didn't have a moment's peace. Even my doctorate in psychology didn't seem to do me much good. Then one day, as I was dressing for work, I reached the turning point. I happened to glance in the mirror, and I saw an all-to-familiar sight—eyes red and puffy from tears of self-pity. Suddenly rage welled up inside of me, and I began shouting at my reflection,* "Enough...Enough...Enough!" *I shouted until I had no more energy (or voice) left.*
>
> *When I stopped, I felt a strange and wonderful sense of relief and calm I had never felt before. Without realizing it at the time, I had gotten in touch with a very powerful part of myself that before that moment I hadn't even known ever existed. I took another look in the mirror and*

smiled as I nodded my head yes. The old familiar voice of doom and gloom was drowned out, at least temporarily, and a new voice had come to the fore—one that spoke of strength and love and joy and all good things. At that moment I knew I was not going to let fear get the best of me. I would find a way to rid myself of the negativism that prevailed in my life. Thus my odyssey began.[2]

In Susan's book *Feel the Fear and Do It Anyway*, she shares two fundamental truths about fear. First, "the fear will never go away as long as you continue to grow." Every step in our maturing process will be met with new challenges and obstacles to overcome. You can't wait until the fear goes away because it never will, which leads to the second truth: "The only way to get rid of the fear of doing something is to go out and do it."[3] Someone once said, "Do the thing you fear the most and the death of fear is certain."

Remember, nobody can keep you from being the person God has called you to be. It is normal to feel the fear but step out anyway as the following poem suggests:

People are unreasonable, illogical, and self-centered:

Love them anyway!

If you do good, people will accuse you of selfish motives:

Do good anyway!

If you're successful, you will win false friends and true enemies:

Succeed anyway!

The good you do today will be forgotten tomorrow:

Do good anyway!

Honesty and frankness make you vulnerable:

Be honest and frank anyway!

The biggest people with the biggest ideas can be shot down by the smallest people with the smallest minds:

Think big anyway!

People favor underdogs but follow only top dogs:

Fight for some underdog anyway!

What you spend years building may be destroyed overnight:

Build anyway!

People need help but may attack if you help them:

Help people anyway!

Give the world the best you've got, and you will get kicked in the teeth:

Give the world the best you've got anyway!

7

Panic Disorder

Fear makes men believe the worst.

—Quintus Rufus,
Alexander the Great IV. x

In her book *Panic Buster*, Bonnie Crandall describes a horrifying moment in her life, a moment that millions of Americans can relate to:

> *I graduated from high school and acquired a good job to start my career in the business world. My life had been normal up to the day I had my first full-blown panic attack. I remember it well.*
>
> *I was working at my bookkeeping machine entering invoices as usual. All of a sudden my hands began to shake. I stared at them. What's wrong with me? I wondered. My heart is pounding like a trip-hammer. I can almost hear it. I feel weak! I'm going to faint, I know it. It's*

> *hard to breathe! Oh, I need more air desperately! What's wrong? Is this a heart attack? Am I dying? I'm only twenty-five. That's too young to have a heart attack!*
>
> *Terror raced through me! I jumped up from my machine. Anything to escape! I staggered out of the office and across the hall to where a friend worked. I sagged into the chair beside her desk.*[1]

After about 20 minutes, Bonnie began to calm down. Still shaken and frightened, she bravely went back to her office. Too drained and confused to focus on her work, however, she took the rest of the day off. But this initial attack was just the beginning:

> *The spells continued. Exhausted from the spells that plagued me, I wasn't sure I could keep up the pace of my job.*
>
> *I sat at my desk and held my head up with one hand. I was so weak. I was continually late for work, but did manage to get the work done. I was drained, both emotionally and spiritually. I'd worry about when and if I'd have another spell. Dread was my constant companion.*
>
> *A storage room in the rear of the factory held empty cartons. I turned one huge carton on its side. I often spent my lunchtime in the carton taking a rest to gather strength for the rest of the day.*[2]

Eventually Bonnie lost her job, and her world began to fall apart. Even after finding a new job, she had to quit after a month due to the continued attacks. Doctors prescribed various medications, but she only felt worse. The panic attacks began occurring in other places besides work, including the grocery store. She was becoming increasingly housebound, trapped in a shrinking world that choked off her work, relationships, and self-esteem.

My world became smaller and smaller. Eventually I had to quit work completely as I became confined to my home. I had gone from panic attacks to agoraphobia, the fear of leaving my home alone. Another three years went by. I simply existed. I felt worthless.[3]

Symptoms

Panic attacks (sometimes called anxiety attacks) are defined in the *Baker Encyclopedia of Psychology* as "very frightening and aversive experiences in which persons are overwhelmed with the physical symptoms of anxiety."[4] Those symptoms generally include some of the following: "racing heartbeat, difficulty breathing—feeling as though you can't get enough air, terror that is almost paralyzing, dizziness, lightheadedness, nausea, trembling, shaking, sweating, choking, chest pains, hot flashes or sudden chills, tingling in fingers or toes like 'pins and needles,' fear that you are having a heart attack, stroke, etc., or that you are going crazy or about to die."[5]

These symptoms are similar to the "fight or flight" body responses to extreme stress and danger. They can occur suddenly, without warning, in seemingly harmless situations. They can even occur while an individual is sleeping, as the following account reveals.[6]

I did not realize I had a problem with fear until I had two surgeries in a short period of time. What a scary time that was for me. All I knew was that I wanted people praying for me. My prayer consisted of Help, God!

I became agitated and shaky inside. My chest began to tighten and as time went by I would wake up every morning at three o'clock with crippling fear. It was as though my thoughts were out of control. I began to have rushes go through my body, and then I would collapse in tears.

If these panic attacks occur frequently (one or more times during any four-week period) and involve at least four of the above symptoms, then the person's affliction is called panic disorder.[7] About 75 percent of panic disorder sufferers are women. It usually has its onset between the ages of 20 and 30, although it can first show up in teenage years and occur in adults over 40. It is rare that the first episodes of panic attacks occur in old age.

Although the first panic attack may come during a time of unusual stress, victims of this problem are often average, emotionally healthy people. The attacks typically reach maximum intensity within one or two minutes from inception and may last (with slowly diminishing symptoms) from 30 minutes to several hours.[8]

It is not uncommon for individuals, after suffering a number of panic episodes, to become increasingly afraid that they are helpless victims of panic. They start avoiding public places and remain at home whenever possible. The sufferer becomes more apprehensive and tense, continually guarding against the possibility of another attack.[9] This fearful, defensive posture causes them to be even more susceptible to panic attacks. Many people with panic disorder still manage to muddle their way through life, coping as best they can.

The fear of having a panic attack causes many people to become agoraphobic. Agoraphobia (literally, "fear of the marketplace") can become so severe that sufferers may quit their jobs, stop going to church, avoid grocery stores and banks, and even dread talking on the telephone. In extreme cases, the individual can become housebound for years.[10] Because the symptoms accompanying a panic attack can come without warning, agoraphobics literally become afraid of fear itself.

Physiological Considerations

In seeking to overcome panic disorder, it is very helpful to understand how the body works and why certain physical symptoms occur. Often those symptoms are so distressing that the panic attack sufferer will believe he or she is in need of emergency medical treatment and will go to the hospital.

There are genuine physical disorders that can cause symptoms that mimic a panic attack, therefore it is wise to undergo a thorough physical examination. If your physician recommends you see another medical specialist, do so. If a physical condition is diagnosed, follow the treatments directed by the doctor. Drug and alcohol use or withdrawal can also result in physical symptoms similar to panic attacks. The use of stimulants, such as caffeine, can be the culprit as well as the side effects of certain prescription medications. Even pregnancy, premenstrual syndrome, and menopause can be at the root of these symptoms.[11]

If there is a legitimate physiological reason for your symptoms, you need medical help. But if no physical reason exists, it would be wise to explore other possible causes. That will help you find the psychological and spiritual assistance you need.

Even when there is no physiological cause for a panic attack, there are still physical effects on the body due to the panic response. For example, more than 80 percent of panic attack sufferers experience a rapid or irregular heartbeat. Any unpleasant sensation in the heart that we can feel is categorized in general as a palpitation.[12]

Assuming there is no legitimate physiological condition warranting medical attention, the critical questions are: "Why am I having this unpleasant physical sensation?" and "How am I going to respond to it?" Let's examine how our body functions. Our nervous system sends a signal from every part of our body to the brain, and the mind interprets the data according to how it has been programmed. The emotional response is immediate. If the mind interprets the data as danger, it immediately sends a signal back to the body. The signal stimulates hormones that engage the sympathetic branch of the autonomic nervous system.[13] The ensuing adrenaline rush is the classic "fight or flight" response protecting you from supposed danger. Physiologically your blood sugar level increases, your eyes dilate, your sweat glands perspire, your heart rate increases, your mouth becomes dry, your muscles tense, your blood flow decreases in the arms and legs and pools in the head and trunk, and your breathing rate and pattern change.[14]

During a panic attack, there is no actual physical enemy to fight so the tension and anxiety we feel continues to build.[15] Eventually we experience so much pent-up emotional energy that the compelling drive is to flee. In a real emergency, our breathing undergoes a significant change in rate and pattern. That is also true during a panic attack. Rather than slow, deep breathing from the lower lungs, we move into rapid, shallow breathing from the upper lungs. This natural and necessary process pumps additional oxygen into the bloodstream, while quickly ridding the body of carbon dioxide during real danger.[16]

If there is no physical activity taking place (and there usually isn't during a panic attack), the body discharges too much carbon dioxide, and we experience hyperventilation: irregular heart rate; dizziness; lightheadedness; shortness of breath; chest pain; blurred vision; numbness or tingling in the mouth, hands, feet; weakness; confusion; inability to concentrate.

The initial physical response to a real or imaginary fear object is to gasp or suck in air. Then instead of exhaling, we try to suck in more air but there is no room for it in our lungs. Having people blow into a paper bag gets them to exhale and return to a normal process of inhaling and exhaling.

Knowing that most of the unpleasant physical symptoms of panic attacks are really the body's God-created means of coping with a perceived emergency takes a lot of the terrifying mystery out of these episodes. What initially seems to be an overwhelming situation over which we have no control becomes a much more manageable problem if we understand what our bodies naturally do.

Suppose you have a minor condition of mitral valve prolapse, which is usually a non life-threatening heart palpitation. Your first experience with it could be frightening because you don't know what it is. You could think you are having a heart attack and the likely response is to panic. After a thorough physical exam you learn that it is only a minor condition. The next time your heart flutters, your "renewed" mind interprets the data differently and there is no panic. Of course, even the first response would be less frightening if your mind had previously been programmed not to fear death.

The Body Responds

Secular therapists talk about the onset of anticipatory anxiety as a key factor in determining whether many panic attacks will occur or not. For example, if a person had a panic attack in a grocery store, he or she will likely struggle with negative thoughts when the need for food shopping arises again. The thought process could be something like this:

> *I've had a panic attack before in a grocery store, what's to keep me from having another one? I don't like waiting in lines, especially with people in front and behind me. What if I start to panic? I won't be able to escape. I may lose control, and I'll make a total fool of myself and have to run out of the store and leave my shopping cart filled with food. People will think I'm absolutely crazy!*

This battle for the mind could go on in the home, while driving to the store, while pulling into the parking lot, or while walking down the aisles. While this person's mind is racing with fearful thoughts and images, what do you think is happening emotionally and physically? Since our emotions are primarily a product of our thoughts, the very same physiological symptoms (pounding heart, rapid and shallow breathing) that accompanied the first panic attack are already beginning to happen again. Why? Because the body responds to how the mind thinks. The body doesn't distinguish between a real or imaginary threat. To quote Dr. R. Reid Wilson:

> Within the Panic Cycle, it is not the body that responds incorrectly. The body responds perfectly to an exaggerated message from the mind. It is not the body that needs fixing, it is our thoughts, our images, our negative interpretation of our experiences that we must correct in order to gain control of panic. If we never told ourselves, in essence, "I'll lose control in that situation," then we would not be flipping on that unconscious emergency switch so often.[17]

Physiological responses to how we think are not foreign to the Bible. The following verses teach that our thoughts and beliefs do have an effect on our physical bodies. "A joyful heart is good medicine, but a broken spirit dries up the bones" (Proverbs 17:22). "For as he thinks within himself, so he is" (Proverbs 23:7). "Trust in the LORD with all your heart, and do not lean on your own understanding. In all your ways acknowledge Him, and He will make your paths straight. Do not be wise in your own eyes; fear the LORD and turn away from evil. It will be healing to your body, and refreshment to your bones" (Proverbs 3:5-8). "Beloved, I pray that in all respects you may prosper and be in good health, just as your soul prospers" (3 John 2).

Our Adequacy Is in Christ

We feel anxious when our perceived needs exceed our perceived resources. We panic when we feel helpless and out of control. Lucinda Bassett, director of the Midwest Center for Stress and Anxiety, shares how her feelings of inadequacy led to crippling fear:

> *I'm afraid I'll lose control. I'm afraid of my father, of God, of what people will think of me. I'm afraid "it" will catch up with me. I'm afraid my parents will embarrass me. I'm afraid I'll embarrass myself. My heart will stop. I'm afraid I'll throw up in front of everybody, and people will talk about me. I'm afraid I'll jump off the balcony. I'm afraid I'll die. I'm afraid I won't. I'm not good enough for my friends. I'm not good enough for God. I'll be found out. I'm afraid of the shadows on the wall. Someone's right outside my window waiting. I'm afraid of myself. I'm not talented enough. I'm not pretty enough. I'll panic. I'm afraid my parents won't love me anymore. I'm afraid I won't get everything done. I'll choke. I'm inadequate. I'm afraid. I'll go crazy. I'm afraid they'll lock me up and no one will care anymore. They won't like me if they really know me. My heart will be broken. I'm not rich enough. I'm not strong enough. I'm not smart enough. No one [would] ever be able to love me if they really knew me. I'm afraid to be myself. I'm afraid I have no self. I'm afraid I might fail. What if I succeed? What if it doesn't happen? What if it does? Why am I so afraid?*[18]

One of the goals of secular therapy is to convince people that they are adequate in themselves to handle their panic attacks. They have no other choice, but the apostle Paul advocates a different answer for the Christian: "Not that we are adequate in ourselves to consider anything as coming from ourselves, but our adequacy is from God, who also made us adequate as servants of a new covenant" (2 Corinthians 3:5,6).

As children of God, we have entered into a new covenant relationship with our heavenly Father. In the flesh we are weak and helpless, but "in Christ" we can do all things through Him who strengthens us (Philippians 4:13). In the flesh we may lose control, but if we walk by the Spirit we will have self-control (Galatians 5:23). "A natural man does not accept the things of the Spirit of God...but we have the mind of Christ" (1 Corinthians 2:14,16). For these reasons Jesus instructs us to "seek first His kingdom and His righteousness; and all these things shall be added to you. Therefore do not be anxious for tomorrow; for tomorrow will care for itself. Each day has enough trouble of its own" (Matthew 6:33,34).

There is one other important spiritual factor that must be considered. Paul says, "Do you not know that your bodies are members of Christ?...Do you not know that your body is a temple of the Holy Spirit who is in you, whom you have from God, and that you are not your own? For you have been bought with a price: therefore glorify God in your body" (1 Corinthians 6:15,19,20). Our bodies are not our own. We, including our bodies, belong to God. So we need to be good stewards of our bodies and submit them to Him as living sacrifices (Romans 12:1).

A Time for Medication

Let's review what we have learned so far. The origin of a panic attack can be a signal to our brain from our physical bodies saying something is wrong. How we interpret that signal is dependent upon how our minds have been previously programmed and what we presently think and believe. The origin of a panic attack can also be a spiritual battle for our minds, which we will discuss later. In cases other than spiritual attacks, how can one overcome panic attacks?

The first consideration is the body and the possible need for medication. To be good stewards of our bodies we should live a balanced life of nutrition, exercise, and rest. But living in decaying bodies and a diseased world may require the additional help of medications. We need medical help when there is something physically wrong with our bodies. Medication can also be helpful in treating symptoms leading up to the panic attack as well as the actual panic attack itself. (Usually this kind of medication is reserved for severe cases to enable patients to have some mental and emotional stability, allowing them to process their issues. In severe cases people are simply too stressed out to handle the truth without first taking medication.)

Many people suffering from panic disorder find help in godly counsel and realize complete resolution without the use of medications. We encourage you to seek the Lord for guidance and godly counsel before you consider medication. Then seek the advice of a qualified medical doctor. There are numerous medications (many of which are used in the treatment of depression as well) available for various anxiety disorders. You should ask about possible side-effects before agreeing to a particular medication.[19]

After acknowledging that "anti-anxiety medications can be a very beneficial tool,"[20] Lucinda Bassett gives the following warning:

> The problem with certain types of anti-anxiety medications is that they give you a false sense of recovery. They alleviate the symptoms, but do nothing to treat the cause, because the cause of your anxiety is very often the way you react and respond to things that are going on in your life."[21]

Medication may bring temporary relief from panic attacks, but they do not alleviate the phobias that may lie behind them nor do they renew your mind. The attacks will likely return when the medication is stopped if no cognitive restructuring has taken place or the physical causes have not been dealt with.

Another potential problem is self-medication. Some chronic sufferers become addicted to prescription drugs or turn to alcohol and illegal drugs to alleviate the emotional pain. Narcotizing one's fears only multiplies the problem, adding another layer to the bondage the individual is already experiencing—chemical dependency. Alcoholism and drug abuse cost businesses $200 billion annually as employees seek to self-medicate their way out of problems.[22] More important than the financial cost is the destruction of their bodies, marriages, and families.

Drugs and alcohol have never cured a problem. They only serve to give the illusion of well-being. When the drug wears off, the harsh realities of life resurface sending the victim into deeper depression, degradation, and despair. The Bible says, "Do not get drunk with wine, for that is dissipation, but be filled with the Spirit" (Ephesians 5:18). (If you or a friend struggle with self-medicating, we encourage you to read Neil's book *Freedom from Addiction*.)

Renewing the Mind

The central nervous system regulates every body function according to how the mind has been programmed. Beyond getting proper medical help, we need to be transformed by the renewing of our minds. The purpose of cognitive therapy is to help sufferers understand how their panic is the result of how they think and what they believe. The emotional response of fear is *always* preceded by a thought, although it can be so rapid that you're hardly aware of the connection. You don't do anything or feel anything without first thinking something.

In addition, certain personality types are more susceptible to panic than others. Dr. Edmund J. Bourne describes four subpersonalities that are most vulnerable to serious bouts with anxiety and panic: the "Worrier," the "Victim," the "Critic," and the "Perfectionist."[23] The "Worrier," Dr. Bourne says, is the most common and forceful subpersonality in anxiety-prone individuals. He describes the Worrier as follows:

> The Worrier creates anxiety by imagining the worst-case scenario. It scares you with fantasies of disaster or catastrophe when you imagine confronting something you fear. It also aggravates panic by reacting to the first physical symptoms of a panic attack. The Worrier promotes your fears that what is happening is dangerous or embarrassing. "What if I have a heart attack?!" "What will they think if they see me?"[24]

Personalities and patterns of thinking have been developed over time, and it takes time to renew the mind. Worriers find it hard to rest in the loving and protective arms of their heavenly Father. They feel that life's problems present a clear and present danger that calls for continual vigilance on their part, lest one be caught off-guard. For instance, at a "fear of flying school," the students were asked if they thought their worrying would help keep the plane in the air. Everyone agreed they had such thoughts. Maybe that is why Jesus asked, "And which of you by being anxious can add a single cubit to his life's span?" (Matthew 6:27). The answer is none, but you can seriously reduce the number of hours by worrying. Isaiah has strong words of comfort to those who put their trust in the Lord, and a sobering word of warning for those who don't:

> For thus the Lord GOD, the Holy One of Israel, has said, "In repentance and rest you shall be saved, in quietness and trust is your strength." But you were not willing, and you said, "No, for we will flee on

> horses," therefore you shall flee! "And we will ride on swift horses," therefore those who pursue you shall be swift. One thousand shall flee at the threat of one man, you shall flee at the threat of five; until you are left as a flag on a mountain top, and as a signal on a hill. Therefore the LORD longs to be gracious to you, and therefore He waits on high to have compassion on you. For the LORD is a God of justice; how blessed are all those who long for Him (Isaiah 30:15-18).

The other three subpersonalities that Dr. Bourne describes also play a key role in determining whether a believer in Christ will have the spiritual fortitude to walk by faith instead of fear. The "Victim" is overwhelmed by a sense of helplessness and hopelessness. Having established a track record of failure, this person sees no reason why his or her string of bad luck should end. According to Dr. Bourne:

> The Victim believes that there is something inherently wrong with you: you are in some ways deprived, defective, or unworthy. The Victim always perceives insurmountable obstacles between you and your goals. Characteristically, it bemoans, complains, and regrets things as they are at present. It believes that nothing will ever change.[25]

The whole message of the cross is that Jesus became the victim so that we can be victors in Him. Though the world may have dealt us a bad hand, we can still be overcomers. "For whatever is born of God overcomes the world; and this is the victory that has overcome the world—our faith. And who is the one who overcomes the world, but he who believes that Jesus is the Son of God?" (1 John 5:4,5).

We overcome the world because Jesus has already done so. We enter into that victory by believing the truth. The person who is convinced that he or she is helpless or hopeless has believed a lie and is consequently unable to walk by faith. How can we be helpless when the Bible says we can do all things through Christ who strengthens us (see Philippians 4:13)? How can we be hopeless when the God of hope is in us and He is able to fill us with all joy and peace in believing, that we may abound in hope by the power of the Holy Spirit (see Romans 15:13)?

Playing the role of the victim can become an excuse for not getting well. Jesus encountered such a man one day in Jerusalem:

> Now there is in Jerusalem by the sheep gate a pool, which is called in Hebrew Bethesda, having five porticoes. In these lay a multitude of those who were sick, blind, lame, and withered, waiting for the moving of the waters; for an angel of the Lord went down at certain seasons into the pool, and stirred up the water; whoever then first, after the stirring up of the water, stepped in was made well from whatever disease with which he was afflicted.
>
> And a certain man was there, who had been thirty-eight years in his sickness. When Jesus saw him lying there, and knew that he had already been a long time in that condition, He said to him, "Do you wish to get well?"
>
> The sick man answered Him, "Sir, I have no man to put me into the pool when the water is stirred up, but while I am coming, another steps down before me."
>
> Jesus said to him, "Arisc, take up your pallet, and walk."
>
> And immediately the man became well, and took up his pallet and began to walk (John 5:2-9).

"Do you wish to get well?" That is not a cruel question; it is a very important one. You can't get well unless you desire it and are willing to make the commitment to do whatever it takes. We have all been victimized, and we can't promise that you won't be again. But we can promise you that you don't have to remain a victim for the rest of your life. Nobody can fix the past. God doesn't even do that, but we can be free from it by the grace of God. That wonderful truth is inherent in the gospel.

The third subpersonality is the "Critic." Their overly sensitive conscience berates themselves and others. They come under mental attack by an unrelenting barrage of thoughts like: "I can't do anything right." "I am so stupid." "Other people don't struggle with this, but look at me!" The Critic never feels good about himself or what he has done. He is discouraged and defeated even before the panic attack hits.

Often echoing the voice of a demanding parent, teacher, coach, or employer, the Critic slaps negative labels on our souls, hindering us from experiencing the joy and freedom of being children of God. Faith is drained away, and we feel constantly put down for not being able to overcome our fears and live a normal life.

Closely akin to the "Critic" is the "Perfectionist." Its modus operandi is not to put you down, but to push you to do better and better.[26] The Perfectionist's favorite expressions are "I should..." "I have to..." and "I must..."[27] They never have any peace of mind because they can never achieve perfection. Their overwhelming need to accomplish more and more makes them driven, stressed, and irritable. They are setting themselves up for an anxiety disorder because they can't stand to fail, especially in public.

The Spiritual Battle for the Mind

There remain key mysteries that the secular world of medicine and psychology have yet to solve. What brings on these attacks in the first place? What causes a person who is normally able to handle stress to suddenly be stricken with a panic attack? Why do people sometimes awaken terrorized from a sound sleep? And why do Christians often find instantaneous freedom from these attacks when they call upon the name of the Lord? These burning questions were on the mind of someone who contacted our ministry:

> *I am wondering if you can help me out with a particular experience that has plagued me and my sleep for the past six or seven years. Although I am a Christian, I have probably experienced about 15 of these panic attacks over the past several years.*
>
> *They are usually associated with a time in which I've given something over to God or committed my ways to His.*
>
> *Here is a little history about my sleeping habits. When I was young I would dream very intense dreams about spirits or things related to the spirit world. I'm not sure why except that I am an artist and have always had a very vivid imagination. Other nights I would dream about the end times and things that happened—very intense dreams also!*
>
> *As I got older these dreams would happen less frequently, but when they did come they came with the same intensity.*
>
> *When I turned 17, I received a calling from God—a very distinct one. Unfortunately, because of my pride and fear, I did not follow that calling. Through the years since then I have received many opportunities to follow that original calling and each time I tried the panic attack would result. Consequently, I would back off from the calling because of the fear of another attack.*
>
> *The panic attack usually started by waking me out of my sleep to either a rushing sound in my ear, many*

people talking incoherently, or many people screaming. By the time this ends (usually in about 5 or 10 seconds) an intense, indescribable, mammoth fear envelopes my whole body.

I really can't describe how intense this fear is. My body becomes physically paralyzed, no movement. I can't talk. I can move my eyes around and can hear, though. Finally a heavy weight seems to rest on my chest and pushes me into my bed. At least that's what it feels like.

This whole experience lasts about a minute, but then I am usually wide awake and scared. I'm not sure what causes this, but I think it may be demonic.

We think so, too. The fact that these attacks occurred around the time she was making a serious move toward God could indicate a spiritual attack. Unfortunately, the scare tactic worked. She backed off from obeying God because of the fear. This is a very common strategy of the enemy. When I first started conducting conferences, I experienced the same kind of attack every evening before the conference began. You begin to wonder about yourself since nobody ever talks about these experiences in most of our churches.

So I began to ask during the conferences how many people have had the following experience: "You were suddenly awakened from a sound sleep with a tremendous sense of fear. You tried to move or say something, but you couldn't. You possibly felt a pressure on your chest or something grabbing your throat." At least a third of the attendees in every conference have had at least one such experience sometime in their lives. Most of them have never shared their experiences. If people did share their experiences with secular counselors, they would likely call it a panic attack. They don't call it a fear attack because they can't identify the object of the fear. We can! This is a spiritual attack, and it can be resolved very easily.

The natural response to fear is to say or do something immediately. Then why couldn't we physically respond? Because we cannot resolve the problem physically. The Bible says, "For though we live in the world, we do not wage war as the world does. The weapons we fight with are not the weapons of the world. On the contrary, they have divine power to demolish strongholds" (2 Corinthians 10:3,4 NIV). God knows the thoughts and intentions of our heart, so we can always call upon the Lord in our minds. The moment we do, we will be able to speak. All we would have to say is "Jesus," and the devil will flee: "At the name of Jesus every knee will bow, in heaven and on earth and under the earth" (Philippians 2:10 NLT). The order of Scripture is critical. First, submit to God inwardly, and then you will be able to resist the devil outwardly (James 4:7).

Spiritual attacks usually occur at night when we are alone and more vulnerable. Being awakened out of a sound sleep heightens our sense of terror as we are caught off guard and easily confused. Scripture is filled with examples of humans being overwhelmed with fear in the presence of angelic beings. Job's friend, Eliphaz, described an experience he had:

> Now a word was brought to me stealthily, and my ear received a whisper of it. Amid disquieting thoughts from the visions of the night, when deep sleep falls on men, dread came upon me, and trembling, and made all my bones shake. Then a spirit passed by my face; the hair of my flesh bristled up. It stood still, but I could not discern its appearance; a form was before my eyes (Job 4:12-16).

The prophet Daniel and his companions were visited by a powerful heavenly messenger and experienced symptoms not unlike those of a panic attack:

> Now I, Daniel, alone saw the vision, while the men who were with me did not see the vision; nevertheless, a great dread fell on them, and they ran away to hide themselves. So I was left alone and saw this great vision; yet no strength was left in me, for my natural color turned to a deathly pallor, and I retained no strength (Daniel 10:7,8).

Several times Daniel was so debilitated by this vision, that the angel had to encourage him by saying, "Do not be afraid" and touched him physically so that he could be strengthened. Daniel's description of how this angelic encounter had affected his breathing is particularly significant in light of the symptoms of panic attacks we discussed earlier. "For how can such a servant of my lord talk with such as my lord? As for me, there remains just now no strength in me, nor has any breath been left in me" (Daniel 10:17).

When Zacharias, John the Baptist's father-to-be, received the news from the angel that he was to be a father he "was troubled when he saw him, and fear gripped him" (Luke 1:12). The shepherds outside of Bethlehem were terribly frightened when the angel of the Lord appeared to them on the first Christmas (Luke 2:9). The guards outside Jesus' tomb "shook for fear of [the angel] and became like dead men" in the early morning of Christ's resurrection (Matthew 28:4).

Human beings react in fear to angels with such regularity that the most common greeting from angel to man is, "Do not be afraid." But it seems like angels (and demons are fallen angels) can turn their fearsomeness on or off at will. For example, Hebrews tells us that we are to show hospitality to strangers because we could "have entertained angels without knowing it" (Hebrews 13:2). Clearly, for whatever reason, those angelic beings cloaked their true identity and didn't invoke a fear response at all. At other times a being that was obviously an angel appeared to the apostles (Acts 5:17-20) and Peter (Acts 12:5-10) and gave them a personal escort out of prison. In each case there is no indication that the men were the least bit afraid.

The point of all this is to realize that the Bible teaches that at times the presence or appearance of angels causes great fear to fall on people, though not always. It is then completely consistent with Scripture to say that a fallen angel (demon), if it chose to do so, could manifest itself to a human being and cause tremendous fear. At other times one could pay attention to a deceiving spirit or spirit guide thinking it is a friend.

How can we discern what is from God? The Bible says, "Humble yourselves, therefore, under the mighty hand of God, that He may exalt you at the proper time, casting all your anxiety upon Him, because He cares for you. Be of sober spirit, be on the alert. Your adversary, the devil, prowls about like a roaring lion, seeking someone to devour" (1 Peter 5:6-8). Lions roar in order to paralyze their prey with fear so they can consume them. Sometimes they will stand over a little burrow and roar. Some little animal will come running out in fear, right into the jaws of death.

But this lion doesn't have any teeth. The devil is defeated and disarmed. All he can do is roar. But his lying demons are paralyzing people in fear. We cannot escape the biblical connection between anxiety (double-mindedness) and the spiritual battle for our minds. We can also see the connection in Ephesians 4:25-27: "Therefore, laying aside falsehood, speak truth, each one of you with his neighbor, for we are members of one another. Be angry, and yet do not sin; do not let the sun go down on your anger, and do not give the devil an opportunity."

We have been clearly warned. "The Spirit explicitly says that in later times some will fall away from the faith, paying attention to deceitful spirits and doctrines of demons" (1 Timothy 4:1). Paul says, "I am afraid, lest as the serpent deceived Eve by his craftiness, your minds should be led astray from the simplicity and purity of devotion to Christ" (2 Corinthians 11:3).

To win this battle for our minds we must take every thought captive to the obedience of Christ. It doesn't make any difference if the thoughts in our minds came from our memory banks, television, another person, the pit, or was an original thought of our own. We take *every* thought captive. If what we are thinking isn't true according to the Word of God, then we shouldn't believe it.

Should we rebuke every negative thought? No! You don't overcome the father of lies by trying not to believe him. You overcome the lies of this world by choosing the truth, and you keep choosing it until your mind is renewed. If you think you are going to panic, you probably will. If you believe in your heart that all things are possible with Christ and that you can do all things through Him who strengthens you, then you can. Whether you think you can or whether you think you can't, either way you are right for, "as he thinks within himself, so he is" (Proverbs 23:7).

The enemies of our sanctification are the world, the flesh, and the devil. There are definite dangers in this world, but Jesus said, "In the world you have tribulation, but take courage; I have overcome the world" (John 16:33). Our flesh is in opposition to the Spirit, but "those who belong to Christ Jesus have crucified the flesh with its passions and desires" (Galatians 5:24). The devil is roaring around like a lion, but you are not alone in your struggle. Peter's advice is to "resist him, firm in your faith, knowing that the same experiences of suffering are being accomplished by your brethren who are in the world" (1 Peter 5:9). Be encouraged by what Jesus said:

> Peace I leave with you; My peace I give to you; not as the world gives, do I give to you. Let not your heart be troubled, nor let it be fearful (John 14:27).

8

Breaking Strongholds of Fear

It is not the lie that passeth through the mind,
but the lie that sinketh in, and settleth in it,
that doth the hurt.

—Francis Bacon
Of Truth

Unless you have experienced the chilling choke hold of fear, you cannot begin to imagine the terror of its presence or the horror of its possible return. All of life as we normally know it can be swallowed up in its fury as it dominates the "picture screen" of the mind and overwhelms the imagination.

The tragedy of fear's cruel dominion is heightened when its victim is a child, a child who may carry this awful burden well into adulthood. The following testimony is one such story:

The mighty river rushes on, headed for its destination. I see my life floating upon the water. I am carried gently and freely. Clouds above me are broken by streaks of sunlight, revealing the secrets and mysteries of the calm river. It's as if for a moment I see a glimpse of God Himself.

Suddenly a storm comes forth, ripping and tearing at the calm, destroying the peace. The storm unjustly attacks and destroys my innocence. Senseless. An abandoned child cries in the night, from deep within, fearful of what is unknown. Tears fall to the ground unseen and unshared, for there is no one else.

The frightened child crouches low, waiting for the storm to pass. But the storm rages out of control, like a vicious animal. The river crashes, beating mercilessly against the cold, hard rocks, and lashes out against the child's bent and trembling body. Greedy fingers of water grab for the lonely, frightened child. Taunting, teasing, terrorizing. The once gentle river now tortures. Foam-lined lips grin hideously and bite ferociously.

The child weeps, now wet and weakened, waiting for someone. No one comes. The dark night has no end and the storm continues its rampage while the child whimpers in fear, clinging to the cold, bare rock, and prays.

This is a story of a woman who was forced into a satanic cult as a young girl. The physical abuse she went through was terrifying. Not long ago, she found her way into two churches, neither of which was equipped to handle the severe bondage in her life. But God has truly begun to answer her prayers as a child, as the end of her testimony reveals:

At this point, terror is a mild word for what I began to experience. Rumors began to fly, people were leaving the church, afraid that my demons would jump on them and their families. One pastor accused me of putting a curse on his family.

The nightmares were terrifying. Flashbacks became a daily occurrence. It seemed hopeless. I was convinced that I was destined to be a child of the demons forever.

Then circumstances led me to a very special Christian counselor. Initially the work he did with me seemed to be failing. My anxiety level was so high and the demonic had much control over me. His attempts at helping me find freedom seemed like jumbled words. Fear dominated my whole life.

Then, Neil, I read one of your books at my counselor's request. Something seemed to click, and we began going through the "Steps to Freedom in Christ." I am reading every word out loud by myself to him.

The struggle is not over. But now for the first time there is hope and a desire to live free in Christ. I no longer want to die. I am beginning to see tragedy turned into opportunity.

Jesus Sets Us Free

No matter what you have been through or are going through, Jesus wants to set you free. That is the reason He came, as Isaiah prophesied:

> The Spirit of the Lord GOD is upon me, because the LORD has anointed me to bring good news to the afflicted; He has sent me to bind up the brokenhearted, to proclaim liberty to captives, and freedom to prisoners; to proclaim the favorable year of the LORD, and the day of vengeance of our God; to comfort all who mourn, to grant those who mourn in Zion, giving them a garland instead of ashes, the oil of gladness instead of mourning, the mantle of praise instead of a spirit of fainting (Isaiah 61:1-3).

Though Christ has ascended into heaven to sit at the right hand of the Father, He continues His ministry of liberation through His people, the church. The truth still sets people free today, and Jesus is the truth. Though composed of imperfect people, the church of the living God is still "the pillar and support of the truth" (1 Timothy 3:15). It is given wisdom through the Word of God, which is truth (John 17:17); it is empowered by the Holy Spirit, who is the Spirit of truth (John 16:13).

The Lord has a specific plan for your freedom. He knows exactly what you need, when you need it, and from where it should come. And when Jesus does the work, He does it right. For when the Son sets you free, you shall be free indeed (John 8:36).

From Fear to Freedom

Though not nearly as terrible a case of childhood fear as our previous story, the following account was a poignant reminder to me (Rich) of the power of fear to control. But more than that, it serves as a demonstration of the tender mercy and grace of God to deliver a child from fear.

> *"Brian has been acting a little strange lately," my wife, Shirley, stated once the kids had left the room. I could tell she was concerned. I had just returned from a ministry trip and was getting the usual "state of the family" update.*
>
> *"In what way?" I replied, putting down the mail I was sorting through. I was concerned, too, since our five-year-old son seems to be vulnerable at times.*
>
> *"Well, he hasn't wanted to eat anything sweet for a few days. And when he was over at a friend's house, he wouldn't even eat ice cream. At least not until they told him there wasn't any sugar in it." She chuckled a little bit at their success in tricking Brian.*

"It sounds like he's afraid of eating sugar. Have they had a dental hygienist or somebody like that at preschool lately?"

There had been someone talking about "sugar bugs" in his class recently, and that had apparently scared him. We decided to wait and see what happened. That night after dinner, Brian refused the cookie that the others got and opted instead for a banana.

"You know, Brian, bananas have sugar in them, too. Natural sugar. It's good for you. In fact, just about everything these days has sugar in it. So to keep from eating sugar, you'd have to stop eating!" I laughed as I finished my "inspired" sermon, fully expecting that Brian would laugh with me and chomp down the banana. I turned back to washing the dishes in the sink, figuring that was the end of this fear of sugar nonsense. The whole thing seemed rather silly. After all, most parents would be overjoyed if their five-year-old stopped eating sugary foods!

A minute or so later, I caught a movement out of the corner of my eye. It didn't register at first, but then I realized that it was Brian. I turned around to see that he was gone from the kitchen table and so was his dessert. I looked in the trash can and there was the uneaten banana.

A little annoyed at Brian's self-will, I marched upstairs to his room. He was sitting on his bed in tears. Softening a bit upon seeing how upset he was, I asked him, "What's wrong, Brian? Why didn't you eat the banana?"

"It has sugar in it."

Frustrated by the irrationality of the whole thing, I left his room, went downstairs and picked up a banana. I took it up to his room, a "brilliant" plan unfolding in my mind.

"Brian, there's nothing to be afraid of. Watch what I do." Breaking the banana in half, I gave one part to him and kept the other. "Daddy is going to eat half of the banana, and you eat the other half, okay?"

He wasn't impressed. As I enthusiastically wolfed down my half, he gingerly took a microscopic bite and promptly spat it out. By that time, I was really frustrated but still undaunted. Another plan formulated in my mind. I went back to the kitchen and grabbed a candy bar. There's no way he'll be able to resist that, I reasoned.

I was wrong! As I chomped down my half, he just stared blankly at me, holding his end of the bargain like it was a mildewed brussels sprout. At wit's end, I slunk downstairs to find Shirley. Totally exasperated, I finally got around to doing what I should have done in the first place.

"Shirley, we need to pray. Brian's fear of sugar is real and serious. Something is very wrong. He wouldn't even eat the candy bar I gave him."

As we prayed, I confessed my frustration. God's peace returned. So did wisdom! The Lord clearly directed me to go back and pray with Brian, seeking the root of his problem, just as I would with an adult.

The Lord moved, and Brian was much calmer. He was able to recall some of the things that had scared him. One by one he, in his five-year-old way, renounced those fears. He said, "I say no to the fear of _______!" Heights, fire, bad dreams, and a few other typical childhood fears came to our minds.

Happy for the progress we made, I was still perplexed as to why he was so fearful of sweets.

"Brian, why are you so afraid of eating sugar?"

"'Cause I'll get a cavity," he answered, choking back the tears.

"No, you won't. We'll brush your teeth, and that won't be a problem at all."

I could tell he still was not convinced. "Brian, do you know what a cavity is?"

He shook his head, tears starting to roll down his cheeks. I then hoped that my clear explanation of the nature, origin and treatment of cavities would do the trick. No dice. So I prayed for more wisdom, and God brought the first breakthrough we needed to help Brian overcome his fear.

"Brian, what do you think will happen to you if you get a cavity?" I asked, sensing that something critical was about to be revealed.

"I'll die."

Bingo! The poor kid had believed the lie that sugar = cavity = death. No wonder he was so afraid of sugar! He had likely misinterpreted something that had been said in his school.

I had Brian renounce the fear of cavities, the fear of death, and also the spirit of fear, affirming that God had not given that to him. He announced that God had instead given him power, love, and a sound mind.

But that wasn't the end of the battle. In school the next day he hardly touched his peanut butter and jelly sandwich. Shirley and I prayed again, this time personally dealing with any fears that we and our parents could have passed on to our children. The Lord then led us to help Brian face his fear head on. The showdown was to be that evening after dinner at the local Dairy Queen®.

I could tell that Brian was nervous after we told him where we were going for dessert. "I'm not hungry for any dessert," he lied, hoping we would leave him alone.

Upon arrival, I purchased everyone's ice cream, including a vanilla cone (his favorite at the time) for

Brian. He watched in silence as everyone else ferociously attacked their dessert. One by one I pointed out to him that his sisters, Michelle and Emily, as well as his mommy and daddy were all eating ice cream. And none of us was getting a cavity. None of us had obviously dropped dead. Still his dessert sat, melted rivulets of ice cream forming small puddles on the table. The "girls" all finished theirs and headed to the rest room. I felt like I had to press the issue to a crisis point with my son.

"Brian, I know you are thinking that if you eat anything with sugar in it, you will die. There's only one way you'll ever know if that little thought in your head is the truth or a lie."

"What's that?" he asked, turning his sad eyes toward me.

"Take a bite."

Rarely have I prayed so fervently. And rarely have I felt such joy as when he leaned over and took a bite.

Relieved, I said quietly, "Did you get a cavity?"

"No," Brian replied, the faintest smile appearing on his face.

"And did you die?" I asked, grinning from ear to ear.

"No." By this time, Brian was smiling, too.

"Then take another bite."

Thankfully, he did. And then he took another and another and another, without any coaxing from me. And then he turned and said something I'll always remember.

"Daddy, I just felt the fear inside of me snap in two, just like a stick."

And it was over. Really over. Not only was the fear broken, but the lie behind it was overcome by truth. Prior to that incident Brian was very fearful. Now he is not afraid at all. Despite his small size, he is one of the most confident, happy boys you would want to meet. A wide grin rarely leaves his face.

Some Important Cautions

There are two reasons why we shared that rather lengthy "home movie." First, to show you what is *not* effective in dealing with a stronghold of fear. Second, this story provides a helpful illustration of breaking down the walls of fear that we will draw upon when we explain the "Phobia Finder."

The futility of trying to resolve an anxiety disorder with mere human reasoning is obvious. In the heat of battle our own ideas can appear quite clever. The temptation is to lean on our own understanding rather than trusting in the Lord with all our hearts. The Lord promises to direct our steps when we acknowledge Him in all our ways (Proverbs 3:5,6). We need the guidance of God to find the root cause of fear and the grace of God to overcome it.

Many of the struggles that children have are simply a matter of growth and are better left to the healing power of time. But we cannot assume that every strange or unusual behavior in the life of a child is just a phase that he or she will outgrow. Debilitating problems like paranoia, lying, abusive behavior, and rebellion have to be resolved. The Lord will give discernment to parents who truly seek it, providing the wisdom to know His path to freedom and healing. The human soul and spirit are remarkably complex, but we have this promise from God's Word:

> For the word of God is living and active and sharper than any two-edged sword, and piercing as far as the division of soul and spirit, of both joints and marrow, and able to judge the thoughts and intentions of the heart. And there is no creature hidden from His

> sight, but all things are open and laid bare to the eyes of Him with whom we have to do (Hebrews 4:12,13).

James provides the biblical basis for finding and maintaining freedom from fear: "But He gives a greater grace. Therefore it says, 'God is opposed to the proud, but gives grace to the humble.' Submit therefore to God. Resist the devil and he will flee from you. Draw near to God and He will draw near to you" (James 4:6-8).

The Key to Freedom

We need to stop submitting to fear and start submitting to God. The word *submit* means to subject oneself to some authority. It was a military term meaning to rank or arrange under. Submitting means letting go of the reins and putting them in the hands of someone who is superior in rank. To submit to God is to come under His authority. It is to acknowledge the omnipresence and omnipotence of our heavenly Father. We are acknowledging Him as the only legitimate fear object when we submit to Him. The essence of humility is to "put no confidence in the flesh" and choose to "be strong in the LORD, and in the strength of His might" (see Philippians 3:3; Ephesians 6:10).

This beginning step of liberation from fear may be the most frightening part of the process for some people. It is like the man who slipped at the edge of a cliff, but managed to hang on to a tree branch for dear life. He could not pull himself up and to lose his grip on the branch meant sudden death. He cried for help and to his relief he heard a voice say, "I will help you."

The desperate man looked up but didn't see anybody. "Who are you?" he asked. "Are you going to help me?"

Then he heard the voice say, "I'm the one who created you, and I will help you because I love you, but you have to let go!"

That is the step of faith that all of us must take in order to be saved. But what alternative do we have? We can try to save ourselves, but eventually we will lose our grip and fall. If hanging on to the reins of life has only resulted in fear and anxiety th[illegible] does that not clearly reveal the futility of such a choice? Could not the presence of anxiety be the very impetus we need in order to submit to God and experience His peace? We have to be brought to the end of our self-sufficiency in order to find our sufficiency in Christ.

True v. False Security

It is far safer to put ourselves into the hands of our all-sufficient heavenly Father than to rely on the false security that comes from relying on our own resources. As God's children we have not been left as orphans, but many live as if they have no heavenly Father at all (see John 14:18). We are like children in an orphanage who can't go to sleep unless we have two pieces of bread—one to fill our stomachs today and one to clutch in our hand for tomorrow. Jesus is the bread of life, and we can cling to Him today and trust Him for tomorrow.

The following parable was written by a dear woman who is learning that her heavenly Father truly does provide and protect:

> *There was once a new tree in a garden full of taller, mature trees. This was the first year the little tree had received a nice covering of leaves, and it was quite comfortable with the leaves it had. So when fall came and its leaves started to turn yellow the little tree was scared! In its fear, it looked around at the other trees and saw that their leaves were also changing color, so it relaxed a little.*
>
> *But then it lost a leaf! The little tree panicked and held on to the rest of its leaves tightly. It looked around again at the other trees and saw that their leaves were falling off too!*
>
> *Why were they letting their leaves get away? They won't be protected from the wind any more, and what*

about the sun? How will they give shade without leaves? The little tree decided it was going to keep its leaves, even if they were now turning brown. The leaves were dead now, but the little tree held on, feeling safe hiding under the shelter of the leaves. Snow fell, and the leaves became heavy, but he still held on.

Soon the weather started to turn warmer and light rains replaced the snowfall. Ah, this was much better, he told himself. Then he noticed the other trees had little green buds on them, and some were starting to flower! He looked at himself and saw that he did not have any signs of change. Pretty soon the other trees had glorious leaves on them, and some had fruit hanging among their branches. Now he was jealous!

So he asked God, "Hey, why did you give the other trees new leaves and fruit, but you did not give me anything?"

God said, "My dear tree, I gave you the same sunshine, I gave you the same rain, and I gave you the same love as the other trees in the garden."

The tree said, "But God, look at me! I am ugly! Why did they get new leaves, and I did not? It's not fair!"

God replied, "Well, my child, you did not get new leaves because you did not let go of the dead ones. You see, the older trees have been through the seasons before. They know that when they let a dead leaf go, I will replace it with a new one when spring comes. Not only that, but I usually give them more than they had before! They sometimes struggle with letting go, just like you. That struggle does not go away when you grow.

"You just have to know that there is a reason why you can't keep your dead leaves. Don't allow fear and pride to trick you into keeping the things of your past.

Besides, you have to admit that it was difficult to hang on to them in the winter! It is easier to let go and let me worry about the new leaves. That is a lesson all new trees have to learn."

The little tree said, "Are you saying that I can be just as beautiful as the other trees?"

God said, "You are already just as beautiful as they are to me. I do not love you any less because of your old leaves. I see what you can be, not what you look like now. But if you truly want to grow, be patient, let go of your leaves as they die, and I will do the rest. I love you."[1]

Resolving Root Issues

Does the prospect of letting go of control of your life scare you? Dead leaves are a sure thing, but the possibility of new leaves doesn't appear as certain unless it is based on the absolute authority of God's Word. At least with dead leaves, you have something to protect you—but dead leaves are only false shields. Jesus wants to set you free and "cleanse your conscience from dead works to serve the living God" (Hebrews 9:14).

We urge you to let go of the dead leaves in your life. Start by going through the "Steps to Freedom in Christ" in the back of this book. It is a thorough spiritual and moral inventory. If possible, work through them with a trusted pastor, counselor, or Christian friend in whose presence you can be open and honest.

The "Steps to Freedom in Christ" is a guide, not a formula. Only Jesus can set us free, but the "Steps" have been a helpful tool for thousands of people who are seeking to experience the freedom Christ purchased for them at Calvary. The "Steps" will help you resolve personal and spiritual conflicts by submitting to God and resisting the devil.

I (Rich) had a conversation with a man attending one of Neil's conferences. He had been raised in a home in which incest was common. As the youngest of 13 children, he had been sexually molested from the time he was 5. Every one of the children and both parents were involved in this depravity. The children believed this was the way all families lived.

He was now in his forties, married, and with a family of his own. The incest had long since ceased, and he himself was not a child abuser, but the fallout from his past still had a hold on him. He was struggling with panic attacks and had become increasingly agoraphobic. He was unable to drive anywhere by himself, and the prospect of traveling to new places terrified him. The fact that he was able to attend the conference was a testimony of the grace of God already at work in his life.

We prayed together, and he went inside to listen to the first message. I didn't see him again until after he had gone through the "Steps to Freedom in Christ" at the very end of the conference. With a huge grin, he testified how Jesus had set him free from the guilt and shame of his past, and that in the process the fear had left him. In fact, he told me that he was going to drive his wife up into the mountains, a place he had longed to see but had previously been afraid to visit.

Seek God First

We cannot overstate how necessary it is to get right with God first. David wrote, "I sought the LORD, and He answered me, and delivered me from all my fears. They looked to Him and were radiant, and their faces shall never be ashamed. This poor man cried and the LORD heard him, and saved him out of all his troubles. The angel of the LORD encamps around those who fear Him, and rescues them" (Psalm 34:4-7).

This was a lesson that Joshua had to learn the hard way. Fresh off their stunning victory over Jericho, Joshua and the Israelites set their sights on the next conquest. The small town of Ai appeared weak compared to the mighty walled city that had just fallen before them. So Joshua dispatched a team of men to spy out the land.

The spies came back confident that only a few thousand men would be needed to take Ai. Joshua listened to their counsel, but neglected to inquire of God. As a result, the small Israelite army was soundly defeated and 36 men lost their lives.

Joshua, being a godly man at heart, fell down before the Lord in mourning. He complained to Him about the defeat, their humiliation, and even the damage done to the great name of God. Joshua was paralyzed by fear and discouragement and uncertain as to what he should do next. God responded by saying:

> Rise up! Consecrate the people and say, "Consecrate yourselves for tomorrow, for thus the LORD, the God of Israel, has said, 'There are things under the ban in your midst, O Israel. You cannot stand before your enemies until you have removed the things under the ban from your midst'" (Joshua 7:13).

If you have successfully resolved your personal and spiritual conflicts by submitting to God and resisting the devil, then you are ready to analyze your fears and work out a responsible course of action. To do so, use the "Phobia Finder":[2]

Phobia Finder

A. Analyze your fear under God's authority and guidance.
   1. Identify all fear objects (What are you afraid of?).
   2. Determine when you first experienced the fear.
   3. What events preceded the first experience?
   4. Determine the lies behind every phobia.

B. Determine the ways you have been living under the control of fear rather than living by faith in God.

1. How has fear:
    a. prevented you from doing what is right and responsible?
    b. compelled you to do what is wrong and irresponsible?
    c. prompted you to compromise your witness for Christ?
2. Confess any active or passive way in which you have allowed fear to control your life.
3. Commit yourself to God to live a righteous and responsible life.

C. Prayerfully work out a plan of responsible behavior.
D. Determine in advance what your response will be to any fear object.
E. Commit yourself to carry out your plan of action in the power of the Holy Spirit.

Analyze Your Fear

Begin the first step in the "Phobia Finder" by praying the following prayer out loud:

> *Dear heavenly Father, I come to You as Your child. I put myself under Your protective care and acknowledge that You are the only legitimate fear object in my life. I confess that I have been fearful and anxious because of my lack of trust and unbelief. I have not always lived by faith in You, and too often I have relied on my own strength and resources. I thank You that I am forgiven in Christ.*
>
> *I choose to believe the truth that You have not given me a spirit of fear, but of power, love, and a sound mind. Therefore, I renounce any spirit of fear. I ask You to reveal to my mind all the fears that have been controlling me. Show me how I have become fearful and the lies I have*

believed. I desire to live a responsible life in the power of Your Holy Spirit. Show me how these fears have kept me from doing that. I ask this so that I can confess, renounce, and overcome every fear by faith in You. In Jesus' name I pray, amen.

The following list may help you recognize some of the fears that have been hindering your walk of faith. On a separate sheet, write down the ones that apply to you, as well as any others not on the list that the Spirit of God has revealed to you. As you prayerfully recall your past, write a brief description of what happened (and when) to trigger that fear.

Fear of Satan
Fear of divorce
Fear of death
Fear of not being loved by God
Fear of never being loved
Fear of not being able to love others
Fear of marriage
Fear of rejection by people
Fear of never getting married
Fear of never having children
Fear of disapproval
Fear of embarrassment
Fear of failure
Fear of being/becoming homosexual
Fear of financial problems
Fear of going crazy
Fear of being a hopeless case
Fear of the death of a loved one
Fear of the future
Fear of confrontation

Fear of being victimized by crime
Fear of losing my salvation
Fear of committing the unpardonable sin
Fear of specific people, animals, or objects

Other specific fears the Lord brings to mind:

We all live by faith, but the real question is, "What or whom do we believe?" You could choose to believe that it would be hopeless to even try overcoming your fears. But that's not true. God is the God of all hope, and there is nothing that is too difficult for Him (see Romans 15:13; Jeremiah 32:17). You could choose to believe that it is safer and wiser to avoid certain strong-willed people, or elevators in stores, or airplanes. You could believe, like Rich's son did, that sugar in foods will kill you. Such false beliefs are not neutral or harmless because whatever is not of faith is sin (Romans 14:23). *The root of any phobia is a belief that is not based in truth.* These false beliefs need to be uprooted and replaced by the truth of God's Word.

Take as much time in prayer as you need to discern these lies because renouncing them and choosing the truth is a critical step toward gaining and maintaining your freedom in Christ. Search the Scriptures for the truth. Seek counsel from mature, godly believers. You have to know and choose to believe the truth in order for it to set you free. Write down the lies you have believed for every fear and the corresponding truth from the Word of God.

Analyzing Your Lifestyle

The next step is to determine how fear has prevented you from living a responsible life, compelled you to do that which is irresponsible, or compromised your Christian witness. Phobias affect how we live and we need to know how. A timid Christian homemaker who fears her pagan husband will likely compromise her witness, which will probably lead to irresponsible behavior. An intimidated employee may lie for her boss even though she knows it is wrong. A teenager may compromise his faith and participate in a crime because he is afraid his friends will reject him.

After you have taken ample time to seek the Lord on these matters, and you feel you have gained the necessary insights into your fear, it is time to experience God's cleansing through confession and repentance: "If we confess our sins, He is faithful and righteous to forgive us our sins and to cleanse us from all unrighteousness" (1 John 1:9; see also Proverbs 28:13). Remember, it is the kindness of God that leads you to repentance (Romans 2:4). Confession is agreeing with God that what you did was sinful. Repentance is the choice to turn away from sin and walk by faith in God.

Express the following prayer for each of the controlling fears that you have analyzed above:

> *Dear Lord, I confess and repent of the fear of ________. I have believed the (state the lie). I renounce that lie, and I choose to believe the truth (state the truth). I also confess any and all ways this fear has resulted in living irresponsibly or compromising my witness for Christ, including ________.*
>
> *I now choose to live by faith in You, Lord, believing Your promise that You will protect me and meet all my needs. In Jesus' trustworthy name I pray, amen.*

After working through every fear the Lord has revealed to you (including their accompanying lies and sinful behavior), pray the following prayer:

> *Dear heavenly Father, I thank You that You are indeed trustworthy. I choose to believe You even when my feelings and circumstances tell me to fear. You have told me not to fear, for You are with me; to not anxiously look about me for You are my God. You will strengthen me, help me, and surely uphold me with Your righteous right hand.*
>
> *I now ask You to show me Your plan of action for living responsibly and facing my fear. I commit myself to do what You tell me to do, knowing that Your grace is sufficient. I pray this with faith in the name of Jesus, my Savior and Lord, amen.*

Most of the lies we have believed come from living in a fallen world, but the god of this world is the father of lies (John 8:44). Part of the purpose of encouraging you to use the "Phobia Finder" to go through the "Steps to Freedom in Christ" and to analyze your fears, is to discern what part the devil may be playing in your struggle with fear and anxiety. That is precisely what happened to this person:

> *Having only been a Christian for five years, I was just coming to understand that many of my experiences of fear and anxiety were not of God, but were of Satan. I couldn't drive over bridges without feeling like I was going to lose control of the steering wheel. I could see myself and my car going over the side, and this totally took over my mind as I came closer to any bridge.*

I would become almost paralyzed by fear, breaking out into a sweat and almost being unable to breathe. I would call for Jesus to get me over and He always did, but still the fear would come back the next time. So I would try and avoid using bridges, or I would just not go where I wanted to.

As a result, I was not enjoying my life to its fullest, as I was living in bondage.

One Sunday in church, a friend of mine came over with a book, plunked it into my lap, and told me to read it. The book was The Bondage Breaker. *I read through it and went through the "Steps to Freedom in Christ" in the back.*

When I first read it, I didn't sleep very well. That first night I dreamed that Satan was taking me from room to room in a large mansion and was showing me everything he said he owned and how he would make it mine. I woke a number of times and found myself repeating Scriptures out loud and calling on the Lord for help.

The second night, I didn't have the dreams, but I woke up about 3 A.M. shaking violently, as if terribly frightened. I felt no inner fear, only this physical manifestation. I fell back asleep and woke up an hour-and-a-half later. As soon as I awoke, I felt very refreshed and calm and sensed the Lord saying to me, "I told you that I would never leave you nor forsake you."

Soon after that I had to cross a bridge. When I came to within 100 feet of it, I loudly said, "In the name of Jesus Christ, I bind you spirit of fear. For Jesus is driving this car now, and I am only the passenger!" I sailed over that bridge and talked happily to my daughter who was in the backseat.

I do not experience that fear any longer, and I know I no longer own it. And it certainly does not own me!

A Responsible Plan of Action

Let's summarize what you have done so far. You have submitted to God and resisted the devil. You have identified your fears and the lies behind them. You understand how those fears have kept you from living a responsible life or compelled you to compromise your witness for Christ. You are now halfway home because a problem well stated is half-solved.

The next step is to face the fear and prayerfully work out a plan to overcome it. Somebody once said, "Do the thing you fear the most and the death of fear is certain." When Rich and Shirley finally discovered the root of Brian's fear, they knew he had to face it. That's why they took him out for ice cream. He wasn't truly free until he took the first few bites. By his own admission, that's when he felt the fear snap in two inside of him.

The woman in the testimony about driving over bridges was exercising faith. By faith she verbally resisted the devil (as Jesus showed us to do when He was tempted in the wilderness), and she declared that Jesus was in charge. Then she drove by faith over the bridge. She broke the back of fear when she called on the name of the Lord and drove across.

Years ago I learned that one of my college students hadn't spoken to her father in six months. The tension in the home was unbearable. I asked her if she would be willing to work out a plan of action to overcome her fear of him. Somehow she needed to break the ice, so I asked her what she thought would happen if she just said, "Hi, Dad," when he came home that night. She wasn't sure, so we considered the possibilities. He could get mad, he could say "hi" back, or he could do nothing. It was the latter possibility that she feared the most.

Then we worked out a plan for each possible response by her father. Then I asked her to commit to saying "hi" that night. She agreed to do that and then call me afterwards. About 7:30

P.M. I got a call from a joyful young lady who reported, "He said 'hi' back!"

Fear is like a mirage in the desert. It seems so real until you move toward it, then it disappears into thin air. But as long as we back away from fear, it will haunt us and grow in size like a giant.

There's a Coast Guard story of an old sea captain who ordered his crew to sea in the midst of a raging storm. A young seaman cried out, "We can't go out; we'll never come back!" To which the captain replied, "We must go out; we don't have to come back!" Fear gets swallowed up when we decide to fulfill our responsibilities.

In Christ we have all been allotted a measure of faith. To exercise that faith we must have sound judgment. To accomplish the goal of complete freedom, we must take that first step in the right direction. If your plan to overcome fear includes confronting other people, it is helpful to determine in advance how you would respond to their positive or negative reactions. In other words the plan shouldn't just include the first step, it should also include possible second and third steps.

Many learned fears should be overcome in bite-size steps. In Dr. Bourne's book *The Anxiety and Phobia Workbook*, he gives many helpful suggestions on *desensitization* from fears, including setting realistic goals.[3] His suggestions on how to overcome the fear of elevators will give you a helpful prototype for making step-by-step progress toward a goal. Each one, as you'll see, is a slightly larger "bite-size" chunk than the one before.

1. Look at elevators, watching them come and go.
2. Stand in a stationary elevator with a trusted friend.
3. Stand in a stationary elevator alone.
4. Travel up or down one floor with your friend.

5. Travel up or down one floor alone, with your friend waiting outside the elevator on the floor where you will arrive.
6. Travel two or three floors with your friend.
7. Travel two or three floors alone, with your friend waiting outside the elevator on the floor where you will arrive.
8. Extend the number of floors you travel, first with your friend with you and then alone with your friend waiting outside the elevator.
9. Travel on an elevator alone without your friend being there.

Depending on the severity of your fear, these steps could take place in one day or over a period of days, weeks, or even months. The main idea is to keep moving forward. If you find yourself beginning to balk in fear, exercise your authority in Christ over any attack of the enemy and make the choice to push through the fear and walk by faith in God.

Most fears are struggles against our own flesh patterns developed in the past. But whenever you sense your fear or panic attack is from the enemy, make the following declaration of your authority over the devil:

> *In the name and authority of the Lord Jesus Christ, I bind all lying spirits causing fear and anxiety in me. I resist Satan and all his evil workers in the name of Jesus, and by His authority I command them to leave my presence. I declare that Satan is already defeated by Jesus at the cross. God has not given me a spirit of fear, but of power, love, and a sound mind. I therefore reject all fear and choose to walk by faith in the Holy Spirit's power, live in the light of God's love, and think with the sound mind of Christ.*

Facing our fears can be one of the toughest things we do, but God has promised to walk with us through it. The following testimony of victory over deep, long-lasting fear shines with the glory of God:

> *My father left home when I was five years old, and so the years that followed were filled with pain and loneliness for me. Our family went to church but didn't know Christ as Savior.*
>
> *When I was eight, my mother purchased three cottages to rent out at a beach resort. My 16-year-old sister took me swimming whenever we had the chance, and I loved it. It was wonderful to leave the city during the summer months.*
>
> *Frequently my future brother-in-law would visit us there at the beach. He enjoyed sneaking up behind me, picking me up, running with me down to the ocean, and throwing me in. Because of the dangerous undertow there, I was terrified. He played this little "game" for many summers, and that is how my fear of water began.*
>
> *I spent the next 30 years of my life making bad choices, which resulted in painful consequences. But after going to a special church service, the Lord wonderfully poured out His grace and mercy, and I received the Lord Jesus as Savior and was saved.*
>
> *As I came to know God more and more, I began to realize that a spirit of fear had been with me most of my life. I prayed and prayed, but still I remained fearful.*
>
> *In the summer of 1998 I was attacked by the enemy like never before. I was afraid to be alone, I trembled every waking moment, and I had constant panic attacks. I even envisioned somebody breaking down my door and harming me. I believed I was losing my mind.*

After three months of this, I sought medical help and was put on Prozac. After two weeks, I threw the medication out and cried out to God to help me. I could no longer go on like this! I told the Lord that I was willing to live for Him, and I wanted nothing more than to serve Him and be used by Him. Soon after my prayer, He gave me His answer.

My husband and I had been directed by God to a new church. Soon after our arrival, the pastor's wife invited me to join her board of women's ministry. With a thankful heart, I quickly accepted. God has given me a gift of mercy, and after much prayer I knew my ministry was to help brokenhearted women.

One of the board's requirements was that I become a member of the church and be water baptized. By immersion! I was certainly willing to become a member, but I knew God was aware of my fear of water and that He would certainly never expect me to get baptized.

Oh how wrong I was! I was reminded of the words of a pastor who had once told me that God will not do all the work of transforming us. He requires our cooperation and participation. We have a part to play, and that part is to meet Him at the place He is working in our lives.

I shared my fear with a dear, loyal friend who gave me some godly counsel. She told me about who I am in Christ and that in Him I had been given authority over Satan, by the power of the shed blood of Jesus. I was, therefore, free to refuse fear and choose faith. In obedience to my heavenly Father, I made the choice to meet Him at His point of working in my life. I would take a step of faith.

On October 24, I went down into the baptismal pool at my church to be baptized by my pastor. As we stood in the pool, we sang "Amazing Grace." I knew angels were all around us, and as I prayed to Jesus for courage, I was able to go under. Almost. My pastor had graciously not put my head under water, knowing my fears.

But when I came up, my husband, who was snapping pictures, yelled out, "Your hair is dry!" God certainly has a wonderful sense of humor.

I knew, however, that I had to go down again, all the way. And I did! My friend who was watching said (during the second time) that I had gone all the way to the bottom of the pool. Total victory!

I had learned that as we draw closer to Christ in total obedience to Him, the enemy tries to intimidate us more than ever. And it is usually at our weakest point. Mine was fear, and it controlled my life.

A few days after my baptism, a peace came over me and it was then that I knew I had overcome fear and replaced it with faith. I am reminded that 2 Timothy 1:7 says, "For God did not give us a spirit of fear, but of power, love and a sound mind."

So now, when the enemy tries to have his way, I remind him of who I am in Christ and I claim the verses in Psalm 91 that say even though a thousand may fall at my side and ten thousand at my right hand, it will not come near me. For I now dwell in the shelter of the Most High!

May the Lord grant you the courage to confront your fears and to know the peace that David must have known when he wrote, "Even though I walk through the valley of the shadow of death, I fear no evil; for Thou art with me" (Psalm 23:4).

9

Building a Stronghold of Faith

A mighty fortress is our God, a bulwark never failing.

—Martin Luther
Ein' feste Burg

Luther's opening line of the great hymn cited above can be translated from the German as, literally, "*an immovable fortress is our God, a good defense and weapon.*" Luther's lyrics could have been inspired by the following words of David, who knew something about the need for protection from enemies: "'I love Thee, O LORD, my strength.' The LORD is my rock and my fortress and my deliverer, my God, my rock, in whom I take refuge; my shield and the horn of my salvation, my stronghold. I call upon the LORD, who is worthy to be praised, and I am saved from my enemies" (Psalm 18:1-3).

David was a man after God's own heart, and so he was able to be honest about his struggles with fear. There were numerous times in his life when fear gripped his soul "and the torrents of ungodliness terrified" him (Psalm 18:4). But David had his roots deep and secure in an even greater reality—the presence and protection of Almighty God. To this man of God, the Lord was his defense and his place of safety.

A Stronghold in God

A stronghold is a well-defended place or system. There are fleshly strongholds (see chapter one), but there are godly strongholds as well. Apart from Christ, we develop our own means of coping with life and defending ourselves. Those fleshly strongholds of the mind are characterized by thoughts raised up against the knowledge of God including doubt, unbelief, fear, and anxiety.

God, however, has given us superior weapons designed to break down fleshly strongholds, including controlling fears and anxieties. Rather than us defending ourselves, however, He wants to become our defense and stronghold. David wrote: "The LORD is a refuge for the oppressed, a stronghold in times of trouble. Those who know your name will trust in you, for you, LORD, have never forsaken those who seek you" (Psalm 9:9,10 NIV).

God is faithful. He never allows His children to be tempted or tested beyond their ability to escape or endure (see 1 Corinthians 10:13). Regardless of the afflictions that we experience in this fallen world, we have the assurance that "the God of all grace, who called you to His eternal glory in Christ, will Himself perfect, confirm, strengthen and establish you" (1 Peter 5:10). So why do people turn to the temporal things of this world to find peace and comfort? Some have little or no knowledge of God, while others, because of negative past experiences with the church or religious people, may have rejected God as being cold, harsh, or uncaring. Some people who have been abused or deeply hurt in the past have wondered, "Where was God when I needed Him?" But according to David, God is always there for us:

> O LORD, you have searched me and you know me. You know when I sit and when I rise; you perceive my thoughts from afar. You discern my going out and my lying down; you are familiar with all my ways. Before a word is on my tongue you know it completely, O LORD. You hem me in—behind and before; you have laid your hand upon me. Such knowledge is too wonderful for me, too lofty for me to attain. Where can I go from your Spirit? Where can I flee from your presence? If I go up to the heavens, you are there; if I make my bed in the depths, you are there. If I rise on the wings of the dawn, if I settle on the far side of the sea, even there your hand will guide me, your right hand will hold me fast. If I say, "Surely the darkness will hide me and the light become night around me," even the darkness will not be dark to you; the night will shine like the day, for darkness is as light to you (Psalm 139:1-10 NIV).

When we are rightly related to God, we will cry out from our hearts, "Abba! Father!" God longs for us to experience that kind of closeness to Him. Even human parents normally desire to be close to their children; how much more then does God, the Perfect Parent, yearn for that kind of intimacy with His children!

The True God

The following exercise will help you renew your mind to the truth of who God really is. Verbally renounce the lies that you may have believed about your heavenly Father, and announce the truths about Him from the Word of God. Work your way down the lists, one-by-one, left to right. Begin each one with the statement in bold print at the top of that list.

The Truth about Our Heavenly Father	
I renounce the lie that my heavenly Father is:	**I announce the truth that my heavenly Father is:**
1. distant and disinterested	1. intimate and involved (Psalm 139:1-18)
2. insensitive and uncaring	2. kind and compassionate (Psalm 103:8-14)
3. stern and demanding	3. accepting and filled with joy and love (Romans 15:7; Zephaniah 3:17)
4. passive and cold	4. warm and affectionate (Isaiah 40:11; Hosea 11:3,4)
5. absent or too busy for me	5. always with me and eager to be with me (Hebrews 13:5; Jeremiah 31:20; Ezekiel 34:11-16)
6. never satisfied with what I do; impatient or angry	6. patient and slow to anger (Exodus 34:6; 2 Peter 3:9)
7. mean, cruel, or abusive	7. loving, gentle and protective (Jeremiah 31:3; Isaiah 42:3; Psalm 18:2)
8. takes all the fun out of life	8. trustworthy; He wants to give me a full life; His will is good, perfect, acceptable (Lamentations 3:22,23; John 10:10; Romans 12:1,2)
9. controlling or manipulative	9. full of grace and mercy (Hebrews 4:15,16; Luke 15:11-16)

I renounce the lie that my heavenly Father is:	I announce the truth that my heavenly Father is:
10. condemning or unforgiving	10. tenderhearted and forgiving; His heart and arms are always open (Psalms 130:1-4; Luke 15:17-24)
11. nit-picking, exacting, or perfectionistic	11. committed to my growth and proud of me as His growing child (Romans 8:28,29; Hebrews 12:5-11; 2 Corinthians 7:4)
I am the apple of His eye! ***Deuteronomy 32:10*** NIV	

Once we have broken the back of unbelief and fear in our lives, we are free to rebuild a stronghold of faith. We keep fear from returning by worshiping God in spirit and truth (see John 4:23,24). We worship Him in spirit when we are born-again and filled with His Holy Spirit. We worship Him in truth by calling upon His name and rightly ascribing to Him His divine attributes.

The Names of God

The more we get to know God, the more we discover His protective care. "The name of the LORD is a strong tower; the righteous runs into it and is safe" (Proverbs 18:10). God's names are descriptive of who He is; they also reveal His character. Every fear we experience ultimately has its antidote in knowing and trusting in God's name. God says "fear not" because He is always with us to protect and guide us:

> Be strong and courageous. Do not be afraid or terrified because of them, for the LORD your God

goes with you; he will never leave you nor forsake you (Deuteronomy 31:6 NIV).

David also said to Solomon his son, "Be strong and courageous, and do the work. Do not be afraid or discouraged, for the LORD God, my God, is with you" (1 Chronicles 28:20 NIV).

Even though I walk through the valley of the shadow of death, I will fear no evil, for you are with me; your rod and your staff, they comfort me (Psalm 23:4 NIV).

The LORD is with me; I will not be afraid. What can man do to me? (Psalm 118:6 NIV).

For I am the LORD, your God, who takes hold of your right hand and says to you, Do not fear; I will help you (Isaiah 41:13 NIV).

God with Us

Time and time again God promises to be with us. In fact, one of the names given to the Messiah is *Immanuel* as prophesied in Isaiah 7:14 and fulfilled in Matthew 1:23: "'Behold, the virgin shall be with child, and shall bear a Son, and they shall call His name Immanuel,' which translated means, 'God with us.'" Jesus is Immanuel, God with us. When He walked on earth, He was God with us in the flesh. Then Jesus sent the Holy Spirit, "another Helper," one who is just like Christ Himself to be with us (see John 14:16).

Picture a stressful, frightening, or anxiety-producing situation. Now picture the Lord Jesus visibly present with you in that same situation. Is there not a greater confidence in your heart as you think of your Lord being there with you? The Lord says, "I will dwell in them and walk among them; and I will be their God, and they shall be My people" (2 Corinthians 6:16).

It would probably be easier to be courageous if Jesus were visibly present with us, but He's not. That is another reason why we need to worship Him—so that we are reminded of His invisible presence. "We walk by faith, not by sight," and "faith is the assurance of things hoped for, the conviction of things not seen" (2 Corinthians 5:7; Hebrews 11:1).

Actually we are better off without Jesus being physically present. In His own words, Jesus said, "But I tell you the truth, it is to your advantage that I go away; for if I do not go away, the Helper shall not come to you; but if I go, I will send Him to you" (John 16:7). It is better to have the indwelling presence of the Holy Spirit than the physical presence of Jesus. If Jesus were physically present by our side, the best we could do is imitate Him, and He would not be omnipresent. But with the Spirit living inside of us, we can actually become like Him, and He is always and everywhere present with us!

God Is Faithful

God is our Father, and we are His children. He is intimately concerned about all our ways. He cannot and will not forget us. It is not unusual, though, in the midst of tough trials to think that God has abandoned us. The prophet Isaiah addressed that fear:

> But Zion said, "The LORD has forsaken me, and the Lord has forgotten me." Can a woman forget her nursing child, and have no compassion on the son of her womb? Even these may forget, but I will not forget you. Behold, I have inscribed you on the palms of My hands; your walls are continually before Me (Isaiah 49:14-16).

If God spoke to Israel of such faithful love, will He not speak to His precious church in the same way? For Jesus indeed has the marks on His palms reminding us for all eternity of the terrible price He paid to redeem us from our sinful way of life. We are the dwelling place of God; we are the temple of the Holy Spirit. Are not our "walls" ever before the eyes of Him whose very dwelling place we are?

God never promised us that His abiding presence means a trouble-free life. Jesus forewarned us that we would have trials and tribulations in this world. But He also promised His peace in the midst of even the worst that the devil or this fallen world can throw at us: "Peace I leave with you; My peace I give to you; not as the world gives, do I give to you. Let not your heart be troubled, nor let it be fearful" (John 14:27). "These things I have spoken to you, that in Me you may have peace. In the world you have tribulation, but take courage; I have overcome the world" (John 16:33).

It is our conviction that every anxiety disorder can ultimately be dissolved by the knowledge and presence of God. That is why the exhortation in Scripture is to "seek the Lord" and "fix your eyes on Jesus" (see Isaiah 55:6; Jeremiah 29:13; Amos 5:4; Hebrews 12:2). We will experience His peace when we keep our eyes of faith trained on God, walking intimately with Him.

When David was fleeing from the relentless pursuit of King Saul, he described his attackers this way: "My soul is among lions; I must lie among those who breathe forth fire, even the sons of men, whose teeth are spears and arrows, and their tongue a sharp sword.... They have prepared a net for my steps; my soul is bowed down" (Psalm 57:4,6). That would be an obvious time to panic, but David's testimony doesn't end there. Psalm 57:7-11 finishes the story:

> My heart is steadfast, O God, my heart is steadfast; I will sing, yes, I will sing praises! Awake, my

> glory; awake, harp and lyre, I will awaken the dawn! I will give thanks to Thee, O Lord, among the peoples; I will sing praises to Thee among the nations. For Thy lovingkindness is great to the heavens, and Thy truth to the clouds. Be exalted above the heavens, O God; let Thy glory be above all the earth.

David's heart was steadfast. He was single-minded, not double-minded. Psalm 86:11 (NIV) puts it this way, "Teach me your way, O LORD, and I will walk in your truth; give me an undivided heart, that I may fear your name." An unwavering, unflinching, undistracted focus of faith on God—that's the key to peace, as Isaiah taught: "The steadfast of mind Thou wilt keep in perfect peace, because he trusts in Thee. Trust in the LORD forever, for in GOD, the LORD, we have an everlasting Rock" (Isaiah 26:3).

Faith v. Fear

Peter demonstrated the contrast between faith and fear in Matthew 14. Once the disciples realized that the person walking on the water toward them was Jesus, and not a ghost, Peter called out, "Lord, if it is You, command me to come to You on the water" (verse 28). Jesus said to him, "Come!" Peter stepped out of the boat and was miraculously walking on the water when he approached Jesus (verse 29). Steadfast of heart and with eyes of faith, he walked toward Jesus. Suddenly he was distracted: "But seeing the wind, he became afraid, and beginning to sink, he cried out, saying, 'Lord, save me!'" (verse 30).

Jesus took hold of His hand and brought Peter safely back to the boat. But there is no mistaking the disappointment in Jesus' words when He said, "O you of little faith, why did you doubt?" (verse 31). As if to drive home His point, the wind stopped immediately upon Jesus' entry into the boat (verse 32). Truly there is no rational reason to fear when Jesus is present.

The following story of faith in the midst of trial bears witness that the Prince of Peace indeed overcomes fear in those who trust Him.

> *When I was a young boy I was terrified of heights. This is not unusual, but when a person is in total terror on the first rung of a ladder, then that might be considered an extreme case.*
>
> *I never really needed to confront this fear in day-to-day living because, as a university student, I rarely thought about it. At one point on a summer job I did realize I needed to confront it or else I was going to lose my job. A foreman pointed to me and to an acetylene torch that needed to be taken to the second story of a building we were demolishing.*
>
> *Unfortunately, the only way there was by ladder. That wouldn't have been bad except that the ladder was 15 feet away in the middle of a pit. The only way to reach the ladder was by a gangplank from the side of the pit.*
>
> *The top was about 30 feet from the bottom of the pit.*
>
> *Fortunately, God had prepared me for that occasion. I had just read a book in which the authors emphasized the verse, "I can do all things through Christ who strengthens me." I spoke the word out loud, grabbed the torch, walked the gangplank and climbed the ladder. I was cured!*
>
> *Later, on the same job, I would climb three stories on nothing but exposed rebar sticking out of the half-demolished walls.*
>
> *Later on in life, I met and married a girl who was afraid of everything. Afraid of succeeding, but afraid of not succeeding. Afraid of having close friends, but afraid of not having any friends. Her whole life was a story of fear. Possibly the root of the fear was her overpowering legalistic parents. Fear was controlling her life.*

Finally it was as if God whacked me on the head with the verse, "God did not grant us a spirit of fear, but of power, love and a sound mind." Standing on that one verse for authority, I asked her if she wanted to be free from that fear. She said, "yes," and so I announced to the spirit that because of that verse it had no place in her life and it was to depart and leave her alone.

That was a seemingly small step, but I can tell you that her whole life and our marriage has never been the same since. We both joke that I am now married to my second wife!

Finally, with regards to anxiety, I suppose we could feel some. We have a very premature daughter, born at 23 weeks, 1 lb. 9 oz. She is in intensive care 60 miles from our town.

Many people ask us why we are so calm. Well, from my perspective, she belongs to God. I'm just looking after her. If she were mine, I would have absolutely no resources for what she needs in order to get well and come home from the hospital. On the other hand, since she belongs to Him, the power that raised Christ from the dead is at God's disposal to intervene in her life to fulfill the advancement of His kingdom. So I have decided to hurl my cares upon Him.

If God said it in the Bible you can stand on one verse and take on the world, the flesh and the devil along with anyone or anything else in all creation and be the victor in Christ.

The Power of God's Word

That kind of trust in God and His Word is what it takes to walk in freedom. Never doubt the power of God's Word. It is "living and active and sharper than any two-edged sword"

(Hebrews 4:12). It is like fire; it is like a hammer that shatters rock (Jeremiah 23:29). It is "inspired by God and profitable for teaching, for reproof, for correction, for training in righteousness; that the man of God may be adequate, equipped for every good work" (2 Timothy 3:16,17). To strengthen your confidence in God and the power of His Word, we encourage you to meditate on Psalms 1, 19, and 119. How courage is the result of trusting God and His Word is evident in the following testimony:

> *Basically, I grew up in a home where both sides of our family had been in the occult for at least three generations in Finland. There were two parts to my life at home—in part A, my father was a Sunday school superintendent at a local fundamental church. But we also celebrated the ceremony of the full moon every month and all the atrocities that are connected with it.*
>
> *The Lord saved me when I was seven years old, and kept me both alive and sane until He brought a dramatic spiritual deliverance to me in 1974. I went from being like the description of the demonized man of the Gadarenes in the Bible, to "an almost normal" person!*
>
> *In regards to fear, right after I found freedom the Lord had me involved in helping others who were trapped in the occult. Satan tried often to blackmail me: "If you help these people, who knows?...you yourself may be dragged back into [what] you have just escaped." I found that I needed to get some "Fearbuster" verses in my heart to combat the enticement to give place to fear.*
>
> *I discovered, "He whom the Son has set free shall be free indeed" (John 8:36), and "No weapon that is formed against you will prosper. This is the heritage of the servants of the Lord, and their vindication is from Me" (Isaiah 54:17).*

Also, for years (probably due to the need for emotional healing) the nights were filled with nightmares and apparitions, with the demonic presence in my bedroom. Again, the ammo of the Word of God was crucial. "When you lie down, you will not be afraid. When you lie down, your sleep will be sweet. Do not be afraid of sudden fear or of the onslaught of the wicked when it comes. For the LORD will be your confidence (at your side), and will keep your foot from being caught" (Proverbs 3:24-26). "I lay down and slept. I awoke, for the Lord sustains me" (Psalm 3:5).

Sometimes, all I could do was quote the verse, "Be anxious for nothing" (Philippians 4:6), and add my own commitment, "I choose to obey that command."

I needed to know the Word of God at all hours of the day and night, so I began memorizing Scripture. It took me 20 years, spending 15 minutes a day, but now I have the entire New Testament and all the psalms memorized. The Lord has always used the truth of His Word to blast away at the intimidation, blackmail, and gut-wrenching fears that the enemy tried to sidetrack me with.

I often think that if there could be only one change in a Christian's life...that of removing anything that had the word fear *connected with it, the change in that person's life would be awesome!*

This brave woman can say with David, "Thou hast magnified Thy word according to all Thy name" (Psalm 138:2)! We discover the names and nature of God through His Word, and through that knowledge faith will grow and peace will come.

Know God's Name

When Melchizedek, the king and priest, blessed Abram, he said, "Blessed be Abram of God Most High, possessor of heaven and earth" (Genesis 14:19). He called God by His *name, El Elyon,* which means the God who is Creator of all things and who is above all other gods. Why should we yield to fear when we can trust in the God who is greater than all things, including fear?

When Moses, the deliverer, was preparing to confront Pharaoh and lead the Israelites from Egypt, God revealed His name: "I AM WHO I AM" (Exodus 3:14). He is the eternal, self-existent, covenant-keeping God. Why should we fear the future when God is eternal and knows the end from the beginning (Isaiah 46:10)? He is the Alpha and the Omega, the first and the last, the beginning and end, who is and who was and who is to come (Revelation 1:8; 22:13).

When the prophet Isaiah spoke of the coming birth of the Messiah, he said, "And His name will be called Wonderful Counselor, Mighty God, Eternal Father, Prince of Peace" (Isaiah 9:6). Why should we be anxious about the decisions we need to make when He is our Wonderful Counselor? Why should we be afraid to step out in faith when our Mighty God is there to provide us with strength? Why should we feel anxious and insecure when our Eternal Father dwells within us? And why let fear and anxiety overwhelm us when the Prince of Peace will never leave us?

Prayerfully meditate on the following names of God. Ask the Lord to show you which of them is the "strong tower" you need today to combat fear and anxiety in your life.

The Fear-busting Names of God

Jehovah-jireh .... The Lord will provide (Genesis 22:14)

El Shaddai .... The One is mighty to shed forth and pour out sustenance and blessing (Genesis 17:1,2)

Jehovah-Sabaoth ... The Lord of the hosts of heaven (Psalm 24:10)

Jehovah-rophe...... The Lord our healer (Exodus 15:26)

Jehovah-shalom .... The Lord is peace (Judges 6:24)
Jehovah-rohi....... The Lord our Shepherd (Psalm 23:1)
Jehovah-shammah.. The Lord is there (Ezekiel 48:35)
Jehovah-nissi .... The Lord is my banner (Exodus 17:15)
Jehovah-tsidkenu ... The Lord our righteousness (Jeremiah 23:5,6)

Studying these names of God in their biblical context may be one of the best faith-building exercises you can do.[1] Romans 12:2 teaches us that we are transformed through the renewing of our minds. In other words, our lives are changed as our minds are changed by the truth.

The name *Jesus* itself is full of grace, truth, and power. His name means "salvation." "God highly exalted Him, and bestowed on Him the name which is above every name, that at the name of Jesus *every knee should bow*, of those who are in heaven, and on earth, and under the earth" (Philippians 2:9,10, emphasis added). We encourage you to make it a regular practice to worship the Lord Jesus with the use of His names. In the process you will find your faith growing and your fear fleeing. We have listed some of these glorious names to help you get started. Just reverently saying these names and thinking about how they relate to your life can be a faith-strengthening act of worship.

The Mighty Names of Jesus

Advocate (1 John 2:1)
Alpha and Omega (Revelation 21:6)
Amen (Revelation 3:14)
Anointed One (Psalm 2:2)
Apostle of our confession (Hebrews 3:1)
Author and perfecter of faith (Hebrews 12:2)
Beginning and end (Revelation 21:6)

Beloved (Ephesians 1:6 KJV)
Branch (Zechariah 3:8)
Bread of Life (John 6:35)
Bright morning star (Revelation 22:16)
Chief cornerstone (Mark 12:10)
Chief shepherd (1 Peter 5:4)
Christ (Matthew 16:16,17)
Counselor (Isaiah 9:6)
Deliverer (Romans 11:26)
Door (John 10:2)
Eternal Father (Isaiah 9:6)
Faithful and True (Revelation 19:11)
First and last (Revelation 20:13)
God (John 1:1,14)
Good Shepherd (John 10:11)
Guardian of souls (1 Peter 2:25)
Head of the church (Colossians 1:18)
Heir of all things (Hebrews 1:2)
High priest (Hebrews 4:14)
Holy One (1 John 2:20)
Horn of salvation (Luke 1:69)
I Am (John 8:58)
Immanuel (Matthew 1:23)
King of Israel (John 12:13)
King of kings (Revelation 17:14)
Lamb (Revelation 13:8)
Life (John 14:6)
Light of the world (John 8:12)
Lion of Judah (Revelation 5:5)

Living stone (1 Peter 2:4)
Lord (John 21:7)
Lord Jesus Christ (1 Peter 1:3)
Lord of lords (Revelation 17:14)
Messiah (John 4:25,26)
Mighty God (Isaiah 9:6)
Our Passover lamb (1 Corinthians 5:7)
Prince of Peace (Isaiah 9:6)
Prophet (Deuteronomy 18:15,18)
Redeemer (Isaiah 59:20)
Resurrection and life (John 11:25)
Righteous One (Isaiah 53:11)
Rock (1 Corinthians 10:4)
Root and offspring of David (Revelation 22:16)
Ruler (Matthew 2:6)
Savior (Luke 2:11)
Son of God (Romans 1:4)
Son of Man (Matthew 24:30)
Teacher (John 13:13)
True Vine (John 15:1)
Truth (John 14:6)
Way (John 14:6)
Wonderful (Isaiah 9:6)
Word of God (Revelation 19:13)

The Holy Spirit

Knowing the true nature of God, the Holy Spirit, is faith-building as well. He is called the Spirit of truth (John 16:13), Spirit of life (Romans 8:2), Spirit of adoption (Romans 8:15), Spirit of the living God (2 Corinthians 3:3), Holy Spirit of promise

(Ephesians 1:13), Spirit of grace (Hebrews 10:29), Spirit of Christ (1 Peter 1:11), and Spirit of glory (1 Peter 4:14).

As we are filled with the Holy Spirit, we are given a heart of praise, thanksgiving, and humility (Ephesians 5:18-21) and the power to be Christ's witnesses (Acts 1:8). We can walk by the Spirit's power and not give in to fleshly desires or legalism (Galatians 5:16-18). We are also gifted for His service and brought into unity with other believers in Christ (1 Corinthians 12). And we can overcome fear with the power, love, and sound mind He gives us (see 2 Timothy 1:7).

Renewing Our Minds

How do words of Scripture renew our minds and transform our lives? The natural man cannot perceive the truth, but we have the mind of Christ (1 Corinthians 2:14-16). On the other hand, the Spirit of God will not do our thinking for us. We must choose to believe the truth and let the Word of Christ richly dwell within us (Colossians 3:16). One effective way to do that is by meditating upon the Word of God. Meditation is a biblical practice, as the following verses reveal:

> How blessed is the man who does not walk in the counsel of the wicked, nor stand in the path of sinners, nor sit in the seat of scoffers! But his delight is in the law of the LORD, and in His law he meditates day and night. And he will be like a tree firmly planted by streams of water, which yields its fruit in its season, and its leaf does not wither; and in whatever he does, he prospers (Psalm 1:1-3).
>
> This book of the law shall not depart from your mouth, but you shall meditate on it day and night, so that you may be careful to do according to all that is written in it; for then you will make your way prosperous, and then you will have success (Joshua 1:8).

The main difference between ungodly meditation and biblical meditation is the object of the meditation. The blessed man's "delight is in the law of the LORD, and in His law he meditates day and night" (Psalm 1:2). After Paul's exhortation to the believers in Philippi to pray instead of worrying, he adds these powerful words: "Finally, brethren, whatever is true, whatever is honorable, whatever is right, whatever is pure, whatever is lovely, whatever is of good repute, if there is any excellence and if anything worthy of praise, let your mind dwell on these things. The things you have learned and received and heard and seen in me, practice these things; and the God of peace shall be with you" (Philippians 4:8,9).

What a promise! Prayerful meditation followed by obedience connects us with the peace of God and the God of peace (Philippians 4:6-9). It's hard to imagine a more encouraging word to one who has been struggling with fear and anxiety. Therefore, it is critical that we approach the Word of God as the life-giving food it is, chewing on it day and night. In prayer, we ask the Lord what it means and how we can apply God's Word to our lives. The more we meditate on the riches of its wisdom and obey what it says, the more it becomes a secure belt of truth around us and a flashing sword in our hand (see Ephesians 6:14,17). The more our faith grows, the more fear flees.

Our Identity in Christ

Knowing God is the most important part of our belief system. Knowing who we are in Christ and how He perceives us is the second most important part of our belief system. How does God view His people? First of all, we are His children (John 1:12), chosen by Him, holy and dearly loved (Colossians 3:12). We have been raised up and seated with Christ so that in the ages to come, God can show us the surpassing riches of grace in kindness toward us (Ephesians 2:6,7). Knowing the love of God and who we are in Christ affects how we live our lives, as 1 John 3:1-3 reveals:

> See how great a love the Father has bestowed upon us, that we should be called children of God; and such we are. For this reason the world does not know us, because it did not know Him. Beloved, now we are children of God, and it has not appeared as yet what we shall be. We know that, when He appears, we shall be like Him, because we shall see Him just as He is. And everyone who has this hope fixed on Him purifies himself, just as He is pure.

God, as the Perfect Parent, loves His children with a love that even the best earthly parent can only hope for. God's love is complete, perfect, and unchanging. He encourages, comforts, strengthens, protects, provides for, and nurtures His children. He delights in us and wants only the best for us. Our response should be to desire to be like Him and purify ourselves, just as He is pure.

But God's love for us is so deep and broad and high and wide that the Father–child relationship cannot completely capture it (see Ephesians 3:17-19). As well as being God's children, Scripture also says that we are Jesus' bride (Revelation 19:7,8).

On the day Shirley and I (Rich) got married, I was a mess. I am so glad that my pastor and groomsmen were there to help me find my way to the front of the church! And when my bride walked down that aisle, beaming with joy, adorned with that flowing white gown, I could barely breathe. Never had I seen such a beautiful sight.

From the moment I had proposed to her, I had been looking forward to that moment. So it is with Christ. For all eternity, Jesus has been waiting for the moment when His precious bride, the church, is presented to Him. Clothed with the clean, bright, white linen of her righteous acts, will not the eyes of our Lord be filled with the deepest of joy? And will not our eyes be filled with wonder at the Groom in all His glory?

The intense, passionate love of a husband for his wife is but a whisper of the love that Jesus Christ has for us, His bride. Consider the apostle Paul's words in Ephesians 5:25-27:

> Husbands, love your wives, just as Christ also loved the church and gave Himself up for her; that He might sanctify her, having cleansed her by the washing of water with the word, that He might present to Himself the church in all her glory, having no spot or wrinkle or any such thing; but that she should be holy and blameless.

Jesus gave Himself up for us, shedding His blood and dying on the cross, and Scripture tells us that there is no greater love possible than laying down your life for a friend (John 15:13). Jesus has already demonstrated His love for us in a way that cannot be surpassed. And yet His love for the church did not end with that one incredible sacrifice on the cross. He continually "nourishes and cherishes" the church, of which every believer is a part (see Ephesians 5:29). Why should we fear or be anxious when we have such a Husband to care for us?

The engagement ring I gave Shirley was a guarantee of the covenant that would be legally binding and consummated seven months later. The Lord Jesus has sealed us with the Holy Spirit of promise, who is the "down payment" of what is to come (Ephesians 1:13,14). The Spirit will remain with us and in us until the time we are safely brought into Jesus' presence.

In addition to being God's children and Jesus' bride, the Bible uses other pictures to show God's deep concern and loving protection over us. We are Jesus' sheep, and He is the Good Shepherd (John 10). We are the body of Christ, and Jesus is the head (1 Corinthians 12:12-28; Colossians 1:18). We are a royal priesthood, and Jesus is the high priest (1 Peter 2:9; Hebrews 7:26,27).

We are a holy nation, and He is the ruler of it (1 Peter 2:9; Isaiah 9:6,7). We are saints, and He is the One who has made us holy (1 Corinthians 1:2; Hebrews 10:10).

Forgiven. Cleansed. Given eternal life. New creations in Christ. Indwelt by the Holy Spirit. Redeemed. Chosen. Declared not guilty. Given the very righteousness of Christ. Gifted by the Spirit. Called into kingdom service. All these things and much, much more God has done for us because of His amazing grace.

The cross was where the work was finished, dealing a death blow to sin and death. The empty tomb was where the work was vindicated, assuring us of eternal life. The presence of Jesus in heaven is where the work will be glorified, consummating our marriage to the Lamb for eternity. Has not God truly demonstrated beyond a shadow of a doubt the extent of His love for His people? Can we not, in light of all this, give ourselves unreservedly into His hands and trust Him to provide for and protect us? In light of this, Paul said, "I urge you therefore, brethren, by the mercies of God, to present your bodies a living and holy sacrifice, acceptable to God, which is your spiritual service of worship. And do not be conformed to this world, but be transformed by the renewing of your mind, that you may prove what the will of God is, that which is good and acceptable and perfect" (Romans 12:1,2).

A Community of Faith

There is more to building a stronghold of faith than our vertical relationship to God. God has provided a great measure of grace and strength through the interpersonal relationships we have with other brothers and sisters in Christ. We cannot fully come to know the love of God apart from His body (1 John 4:12). A stronghold of faith develops best in a *community* of faith. We need to be in fellowship with other believers for accountability and edification:

> Take care, brethren, lest there should be in any one of you an evil, unbelieving heart, in falling away from the living God. But encourage one another day after day, as long as it is still called "Today," lest any one of you be hardened by the deceitfulness of sin... (Hebrews 3:12,13).
>
> Let us hold fast the confession of our hope without wavering, for He who promised is faithful; and let us consider how to stimulate one another to love and good deeds, not forsaking our own assembling together, as is the habit of some, but encouraging one another; and all the more, as you see the day drawing near (Hebrews 10:23-25).

Encouragement is a great need for people struggling with fear and anxiety. Much of life in this world discourages us or takes courage out of us. To put courage in, God has given us each other. No congregation is perfect—but God is and He delights to work through imperfect people. Neglecting fellowship with other Christians makes us greatly susceptible to having our hearts hardened by sin's deceitfulness, and we are at risk of falling away from the living God.

But when we experience the encouragement of other believers, we find ourselves strengthened to hold fast the confession of our hope without wavering. We are stimulated to love and good deeds; we are given the courage to walk by faith instead of fear.

Satan's strategy is to "divide and conquer," so he tries to isolate us and cut us off from the encouraging fellowship of other believers. God never intended or expected us to live the Christian life alone. Make the choice today to become involved in Christian fellowship if you are not already doing so. The need for fellowship with other believers will become more and more critical as time goes on (Hebrews 10:25).

We need to know that we are not alone in our fight against fear. God has created us with a need for Him and one another, and we will be more safe and secure within the context of close human relationships. Use the following list of "who we are" and the group resolution following to strengthen your corporate identity and ties with other believers:

Who Are We?

We are brothers and sisters in Christ (1 John 3:14).

We are growing into a holy temple in the Lord (Ephesians 2:19-21).

We are being built together into a dwelling of God in the Spirit (Ephesians 2:22).

We are a chosen race (1 Peter 2:9).

We are a royal priesthood (1 Peter 2:9).

We are a holy nation (1 Peter 2:9).

We are a people for God's own possession, called out of darkness, into His marvelous light, called to proclaim His excellencies (1 Peter 2:9-10).

We once were not a people, but now we are the people of God (1 Peter 2:10).

We once had not received mercy, but now we have received mercy (1 Peter 2:10).

We are the body of Christ, and individual members of it (1 Corinthians 12:27).

We all suffer when one of our members suffers (1 Corinthians 12:26).

We all rejoice when one of our members rejoices (1 Corinthians 12:26).

We need each other and are interdependent just as the parts of the human body need each other (1 Corinthians 12:14-27).

We have different gifts, but the same Spirit (1 Corinthians 12:4).

We have different ministries, but the same Lord (1 Corinthians 12:5).

We have different results, but the same God who is working in all things (1 Corinthians 12:6).

We are already one in the Spirit in the bond of peace (Ephesians 4:3).

We are the bride of the Lamb, Jesus Christ (Revelation 21:2,9).

We, therefore, renounce any spirit of isolation, division, or competition. We rejoice that we are one body—having one Spirit, one hope of our calling, one Lord, one faith, one baptism, and one God the Father who is over all and through all and in all. Therefore, we resolve by God's grace to consider how to stimulate one another to love and good deeds, encouraging one another day after day. We resolve to accept one another in Christ, just as we have been accepted by God in Christ. We resolve by the power of the Holy Spirit to exercise the spiritual gifts given to us, speaking the truth in love so that we can grow up in all aspects into Him, who is the head, even Christ. In so doing, we know that the whole body, being fitted and held together by that which every joint supplies, according to the proper working of each individual part, causes the growth of the body for the building up of itself in love (see Ephesians 4:1-16; Hebrews 10:24,25; Romans 15:7).

We conclude this chapter with a word of encouragement to you as you think about your relationship to your heavenly Father. Right now:

Somebody is thinking of you
Somebody is caring about you
Somebody is caring for you
Somebody longs for you
Somebody wants to talk to you
Somebody wants to be with you
Somebody wants to listen to you
Somebody wants to hold your hand
Somebody is protecting you
Somebody is working for your good
Somebody is celebrating your successes
Somebody wants to give you a gift
Somebody thinks you are a gift
Somebody wants to hold you in His arms
Somebody wants to make you the best you can be
Somebody is on your side and is pulling for you today
Somebody loves you
Somebody wants to laugh with you
Somebody wants to cry with you
Somebody wants to tell you how much He cares
Somebody wants to share His life with you
Somebody wants to be your friend
Somebody died to make that friendship possible
Somebody loves you for who you are
Somebody wants you to know that He is there for you
Somebody is always thinking about you
Somebody believes in you
Somebody wants you to trust Him...today

10

The Fear that Dispels All Other Fears

> To love and admire anything outside yourself is to take one step away from utter spiritual ruin; though we shall not be well so long as we love and admire anything more than we love and admire God.
>
> —C.S. Lewis
> *Mere Christianity*

Have you ever had one of those discovery moments when suddenly your eyes are opened to the truth in a new way? I did a number of years ago. I was studying through the books of Psalms and Proverbs in my devotional time and kept encountering the phrase, "the fear of the Lord." I read that "the fear of the Lord is the beginning of knowledge; fools despise wisdom and instruction" (Proverbs 1:7) and "the fear of the LORD is the beginning of wisdom, and the knowledge of the Holy One is understanding" (Proverbs 9:10).

The new insights I began to gain from studying the Scriptures were life-changing, since I previously had not understood what the fear of the Lord meant. If the fear of the Lord really is the beginning of knowledge and wisdom, then it is imperative that we all come to understand what it means.

An Enduring Truth

When was the last time you heard a sermon on the "fear of the Lord" or read a book on the subject? Maybe it's been a long time; maybe this is the first time. But the fear of the Lord isn't an outdated concept belonging in the dusty archives of hellfire and brimstone preachers: "The fear of the LORD is clean, enduring forever" (Psalm 19:9). This important theme occurs consistently throughout Scripture, from Genesis 20:11 to Revelation 19:5.

Fearing God is not a law-based principle, but rather it is an eternally enduring aspect of our relationship to God. Isaiah foretold that the fear of God would rest on Jesus the Messiah, and He was the One in whom grace and truth were realized (John 1:17). Isaiah prophesied, "Then a shoot will spring from the stem of Jesse, and a branch from his roots will bear fruit. And the Spirit of the LORD will rest on Him, the spirit of wisdom and understanding, the spirit of counsel and strength, the spirit of knowledge and the fear of the LORD. And He will delight in the fear of the LORD" (Isaiah 11:1-3). The Lord Jesus was not only characterized by the fear of the Lord, He *delighted* in the fear of the Lord. It is safe to say, then, that He still delights in it. Whatever Jesus delights in ought to be of great interest and importance to us.

What does it mean to "fear the Lord"? Does it mean that we are supposed to be afraid of God? Doesn't "perfect love cast out fear" (see 1 John 4:18)? How can we love God and fear Him at the same time? And how does the fear of God dispel all other (unhealthy) fears?

Defining the Fear of God

The following verses from the psalms will help us formulate a definition of what it means to fear the Lord:

> You who fear the LORD, praise Him; all you descendants of Jacob, glorify Him, and stand in awe of Him, all you descendants of Israel (Psalm 22:23).

> Let all the earth fear the LORD; let all the inhabitants of the world stand in awe of Him. For He spoke, and it was done; He commanded, and it stood fast. The LORD nullifies the counsel of the nations; He frustrates the plans of the peoples. The counsel of the LORD stands forever, the plans of His heart from generation to generation (Psalm 33:8-11).

> You alone are to be feared. Who can stand before you when you are angry? From heaven you pronounced judgment, and the land feared and was quiet—when you, O God, rose up to judge, to save all the afflicted of the land (Psalm 76:7-9 NIV).

> My flesh trembles in fear of you; I stand in awe of your laws (Psalm 119:120 NIV).

To fear God is to be awestruck with God's character and Word. It is a state of deep reverence that can cause us to tremble before Him because of His righteous judgments. The fear of the Lord is also joyful praise and worship of His glory, resulting in humble obedience to His will. "Holy fear...is God-given, enabling men to reverence God's authority, obey His commandments, and hate and shun all form of evil."[1]

The apostle John gives us a vivid picture of what it means to fear the Lord. He was "in the Spirit on the Lord's day" when he heard a voice behind him like a loud trumpet (Revelation 1:9,10). When he turned around, he saw a vision of the reigning Christ that overwhelmed him:

> And having turned I saw seven golden lampstands; and in the middle of the lampstands one like a son of man, clothed in a robe reaching to the feet, and girded across His breast with a golden girdle.

> And His head and His hair were white like white wool, like snow; and His eyes were like a flame of fire; and His feet were like burnished bronze, when it has been caused to glow in a furnace, and His voice was like the sound of many waters. And in His right hand He held seven stars; and out of His mouth came a sharp two-edged sword; and His face was like the sun shining in its strength. And when I saw Him, I fell at His feet as a dead man (Revelation 1:12-17).

John knew and loved Jesus with all his heart. He had spent three years with Him, witnessing His miracles and His loving, gracious heart. But he had never seen the Lord Jesus like this. All John's strength was drained from his body as he collapsed in holy fear. He needed a touch and a word from Jesus Himself in order to revive. "And He laid His right hand upon me, saying, 'Do not be afraid; I am the first and the last, and the living One; and I was dead, and behold, I am alive forevermore, and I have the keys of death and of Hades'" (Revelation 1:17,18).

John needed to see Jesus in a new light and so do we. He had known Jesus as the miracle-working Messiah who displayed His tender mercies. But now John saw Him as the Creator God, Judge of the earth, and Head of the church. In the mind of John, the gentle Jesus suddenly became the great "I AM."

It is hard for us to grasp the greatness of God. Many people prefer to think of Him as a kindly old grandfather who winks at sin and dutifully hands out treats whenever they ask for them. Such a distorted concept of God will cause no one to fear Him. Job's friend, Elihu, however, painted a picture of God that should help us learn to fear Him:

> For as we cannot look at the sun for its brightness when the winds have cleared away the clouds,

> neither can we gaze at the terrible majesty of God breaking forth upon us from heaven, clothed in dazzling splendor. We cannot imagine the power of the Almighty, and yet he is so just and merciful that he does not destroy us. No wonder men everywhere fear him! (Job 37:21-24 TLB).

Psalm 33 teaches that God spoke and propelled billions of galaxies into existence. They remain in place by the word of His power (Hebrews 1:3). Mighty leaders and nations make their plans, and God effortlessly thwarts them, revealing to the world that He is the ruler over the realm of mankind (Daniel 4:17). Nations that vie for world power and domination are as a speck of dust or drop of water to Him (Isaiah 40:15).

"The heavens are telling of the glory of God, and their expanse is declaring the work of His hands" (Psalm 19:1). The God of all creation has a way of rekindling our awe of Him. A violent thunderstorm crashes upon us in the middle of the night. A snow-capped peak rivets our attention as we round a curve in the road. A totalitarian government suddenly topples, opening the doors wide for the gospel. A child is born. A family member is saved.

Unusual "natural" events invade the humdrum of life and provide vivid opportunities for knowing the fear of God. Yet even when life is quite routine, the trained eye of faith has learned to experience the Almighty in the ordinary and can worship Him for the dew as well as the downpour.

Knowing and Fearing God

The Word of God provides us with constant reminders of His awesome wonders. Every book of the Bible reveals His glory. Although any one of God's attributes or acts could prompt people to revere Him, the following Scriptures give examples for our instruction.

> Who will not fear you, O Lord, and bring glory to your name? For you alone are holy. All nations will come and worship before you, for your righteous acts have been revealed (Revelation 15:4 NIV).

> God blesses us, that all the ends of the earth may fear Him (Psalm 67:7).

> Who knows the power of your anger? For your wrath is as great as the fear that is due you (Psalm 90:11 NIV).

> If you, O LORD, kept a record of sins, O LORD, who could stand? But with you there is forgiveness; therefore you are feared (Psalm 130:3,4 NIV).

God is so awesome in majesty, glory, splendor, and holiness that human language falls woefully short in describing the glory of the Lord. But in the hearts of those who fear Him there is an unspoken language of faith, a bowing down with humility before One infinitely greater and more magnificent than self. Ethan the psalmist revealed that God is even feared by the spiritual beings who surround Him:

> The heavens praise your wonders, O LORD, your faithfulness too, in the assembly of the holy ones. For who in the skies above can compare with the LORD? Who is like the LORD among the heavenly beings? In the council of the holy ones God is greatly feared; he is more awesome than all who surround him. O LORD God Almighty, who is like you? You are mighty, O LORD, and your faithfulness surrounds you (Psalm 89:5-8 NIV).

Almost all children have heroes they idolize. They would widen their eyes and be stunned to silence if their heroes entered the room. They would hardly be able to speak if their heroes actually talked to them. But the reality of life is that they are just mortals with feet of clay like the rest of us. Not so with God! The sheer magnitude of His glory and greatness does not diminish over time. Familiarity does not breed contempt of the Almighty. The holy angels, who have been in His presence for thousands of years do not cease day and night to proclaim, "Holy, Holy, Holy, is the LORD God the Almighty, who was and who is and who is to come" (Revelation 4:8).

A Sanctuary

There is more to God than power and majesty that moves people to fear Him. God's kindness in blessing us, His faithfulness to provide, and His forgiveness of our sins should also move us to stand in awe of Him. Because He has the power to forgive we fear Him.

Normally we shun any fear object and dread being in its presence. That would also be true of God if He were cruel and unforgiving. Why would anyone want to approach a god like that? We might try to appease his wrath, but we would not be likely to draw near to him if we feared punishment for wrongdoing.

For that reason some Bible translators have preferred to use the word "reverence" instead of fear. We revere God in the sense that we have the ultimate respect for Him, but it goes deeper than that. We also fear God because He has the power to judge and His attributes make Him the only legitimate fear object (He is both omnipresent and omnipotent). This healthy and balanced knowledge of God provides for us a sanctuary from all unhealthy fears. "You are not to say, 'It is a conspiracy!' in regard to all that this people call a conspiracy, and you are not to fear what they fear or be in dread of it. It is the LORD of hosts whom you should regard as holy. And He shall be your fear, and He shall be your dread. Then He shall become a sanctuary" (Isaiah 8:12-14).

Fortunately for all of us, our God is indeed a forgiving God; therefore, we love and worship Him. His grace and mercy inspire us to stand in grateful awe of the Lord Jesus' shed blood and death on the cross. The fear of the Lord (unlike other fears) moves us to run *to* Him, experiencing His cleansing and renewal. Then He indeed becomes our place of safety and worship.

In the Old Testament, the term *sanctuary* referred to the tabernacle of Moses and later to the temple of Solomon. A sanctuary was the place where God manifested His presence to His people. It was a holy place of communion with the Almighty. No matter what might happen to the nation, the city of Jerusalem, or even its magnificent temple, God was assuring Isaiah that His presence would always be a sanctuary for His people. He would be present and available 24 hours a day, 365 days a year for those who feared Him.

The fear of the Lord was the door that opened that sanctuary, which is not a physical location or building at all. It is the presence of God! New Testament believers find their sanctuary "in Christ," which is a spiritual position, not a physical location.

Fear v. Being Afraid

God is far superior to all other fear objects, but He is also kind and good. He is to be feared, but God does not want us to be afraid of Him. When Jesus touched John, He said, "Do not be afraid" (Revelation 1:17). God is our "Abba, Father" (Galatians 4:6). He delights in His children, quieting us in His love and rejoicing over us with shouts of joy (Zephaniah 3:17). It would grieve the heart of our heavenly Father if we fearfully run away from Him or slink away in suspicion and mistrust. Even when we sin, His love for us does not change. The Bible says the kindness of God led you to repentance, not the craven fear of His wrath (see Romans 2:4).

My son, Brian, has always loved his daddy (Rich). Even as a toddler, he would be the first to greet me when I would come home from a ministry trip. Even when I was gone for just a few hours, he would run across the kitchen with his arms stretched out, wanting me to pick him up and hug him. Unfortunately, sometimes he would be carrying a ten-pound payload in his diaper. As he ran toward me, my sense of smell would warn me of what was coming, if you catch my drift!

Was he afraid to come rushing into daddy's hug because he was messy? No way! And was I hesitant to pick him up and love on him just because he was stinky? Even though I was aware of his condition, I would scoop him up, loaded diaper and all, and hug him and kiss him.

There is no way I would leave him in that dirty diaper because the mess he made was unhealthy for him and unpleasant to me. So I would gently put him down on the carpet, clean him up, and put a clean diaper on him. Then I would file the old diaper under "toxic waste."

We are most tempted to run from God when we feel dirty or defiled, but that is the time when we need Him the most. When Adam sinned, he tried to hide from God. It was God who first came to Adam after the fall, and it is God who takes the initiative to come to us. Now that we are "in Christ," our sins are forgiven. We are no longer sinners in the hands of an angry God; we are saints in the hands of a loving God. Therefore, "let us draw near with a sincere heart in full assurance of faith, having our hearts sprinkled clean from an evil conscience and our bodies washed with pure water" (Hebrews 10:22).

A Deep Purifying Work

God is a forgiving God, and He is also a purifying God. He will do a deeper work in our lives beyond salvation. He will take us far beyond simple survival to real *revival.* This purifying process may be painful at times, but it is always for our good. God is in the process of conforming us to His image. His ultimate concern is to purify the church.

The apostle Peter wrote, "For it is time for judgment to begin with the household of God; and if it begins with us first, what will be the outcome for those who do not obey the gospel of God? And if it is with difficulty that the righteous is saved, what will become of the godless man and the sinner?" (1 Peter 4:17,18).

The judgment on God's people comes by way of discipline: "If you are without discipline, of which all have become partakers, then you are illegitimate children and not sons" (Hebrews 12:8). "He disciplines us for our good, that we may share His holiness" (Hebrews 12:10). The purifying work of God should not drive us away from Him in fear but draw us toward Him in faith. "Therefore, let those also who suffer according to the will of God entrust their souls to a faithful Creator in doing what is right" (1 Peter 4:19).

The writer of Hebrews provides a powerful picture of our relationship under grace as opposed to the terror-stricken aversion of God that Moses and the Israelites experienced under law:

> For you have not come to a mountain that may be touched and to a blazing fire, and to darkness and gloom and whirlwind, and to the blast of a trumpet and the sound of words which sound was such that those who heard begged that no further word should be spoken to them. For they could not bear the command, "If even a beast touches the mountain, it will be stoned." And so terrible was the sight, that Moses said, "I am full of fear and trembling."
>
> But you have come to Mount Zion and to the city of the living God, the heavenly Jerusalem, and to myriads of angels, to the general assembly and church of

> the first-born who are enrolled in heaven, and to God, the Judge of all, and to the spirits of righteous men made perfect, and to Jesus, the mediator of a new covenant, and to the sprinkled blood, which speaks better than the blood of Abel (Hebrews 12:18-24).

Anyone who would seek to keep God's people today under a heavy burden of impending wrath and punishment is misguided at best and deceptive and controlling at worst. The difference between living under the law and living under grace is like the difference between night and day: despair versus joy, death versus life, wrath versus forgiveness. The law came through Moses; grace and truth through Jesus Christ (John 1:17).

But the message of the new covenant does not negate the principle of fearing God. Nor does it mean that God is unconcerned for the purity of His bride. The writer of Hebrews shares what the church can expect and what our response should be:

> See to it that you do not refuse Him who is speaking. For if those did not escape when they refused him who warned them on earth, much less shall we escape who turn away from Him who warns from heaven. And His voice shook the earth then, but now He has promised, saying, "Yet once more I will shake not only the earth, but also the heaven."
>
> And this expression, "Yet once more," denotes the removing of those things which can be shaken, as of created things, in order that those things which cannot be shaken may remain. Therefore, since we receive a kingdom which cannot be shaken, let us show gratitude, by which we may offer to God an acceptable service with reverence and awe; for our God is a consuming fire (Hebrews 12:25-29).

Have you ever wondered why you struggle with controlling fears and anxieties? Perhaps it is because your trust has been in something created, something that can be shaken. And when God shakes the world, as Hebrews says He will, you shake with it! Putting our faith in anything other than God is *false security* that will become *insecurity* as God shakes the foundation of this world. Fear and anxiety will be the inevitable results.

We will all discover in the days ahead whether our trust is truly in Him or in our own natural resources. By shaking the world, God is rattling the bars on our "fear cage," exposing our insecurities. Why? So that we will come to understand that we have become prisoners of our own fears and anxieties, and God alone has the truth to set us free.

We should not be afraid of this purifying work of God. We should be thankful because He is stripping away our self-sufficiency in order for us to be fully clothed in Christ. We will only be secure in the unshakable kingdom of Jesus. It's kind of like the wood sculptor that was asked how he was able to carve such beautiful birds. Picking up one of his masterpieces, the sculptor smiled at the man and replied, "It's simple. I just cut away everything that doesn't look like the bird." God is cutting away everything in us that doesn't look like Jesus.

The Judgment Seat of Christ

Every believer will someday appear before the judgment seat of Christ. This is not a judgment for sins, for we have already been forgiven of all our sins and made alive together with Christ. Jesus "canceled out the certificate of debt consisting of decrees against us and which was hostile to us; and He has taken it out of the way, having nailed it to the cross" (Colossians 2:14). "There is therefore now no condemnation for those who are in Christ Jesus" (Romans 8:1). The believer's final judgment is for works in order to receive rewards, as 1 Corinthians 3:11-15 teaches:

> For no man can lay a foundation other than the one which is laid, which is Jesus Christ. Now if any man builds upon the foundation with gold, silver, precious stones, wood, hay, straw, each man's work will become evident; for the day will show it, because it is to be revealed with fire; and the fire itself will test the quality of each man's work. If any man's work which he has built upon it remains, he shall receive a reward. If any man's work is burned up, he shall suffer loss; but he himself shall be saved, yet so as through fire.

For believers in Christ, where we spend eternity has already been decided, but how we spend eternity is still to be judged according to our faithfulness. We have only one life and it will soon be past; only what's done for Christ will last. Whatever we have done in the flesh will not last. Work done for our own glory, in our own strength, will be burned up. That which we have done for the glory of God is like gold, silver, and precious jewels. It will stand the test of fire, and we will be rewarded. Knowing that we will be held accountable before God is a powerful motivating force:

> Therefore also we have as our ambition, whether at home or absent, to be pleasing to Him. For we must all appear before the judgment seat of Christ, that each one may be recompensed for his deeds in the body, according to what he has done, whether good or bad. Therefore knowing the fear of the Lord, we persuade men, but we are made manifest to God; and I hope that we are made manifest also in your consciences (2 Corinthians 5:9-11).

Knowing we will be held accountable should motivate us to please God and live a righteous life. It is a sobering reality that we will all stand before God one day and give an account for every deed done and every word spoken. How we live life on earth will determine our rewards in heaven. Peter's words are good counsel for daily living in light of eternity:

> Therefore, gird your minds for action, keep sober in spirit, fix your hope completely on the grace to be brought to you at the revelation of Jesus Christ. As obedient children, do not be conformed to the former lusts which were yours in your ignorance, but like the Holy One who called you, be holy yourselves also in all your behavior; because it is written, "You shall be holy, for I am holy." And if you address as Father the One who impartially judges according to each man's work, conduct yourselves in fear during the time of your stay upon earth (1 Peter 1:13-17).

We long to see Jesus face to face and hear Him say, "Well done, good and faithful servant! You have been faithful with a few things; I will put you in charge of many things. Come and share your master's happiness" (Matthew 25:21 NIV). As a child, I didn't fear the rod of discipline from my father. I feared the accountability. It was an issue of shame, not guilt. In a similar fashion, I don't want to stand before God someday and regret the way I lived my life as a believer. Whether in loss or in reward, we have the confidence that He loves us and will remember our sins no more.

Loving and Fearing God

It may be difficult at first to understand how we can love God and fear Him at the same time. At first glance we might even think that 1 John 4:16-18 is saying that the love of God eliminates the fear of God:

> And we have come to know and have believed the love which God has for us. God is love, and the one who abides in love abides in God, and God abides in him. By this, love is perfected with us, that we may have confidence in the day of judgment; because as He is, so also are we in this world. There is no fear in love; but perfect love casts out fear, because fear involves punishment, and the one who fears is not perfected in love.

God's love for us and our love for Him does not negate the fear of God. Perfect love casts out the *fear of punishment* for our sins. Too many Christians live in fear of punishment; they live as though the hammer of God will fall upon them if they make even the slightest mistake.

Dear Christian, the hammer fell! It fell on Christ. The punishment we deserved has already fallen on Christ. That is the good news. But John is not saying that God's love casts out the fear of Himself. In fact, this same biblical author records an angel commanding people on earth to fear God:

> And I saw another angel flying in midheaven, having an eternal gospel to preach to those who live on the earth, and to every nation and tribe and tongue and people; and he said with a loud voice, "Fear God, and give Him glory, because the hour of His judgment has come; and worship Him who made the heaven and the earth and sea and springs of water" (Revelation 14:6,7).

Loving God and fearing God are not mutually exclusive. Both are needed for a healthy spiritual life. They reflect the justice and mercy of God, which are opposite sides of the same coin. If we loved God without fearing Him, we could easily slip into laziness or license. If we feared God without loving Him we could easily become legalistic. The following Scriptures provide the biblical balance of both fearing and loving God:

> For as high as the heavens are above the earth, so great is His lovingkindness toward those who fear Him.... Just as a father has compassion on his children, so the LORD has compassion on those who fear Him (Psalm 103:11,13).

> Let those who fear the LORD say: "His love endures forever" (Psalm 118:4 NIV).

> The LORD delights in those who fear him, who put their hope in his unfailing love (Psalm 147:11 NIV).

A Healthy Reverence

Let us illustrate how we can both love and fear our heavenly Father at the same time. Many of us have been blessed with fathers, mothers, aunts, uncles, grandparents, pastors, teachers, or coaches who loved us dearly and believed in us deeply. Possibly they would have even given their lives for ours had they been faced with that decision.

As we reflect on that relationship, we also had a great respect for them. Their characters were reflections of the kinds of qualities we admired. Consequently, we had a strong motivation to please them. To do something that was dishonoring to them or which abused their trust was unthinkable. There was a very real sense in which we feared them.

Like most sons, I admired my father greatly growing up. He was tall and strong, kind and giving, involved with my life but not controlling. But I also knew that if I gave my mom any problems, I'd have to answer to my father and face his strong, firm, and loving hand of discipline.

When I was about ten years old, I was involved in Little League baseball, and my father was a faithful fan and follower of my "career." He was the first one to congratulate me when I pitched a no-hitter (though I walked eight batters!).

During those preteen years I went through different phases where I wanted to own exotic or unrealistic pets. Since we lived on a quarter-acre lot in suburban Philadelphia, our options were limited. Whatever I saw on TV, I wanted. One day it was a raccoon, the next it was a fox, then it was a dolphin, and so on. At one point I was sold on getting a horse. I had no idea how much a horse cost, though I knew it was more than I had. So I concocted a plan to give the "horse fund" a running start.

My father was paid on Thursday nights and after cashing his check, would turn the money over to my mother, the family accountant. One evening my parents were watching TV in the living room. My father had just turned over his pay, in $20 bills, to mother, and they were inside her purse by the phone in the hall. No one was around.

Quietly, I pulled one of those twenties out of the purse and took it to my room. After school the next day I found a white envelope, put the money in it, stuffed it in my pocket, and took it down to the woods where I often played. Once I got there, I dragged the envelope around in the dirt to make it look like it had been there for some time.

Running home about an hour later, I burst in the door and announced the treasure that I had "found." My mother was excited for me, encouraging me to use that money toward my horse.

So far, so good. The crime of the century had been pulled off and no one was even suspicious. I never counted on my conscience betraying me, however. Hour by hour, I felt worse and worse. Finally, after baseball practice on Saturday afternoon, I couldn't stand it any more.

My father was sitting on a little hill waiting for me to finish. The closer I got to him, the worse I felt. How could I have stolen from my own parents? How could I have betrayed their trust and taken advantage of them like that? I was miserable. I didn't want to face them because I felt such shame, but I knew I could never be happy unless I told the truth.

When I reached my father, I burst into tears and confessed the whole crime. He put his arms around me and hugged me. I can still remember the sweetness of being accepted despite my stealing and lying.

After hugging me, my father floored me as he looked me in the eye and said, "Son, your mother and I knew you had stolen the money you said you'd found."

"You did?" My eyes bulged with shock. I thought they had suspected nothing.

He nodded sadly. "Yes, son, we knew. We were just waiting for you to come and tell us."

That did it. The floodgates of tears blew wide open. I had sinned. I had been discovered. But I had been loved anyway. And you better believe I never stole a thing from them again.

Revival Before a Holy God

The closer we get to our heavenly Father, the more we are aware of how far short we fall of His glory (see Romans 3:23). Although few people have seen God the way Isaiah did, many of us can relate to the conviction he experienced:

> In the year of King Uzziah's death, I saw the Lord sitting on a throne, lofty and exalted, with the train of His robe filling the temple. Seraphim stood above Him, each having six wings; with two he covered his face, and with two he covered his feet, and with two he flew. And one called out to another and said,

> "Holy, Holy, Holy, is the LORD of hosts, the whole earth is full of His glory."
>
> And the foundations of the thresholds trembled at the voice of him who called out, while the temple was filling with smoke.
>
> Then I said, "Woe is me, for I am ruined! Because I am a man of unclean lips, and I live among a people of unclean lips; for my eyes have seen the King, the LORD of hosts" (Isaiah 6:1-5).

The prophet Isaiah, a godly man worshiping in the temple, was brought face to face with his own sin in the presence of the Holy One. He cried out in holy fear as we all would. After the fear of God gripped him, the forgiving love of God touched him through one of His angels: "Then one of the seraphim flew to me, with a burning coal in his hand which he had taken from the altar with tongs. And he touched my mouth with it and said, 'Behold, this has touched your lips; and your iniquity is taken away, and your sin is forgiven'" (Isaiah 6:6,7).

Isaiah experienced a personal revival. A revival that brought a fresh cleansing from sin. A revival that brought a new commission for service (Isaiah 6:8-13). Revival in an individual, group, or nation is always accompanied by the love and fear of God together. There is a deep brokenness and groaning over sin in view of the righteousness of God. Brokenness is followed by repentance, which is granted by the kindness of God. The psalmist captures this "marriage" of the fear and love of God in revival:

> Will you [God] not revive us again, that your people may rejoice in you? Show us your unfailing love, O LORD, and grant us your salvation. I will listen to what God the LORD will say; he promises peace to

> his people, his saints—but let them not return to folly. Surely his salvation is near those who fear him, that his glory may dwell in our land.
>
> Love and faithfulness meet together; righteousness and peace kiss each other. Faithfulness springs forth from the earth, and righteousness looks down from heaven (Psalm 85:6-11 NIV).

Following a recent outpouring of God's Spirit among college students, one participant in the revival captured the spirit of it in a written testimony:

> *Deeply emotional religious displays always seemed like a tidal wave to me—a massive, powerful, all-enveloping rise, and a quick, heavy crash to the sand again, with no lasting effect. However, this was more than emotion. It involved hearts in a spiritual sense—more than just an emotional sense. I felt the deep sincerity of it, the movement of the Lord in the hearts and spirits of His people.*
>
> *I cried, moved by a grief that gave me a glimpse of the terrible and beautiful sadness that must rend the Lord's heart when He looks down and sees us hurting so badly because of sins we committed and wrong choices we made. Our sins must hurt the Lord so much more because He has a fuller, holier love for the world and the community than I could ever have.*
>
> *[The praise service, after the public confession was over,] was a bandaging of the wounds which were opened during the week. It was a time of victory and a time of praise for the grace God pours out on us so freely like ointment, bathing us with Jesus' blood and purifying us as white as freshly fallen snow.*

> *It was a practice for eternity, when as a body, all Christians will glorify the Lord forever.*[2]

Dispelling All Other Fear

Such a holy fear came upon the students attending the revival meetings that many of them waited in line for hours to publicly confess their sins before hundreds of their fellow students! These were the same students who only days before would likely have shuddered at the thought of airing their dirty laundry in such a way. What caused such a change? *The fear of God!* The fear of God brings a hatred of evil and a turning away from it (Proverbs 8:13; 16:6). Those who once were afraid to admit their wrongdoings can't bear to live in sin any longer.

The fear of embarrassment, the fear of disapproval, the fear of rejection, the fear of failure (or being perceived as a failure), the fear of man, and so on dissolve away when we fear God more than any other fear object. It is indeed the one fear that dispels all other fears.

When our eyes are opened to God as He truly is, nothing else really matters. Running to Him as the holy, forgiving, loving sanctuary that He is becomes an all-consuming passion and priority. Pride, guilt, shame, and fear are swept clean by the fear of God and replaced with humility, forgiveness, affirmation, and faith. All this happens when we have a truth encounter with the living God.

Another account of the fear of God delivering us from all other fears is revealed in the following testimony of the revival at Wheaton College in 1950. This is an excerpt of a letter from psychiatrist and professor of psychology, Philip B. Marquart, M.D., to Dr. David Howard:

> Now here are some of the astounding psychological facts [coming out of the revival].... Several dozen cases of emotional problems melted away in

> revival. I lost all my student counseling interviews. One by one they came around and declared that they were cured. So I merely asked them to return once more to give their testimony—which I wrote down in my revival notebook. That means that if we had continuous revival all over the world, believers would need psychiatry much less than they do. I began to wonder whether the Lord wasn't rejecting, for me, the idea of psychiatry of any kind.
>
> Then I began to get an avalanche of new patients. Most of them were under conviction—and in conviction it is possible to get every kind of mental abnormality, as long as they resist.
>
> One student who had scoffed at the revival became beset with a serious phobia—a fear that he might be catching epilepsy. This phobia was the punishment for his scoffing. Secular methods were of no avail.
>
> Finally I led him to confess to the Lord. Here he resisted. He had scorned the revival in the first place because he was against confession. As soon as he confessed, his phobia left him.[3]

The power and freedom in Christ has not lessened over the years. Christian leaders all over the world are praying for revival and believing God for a mighty outpouring of His Spirit. An unprecedented movement of prayer is taking place worldwide. David Bryant says that "prayer is laying the runway so that God can land." We are filled with that same sense of anticipation and urgency. We need revival in our churches and another great awakening in our nation.

You can begin to have revival right now in your heart. In the fear of the Lord, submit to Him and resist the devil. "Humble yourselves in the presence of the LORD, and He will exalt you" (James 4:10). Prayerfully go through the "Steps to Freedom in Christ" at the end of this book.

You will not be fearful of any other fear object or be anxious for tomorrow *if* you choose to believe that your omnipresent and omnipotent heavenly Father is with you. He promises to never leave you or forsake you. Fear the Lord, and you will fear nothing else.

11

Recovering the Fear of God

> For the church in the West to come alive, it needs to resolve its identity crisis, to stand on truth, to renew its vision... and more than anything else, it needs to recover the fear of the Lord.
>
> —Charles Colson
> *The Body*

"You can't tell me what to do! You're not the boss of my life!" Those uncharacteristically harsh words from my eldest daughter, Michelle, were leveled at her mother. I (Rich) was angered by the defiance that this normally sweet seven-year-old girl had expressed. Shirley, trying hurriedly to get Michelle dressed and on the bus for school, didn't have time to deal with our daughter's behavior at that moment. That would have to wait.

"We really need to get her to bed earlier," Shirley stated emphatically as she told me about the incident.

"That's true. She's really tired. That may explain why she was nasty to you, but it doesn't excuse her behavior."

I made a mental note to talk to Michelle when she got home, praying for the wisdom to know how to handle the situation and for our daughter's heart to be tender. Unknown to me, God was doing some tenderizing in my own heart to prepare me for the confrontation.

Somewhere around five o'clock, Michelle wandered into my upstairs office. I was doing some editing on this book, but I put it down when she came in. I knew that this was God's moment for me to talk to her. So I had her sit down.

Never have I seen her eyes so wide and so glued to my face as when I began to gently express my disappointment with her words and attitude toward her mother. I reminded her that the Bible says to honor your father and your mother, and that I expected her to show the same respect to her mother that she gave me.

I had considered spanking her for what she did, and I told her so. When she heard the dreaded "s" word, I could see her tense up. But then I told her that I was not going to get out the paddle...this time. She perceptibly relaxed. But I firmly warned her that the next time, if there was a next time, she would be disciplined more severely.

By this time I could see her eyes filling with tears. Involuntarily, I felt mine doing the same. Knowing that she was ready to deal with her sin, I told her to go to her room and talk to Jesus about what she had done. Then I instructed her to apologize to her mother.

As she got up, the tears were streaming down her face. I changed my mind. "On second thought, honey, why don't you just come over here with daddy and talk to Jesus right here."

Without hesitation, she climbed up in my lap and I wrapped my arms around her like a nice, warm quilt. She prayed and confessed her wrong behavior and bad attitude to the Lord, all in the safe protection of her daddy's (and heavenly Father's) arms. When she finished I turned her around so that she could face me. I was crying; she was crying. The tenderness of the moment was profound.

Before sending her off to find her mother, I said, "Sweetheart, your tender heart toward God is so good. When I look at your face, I can see Jesus in you." Another kind of tear rolled down her cheek. Not a tear of sadness and repentance this time, but a tear of joy. She had messed up, been caught, been disciplined, but she was still loved. Deeply loved.

Living a Holy Life

Even at her young age, I can see that Michelle is learning to fear God. Right now a large part of her development is being accountable to her father and mother. The fear of being held accountable for her attitudes and actions makes her very aware of our presence and the authority we have as parents. Such a fear causes her heart to burst with a hatred of evil and a yearning to be restored to fellowship with us. The healthy fear she now has of our authority must increasingly be directed toward God as she matures.

Paul expressed that desire toward his spiritual children: "So then, my beloved, just as you have always obeyed, not as in my presence only, but now much more in my absence, work out your salvation with fear and trembling; for it is God who is at work in you, both to will and to work for His good pleasure" (Philippians 2:12,13). King David also longed to see his children know the fear of the Lord: "Come, you children, listen to me; I will teach you the fear of the LORD" (Psalm 34:11). Solomon, David's most famous child, passed on his father's teaching: "Do not let your heart envy sinners, but always be zealous for the fear of the LORD" (Proverbs 23:17 NIV). Fearing God is not a developmental phase we pass through. The fear of the Lord is a permanent part of our walk with God, fervently springing from hearts that yearn to be near God and to be like Him.

The lifestyle of the one who fears God is radically different from the behavior of the one who is controlled by other fears.

Everyone has sinned, but God-fearing people are characterized by genuine righteousness. They don't tolerate sin or compromise with the world. When disciplined, they quickly repent and change the way they live. One young man in Sunday school summarized the fear of the Lord by saying, "The fear of the LORD is believing He means what He says!"

This pursuit of righteousness is not motivated by the fear of punishment because "there is therefore now no condemnation for those who are in Christ Jesus" (Romans 8:1). Rather, it is born out of a reverence for God and a longing for an intimate Father/child relationship, which is our heritage in Christ:

> For we are the temple of the living God; just as God said, "I will dwell in them and walk among them; and I will be their God, and they shall be My people. Therefore, come out from their midst and be separate," says the Lord. "And do not touch what is unclean; and I will welcome you. And I will be a father to you, and you shall be sons and daughters to Me," says the Lord Almighty. Therefore, having these promises, beloved, let us cleanse ourselves from all defilement of flesh and spirit, perfecting holiness in the fear of God (2 Corinthians 6:16–7:1).

Phobias Breed Sin

In contrast to the God-fearing person, the one controlled by other fears is driven into irresponsible and irrational behavior. Adam and Eve were driven by fear to hide from God (Genesis 3:8-10). Abraham was afraid that Abimelech would take his wife, Sarah, and kill him. So he lied to save his own life, saying Sarah was his sister (Genesis 20:1-13). When confronted by the pagan king, Abraham tried to rationalize his sinful behavior. Later on, his son, Isaac, would also fear for his life and commit the same sin.

Isaac's son, Jacob, schemed, lied, and tried a bribe when confronted with the fearful prospect of facing his brother Esau (Genesis 32). Saul tried to murder David because he was afraid of him. David had become more popular than Saul, and the Lord was with David (1 Samuel 18:12,15,29).

The prophet Samuel had told Saul to wait seven days in Gilgal and then he would meet him there and offer sacrifices. A week passed, but Samuel was delayed. So Saul decided to take matters into his own hands and offer the sacrifices himself, thus disobeying God. Finally Samuel arrived and confronted Saul:

> But Samuel said, "What have you done?" And Saul said, "Because I saw that the people were scattering from me, and that you did not come within the appointed days, and that the Philistines were assembling at Michmash, therefore I said, "Now the Philistines will come down against me at Gilgal, and I have not asked the favor of the LORD," So I forced myself and offered the burnt offering (1 Samuel 13:11,12).

Why did Saul sin? Because he feared man more than he feared God. Saul's disobedience disqualified him for spiritual leadership, and his flesh pattern of fear continued to surface. Later on, Saul confessed, "I have sinned; I have indeed transgressed the command of the LORD and your words, because I feared the people and listened to their voice" (1 Samuel 15:24).

Ten of the 12 spies who investigated the promised land were terrified of the giants and their fortified cities. Only Joshua and Caleb believed God and urged the people to claim the land He had given them. Unfortunately, the fearful report of the 10 swayed the whole Israelite nation into a rebellion against the Word of the Lord. Their disobedience cost all but Caleb and Joshua a sandy grave in the wilderness (Numbers 13;14).

Lying. Scheming. Controlling. Anger. Hatred. Rebellion. Passivity. Withdrawal. Such are the characteristics of the man or woman who is controlled by phobias. But the one who fears God is faithful and finds that in keeping God's commands there is great reward:

> The fear of the LORD is clean, enduring forever; the judgments of the LORD are true; they are righteous altogether. They are more desirable than gold, yes, than much fine gold; sweeter also than honey and the drippings of the honeycomb. Moreover, by them Thy servant is warned; in keeping them there is great reward (Psalm 19:9-12).

Benefits of Fearing God

Scripture promises that the fear of God will bring a treasure of great blessing to our lives. Consider the following benefits to the one who fears God:

Guidance in life: "Who is the man who fears the LORD? He will instruct him in the way he should choose" (Psalm 25:12).

Intimacy with God: "The secret of the LORD is for those who fear Him, and He will make them know His covenant" (Psalm 25:14).

Preservation in trial: "Behold, the eye of the LORD is on those who fear Him, on those who hope for His lovingkindness, to deliver their soul from death, and to keep them alive in famine" (Psalm 33:18,19).

Provisions for life: "O fear the LORD, you His saints; for to those who fear Him, there is no want. The young lions do lack and suffer hunger; but they who seek the LORD shall not be in want of any good thing" (Psalm 34:9,10).

God's love: "For as high as the heavens are above the earth, so great is His lovingkindness toward those who fear Him" (Psalm 103:11).

God's compassion: "Just as a father has compassion on his children, so the LORD has compassion on those who fear Him" (Psalm 103:13).

Physical health: "Do not be wise in your own eyes; fear the LORD and turn away from evil. It will be healing to your body, and refreshment to your bones" (Proverbs 3:7,8).

Wisdom and knowledge: "The fear of the LORD is the beginning of wisdom, and the knowledge of the Holy One is understanding" (Proverbs 9:10).

Life and peace: "The fear of the LORD leads to life, so that one may sleep satisfied, untouched by evil" (Proverbs 19:23).

Prosperity: "The reward of humility and the fear of the LORD are riches, honor and life" (Proverbs 22:4).

The Bible is full of promises from God for the person who fears the Lord. Every one of them provides an antidote for the poison of controlling fears and anxieties. "For as many as may be the promises of God, in Him [Christ Jesus] they are yes; wherefore also by Him is our Amen to the glory of God through us" (2 Corinthians 1:20). God's promises are true for all who are "in Christ." As believers, we simply respond to God in faith, saying "amen" to the blessings that are already ours.

Consequences of Not Fearing God

The consequences of not fearing God are sobering. You can read about them in this morning's newspaper. Notice how Paul described those who have no fear of God:

> There is none righteous, not even one; there is none who understands, there is none who seeks for God; all have turned aside, together they have become useless; there is none who does good, there is not even one. Their throat is an open grave, with their tongues they keep deceiving, the poison of asps is under their lips; whose mouth is full of cursing and bitterness; their feet are swift to shed blood, destruction and misery are in their paths, and the path of peace have they not known. There is no fear of God before their eyes (Romans 3:10-18).

An article in *Christianity Today* entitled "America the Brutal," explained why we have become a culture of violence:

> Violence in American society reflects a lack of the fear of God. The carnage in our cities raises a crucial question: Where is God? Or, more precisely, where is the sense of the holiness and awesomeness of God to whom one must give account? The Bible calls this sense the "fear of God." It does not mean fear in our usual sense of being afraid.
>
> It means rather to quake or tremble in the presence of a Being so holy, so morally superior, so removed from evil, that in His presence, human boasting, human pride, human arrogance vanish as we bow in speechless humility, reverence, and adoration of the One beyond understanding.

For this reason, Proverbs declares, "The fear of the Lord is the beginning of wisdom." Any correct understanding of the human condition begins with a sense of the presence of God in human affairs. When the fear of God is missing, evil, corruption, and violence prevail....

The psalmist says, "Transgression speaks to the wicked deep in their hearts" (Psalm 36:1). Why? "There is no fear of God before their eyes." Abraham went down to Egypt and feared for his life. He declared, "I thought, 'There is no fear of God at all in this place, and they will kill me'" (Genesis 20:11).

Where God is not feared, life is cheap.[1]

Developing the Fear of God

Fearing God and seeking God go hand in hand in Scripture. Psalm 34:8-10 says: "O taste and see that the LORD is good; how blessed is the man who takes refuge in Him! O fear the LORD, you His saints; for to those who fear Him, there is no want. The young lions do lack and suffer hunger; but they who seek the LORD shall not be in want of any good thing." What can we do to draw closer to God?

1. *Seek first the kingdom of God (Matthew 6:33)*

In western culture we are conditioned to seek every natural explanation and solution first, and if none can be found, then there is nothing left to do but pray. But that is not the order of Scripture. Jesus said, "For all these things the Gentiles eagerly seek; for your heavenly Father knows that you need all these things. But seek first His kingdom and His righteousness; and all these things shall be added to you. Therefore do not be anxious for tomorrow..." (Matthew 6:32-34).

Whenever you sense the slightest fear or anxious thought, turn to God in prayer as Paul advised: "Be anxious for nothing, but in everything by prayer and supplication with thanksgiving let your requests be made known to God" (Philippians 4:6). It sounds so simple, but it is not our natural response to fear and anxiety. If you have an anxious thought, then take that thought captive in obedience to Christ (2 Corinthians 10:5). If what you are thinking is not true according to Scripture, then don't believe it.

We have to recondition ourselves to seek God first. We have seen the need for this often when counseling Christian people with anxiety disorders. They seem to have no awareness of God's presence, nor any practice of calling upon Him in prayer. They don't realize they have a choice. Their emotional response of fear to anxious thoughts appears sudden and uncontrollable. But they do have a choice. *Everybody has a will that can be exercised.* We can choose how we think and who we turn to for help.

Joel prophesied, "And it will come about that whoever calls on the name of the LORD will be delivered" (Joel 2:32). If people knew they had all the Lord's resources at their disposal, they would certainly call upon Him first: "How great is your goodness, which you have stored up for those who fear you, which you bestow in the sight of men on those who take refuge in you" (Psalm 31:19 NIV).

2. *Discern the fear of God from Scripture*

If we truly know God and His Word, we have a balanced understanding of what it means to fear the Lord. Notice the verbs that are used in the following exhortation from King Solomon:

> My son, if you will receive my sayings, and treasure my commandments within you, make your ear attentive to wisdom, incline your heart to understanding; for if you cry for discernment, lift your voice

> for understanding; if you seek her as silver, and search for her as for hidden treasures; then you will discern the fear of the LORD, and discover the knowledge of God (Proverbs 2:1-5).

Receive. Treasure. Make your ear attentive. Incline your heart. Cry out. Lift your voice. Seek. Search. This is not a description of passivity, but of a passionate pursuit of the truth. We treasure the commandments of God when we know they are protective and not restrictive. Truth can't set us free unless we know the truth. Therefore, "be diligent to present yourself approved to God as a workman who does not need to be ashamed, handling accurately handling the word of truth" (2 Timothy 2:15).

George Massie founded the Gold Prospectors Association of America back in the 1960s in the hopes of striking it rich. After years of searching, one day he did. George was dredging up gravel from a riverbed when he struck a huge boulder. Convinced there was gold under the rock, he worked arduously to move it.

He attached cables and air-filled 55-gallon drums to the boulder. Finally the water buoyed up the rock and it floated out of its hole. Under that massive rock were 800 ounces of gold nuggets. The boulder that laid the golden eggs "hatched" more than $600,000 worth of gold for Massie.

What would you do if you knew for sure that a vein of pure gold ran under your backyard? If you knew that an investment of time and energy would net you a treasure that would provide for your material needs the rest of your life, would you take the risk? Wouldn't the long hours of hard work and temporary sacrifice be worth the effort to gain such treasure?

Recall again the blessings that come from knowing the fear of the Lord: intimacy with God, guidance, wisdom, knowledge, preservation and protection during times of trial, provisions for life, God's abundant love and compassion. Can gold guarantee those things? If we would zealously search for treasures on earth, how much more should we zealously search for treasures from heaven?

When Solomon was given the chance to ask God for one thing, what did he choose? "Give thy servant an understanding heart." And God commended him for his choice: "It was pleasing in the sight of the Lord that Solomon had asked this thing" (1 Kings 3:9,10).

In the crisis of any decision, isn't wisdom what you need? Consider any worry you have over the future or finances. Wouldn't the wisdom of God dispel all confusion and distraction of thought? Most of our struggles with fear and anxiety would disappear if we drew upon the wisdom of God. Remember, the fear of the Lord is the beginning of wisdom. Solomon taught the value of wisdom when he wrote:

> How blessed is the man who finds wisdom, and the man who gains understanding. For its profit is better than the profit of silver, and its gain than fine gold. She is more precious than jewels; and nothing you desire compares with her. Long life is in her right hand; in her left hand are riches and honor. Her ways are pleasant ways, and all her paths are peace. She is a tree of life to those who take hold of her, and happy are all who hold her fast (Proverbs 3:13-18).

In John 17:15-17 (NIV), Jesus said, "My prayer is not that you take them out of the world but that you protect them from the evil one. They are not of the world, even as I am not of it. Sanctify them by the truth; your word is truth." We do not overcome the father of lies by research or human reasoning, but by revelation. Jesus also said, "If you abide in My word, then you are truly disciples of Mine; and you shall know the truth, and the truth shall make you free" (John 8:31,32).

In the book of Romans, Paul reminds us of the power of the Word of God to strengthen us:

> For whatever was written in earlier times was written for our instruction, that through perseverance and the encouragement of the Scriptures we might have hope. Now may the God who gives perseverance and encouragement grant you to be of the same mind with one another according to Christ Jesus; that with one accord you may with one voice glorify the God and Father of our Lord Jesus Christ (15:4-6).

It takes time to overcome phobias and deep-seated anxieties. You will be tempted to think the battle is too hard and not worth the effort. Those are the times when you need perseverance and encouragement to not give up. The Scriptures promise to bring hope in times like that. Galatians 6:9 says, "And let us not lose heart in doing good, for in due time we shall reap if we do not grow weary."

3. *Practice the presence of God*

As a child I attended a Ringling Brothers and Barnum & Bailey circus. In those days they raised the big top with elephants. People were allowed to watch the process, and it was exciting to see. It was part of the "Greatest Show on Earth." In the presence of strangers and elephants, I didn't sense any fear so long as my father was with me.

In my curiosity, I wandered off from my family and suddenly found myself alone. I started to panic when I realized that my provider and protector father wasn't there.

Our spiritual growth and protection require the presence and power of God. The more we practice the presence of God, the less fear and anxiety we will experience. Begin your day by putting on the armor of God. The first instruction is to "be strong in the Lord, and in the strength of His might" (Ephesians 6:10). A spiritual battle requires spiritual power. The devil wants us to lean on our own understanding and live according to the flesh because in the flesh we are no match for him. But if we walk by faith in the power of the Holy Spirit, we will not carry out the desires of the flesh (Galatians 5:16-18). God is "able to do exceeding abundantly beyond all that we ask or think, according to the power that works within us" (Ephesians 3:20). That power is unleashed when we are filled with the Holy Spirit and abide in Christ (see Ephesians 5:18; John 15:1-5).

No matter where we go, God is always there. Practice His presence by learning to "pray without ceasing" (1 Thessalonians 5:17). Whenever any crisis occurs, stop and pray. When you begin to worry about tomorrow, stop and pray. When you are intimidated at work or play, stop and pray. When you stop and seek the Lord in prayer, He will deliver you from your fears (Psalm 34:4).

To have a biblical fear of God is to have an awareness of His presence in the face of lesser fear objects. The God-fearing person has learned the futility of life lived in the energy of the flesh and agrees with Solomon who wrote: "I know that everything God does will remain forever; there is nothing to add to it and there is nothing to take from it, for God has so worked that men should fear Him" (Ecclesiastes 3:14).

4. *Worship the Lord*

The Father is seeking people to worship Him in spirit and truth (John 4:23,24). David said, "You who fear the LORD, praise

Him; all you descendants of Jacob, glorify Him, and stand in awe of Him, all you descendants of Israel" (Psalm 22:23). An act of worship is to ascribe to God His divine attributes. We praise God for who He is, and we do this for our sake. God doesn't need us to tell Him who He is, but we need to keep His divine attributes constantly before us.

The form of worship isn't important so long as your worship of God is prompted by the Holy Spirit and in accordance with the truth of God's Word. You are worshiping God when you sing hymns or when you play a praise tape in your car. You can worship God by shouting praises to Him in the forest or bowing in silence before Him in your bedroom at home. You are worshiping God when you "do your work heartily, as for the Lord rather than for men" (Colossians 3:23). You can worship God anywhere at anytime in the quietness of your heart. You can worship God formally or informally, but never irreverently.

Nothing dispels a cloud of despair over our lives like uninhibited praise and worship of the King. He is worthy of it, and we need to do it. Worship reminds us of who God is and who we are in relation to Him. Pride crumbles and humility flourishes in the heart of worship. Worship is like a spiritual greenhouse in which the fear of God and love of God blossom. And as delightful as personal worship is, corporate worship is even better!

Few commands are repeated more often in Scripture than "praise the Lord." Three of the shortest commands in the Bible should always be on the lips of those who continuously worship God: "Rejoice always; pray without ceasing; in everything give thanks; for this is God's will for you in Christ Jesus" (1 Thessalonians 5:16-18). The writer of Hebrews says, "Through Him [Jesus] then, let us continually offer up a sacrifice of praise to God, that is, the fruit of lips that give thanks to His name" (Hebrews 13:15).

The Moabites and Ammonites were attacking King Jehoshaphat and the army of Judah. "And Jehoshaphat was afraid and turned his attention to seek the LORD; and proclaimed a fast throughout all Judah" (2 Chronicles 20:3). The people of God came together and worshiped the Lord saying, "O LORD, God of our fathers, are you not the God who is in heaven? You rule over all the kingdoms of the nations. Power and might are in your hand, and no one can withstand you" (2 Chronicles 20:6 NIV).

Crying out to God in desperation, they stood before the LORD, waiting for His word (2 Chronicles 20:13). God's Spirit came upon Jahaziel and he said, "Do not be afraid or discouraged because of this vast army. For the battle is not yours, but God's....Do not be afraid; do not be discouraged. Go out to face them tomorrow, and the LORD will be with you" (2 Chronicles 20:15,17 NIV).

In response to the word of God, all the people worshiped God (2 Chronicles 20:18). Worship became their battle plan to defeat the enemy. "And when he [Jehoshaphat] had consulted with the people, he appointed those who sang to the LORD and those who praised Him in holy attire, as they went out before the army and said, 'Give thanks to the LORD, for His lovingkindness is everlasting.' And when they began singing and praising, the LORD set ambushes against the sons of Ammon, Moab, and Mount Seir, who had come against Judah; so they were routed" (2 Chronicles 20:21,22).

Worship brings to our minds the awareness of God's presence and fear flees! When the first hint of fear or anxiety comes into your mind, worship God. One time I was battling oppressive thoughts about my children being kidnapped and tortured by evil people. Taking a walk on a quiet country road I prayed about my mental battles and even renounced the enemy's attack. But it wasn't until I worshiped God and praised Him in song that the heaviness lifted. Fear fled and faith flowed in the presence of God.

God is the ultimate fear object because He is everywhere present and all powerful. Satan is a defeated foe, but he wants to be feared because he wants to be worshiped like God. He even tempted Jesus to worship him in the wilderness—he offered to give the kingdoms of this world to Jesus in exchange for one act of worship. Jesus responded, "Begone, Satan! For it is written, 'You shall worship the LORD your God, and serve Him only' " (Matthew 4:10). Our response to Satan ought to be the same as Jesus' was!

The devil craves worship as the god of this world, but the Lord is our God and this world is not our home. Our research has revealed that many Christians have sensed an evil presence in their rooms that frightened them. Not knowing their identity or authority in Christ, they trembled before that demonic presence. To cower in fear before Satan is a twisted form of worship and is exactly what he wants. Satan is worshiped because he is feared.

Many parents have heard their children say, "There was something in my room last night!" A wise parent reminds the children that God was there. But the child might respond: "No, there was something else!" But God indeed was there, and if our children knew that they would submit to God and resist the devil—and the devil would flee from them. Such a courageous stand is an act of worship and would teach our children forever that "greater is He who is in you than he who is in the world" (1 John 4:4).

5. ***Fellowship with other believers***

The fear of God affects how we relate to others, as the following verses indicate:

> Do not curse the deaf or put a stumbling block in front of the blind, but fear your God. I am the LORD (Leviticus 19:14 NIV).

> Do not take advantage of each other, but fear your God. I am the LORD your God (Leviticus 25:17 NIV).

> Come, you children, listen to me; I will teach you the fear of the LORD. Who is the man who desires life, and loves length of days that he may see good? Keep your tongue from evil, and your lips from speaking deceit. Depart from evil, and do good; seek peace, and pursue it (Psalm 34:11-14).

> Slaves, in all things obey those who are your masters on earth, not with external service, as those who merely please men, but with sincerity of heart, fearing the Lord. Whatever you do, do your work heartily, as for the Lord rather than for men; knowing that from the Lord you will receive the reward of the inheritance. It is the Lord Christ whom you serve (Colossians 3:22-24).

The fear of the Lord changes your perception of the work you do and the people you meet. Your work becomes more than a means of paying bills; it becomes an opportunity to worship and serve God. Individuals and groups that you previously rejected, made fun of, or took advantage of are now seen in a whole new light. They are no longer "losers," but rather men and women deeply loved by God.

We were never intended by God to live the Christian life alone. We absolutely need God, and we necessarily need each other. We are to be "subject to one another in the fear of Christ" (Ephesians 5:21). The bondage of fear selfishly chokes out our love for others. As we resolve our personal and spiritual conflicts, we are unlocked from self-centered living and loosed to meet the needs of others. Convinced that God will take care of us, we are free to serve.

God is interested in doing far more than simply taking away our fears and anxieties. We have been set free for a purpose. God wants to do more than lift us out of the miry clay. He wants to set our feet on a rock, so we can build our house (life) on a firm foundation (Psalm 40:2). Jesus is the Rock, and we are to build our lives on Him and His Word (Matthew 7:24,25). A rock-solid security in Christ is the necessary prerequisite for sincere and humble service to others. The writer of Hebrews admonishes us to gather strength from other believers:

> Let us hold fast the confession of our hope without wavering, for He who promised is faithful; and let us consider how to stimulate one another to love and good deeds, not forsaking our own assembling together, as is the habit of some, but encouraging one another; and all the more as you see the day drawing near (Hebrews 10:23-25).

6. *Be committed to doing the will of God*

Crippling fears and anxieties draw us away from the will of God and from living a responsible life. God's will for our lives is good, acceptable, and perfect (Romans 12:2). The problem is that we don't always know what is good for us. What appears to be good for us now may not be years later or in eternity. That is why we need to trust God that His will for our lives is better than anything we could plan.

Suppose God's will for your life is on the other side of a closed door. You couldn't help but wonder what it is. But why do you want to know? So you can decide whether or not you are willing to go through the door? If you really want to know and do God's will, you have to resolve an issue on this side of the door. If God is your God, then He has the right to decide what is on the other side of the door. If you haven't given Him that right, then you are acting as your own god.

What gives us the courage to open the door and walk through it is the conviction that God is good and His will for our lives is good. There is no safer place to be than in the center of His will, no matter how difficult it might initially appear to be. In order to know God's will, we have to deny ourselves, take up our cross, and follow Jesus (Matthew 16:24). Jesus said, "If any man is willing to do His will, he shall know of the teaching, whether it is of God or whether I speak from Myself" (John 7:17).

7. *Develop an attitude of gratitude*

We have so much to be thankful for. We all deserved eternal damnation, but God gave us eternal life. Our sins are forgiven, God will supply all our needs, and we shall see Him face to face in eternity. We have the assurance that God was faithful yesterday, He is faithful today, and He will be faithful tomorrow (Hebrews 13:8). The psalmist tells us how we are to come before His presence:

> O come, let us sing for joy to the LORD; let us shout joyfully to the rock of our salvation. Let us come before His presence with thanksgiving; let us shout joyfully to Him with psalms. For the LORD is a great God, and a great King above all gods, in whose hands are the depths of the earth; the peaks of the mountains are His also. The sea is His, for it was He who made it; and His hands formed the dry land.
>
> Come, let us worship and bow down; let us kneel before the LORD our Maker. For He is our God, and we are the people of His pasture, and the sheep of His hand (Psalm 95:1-7).

One of the keys that unlocks prayer is to come before God with thanksgiving. If we are going to pray by the Spirit, then we need to be filled with the Spirit. Thankfulness is the result of the Spirit-filled life: "always giving thanks for all things in the name of our Lord Jesus Christ to God, even the Father" (Ephesians 5:20). Notice in the following verses how prayer and thanksgiving are intertwined:

> Be anxious for nothing, but in everything by prayer and supplication with thanksgiving let your requests be made known to God (Philippians 4:6).

> Devote yourselves to prayer, keeping alert in it with an attitude of thanksgiving (Colossians 4:2).

> Pray without ceasing; in everything give thanks; for this is God's will for you in Christ Jesus (1 Thessalonians 5:17,18).

8. ***Keep a daily journal***

Throughout the Israelites' wanderings in the wilderness, they were exhorted by God through Moses to remember what God had done. To do so was to create a record of God's faithfulness so that future fears could be easily overcome. Here is one example: "If you should say in your heart, 'These nations are greater than I; how can I dispossess them?' you shall not be afraid of them; you shall well remember what the LORD your God did to Pharaoh and to all Egypt" (Deuteronomy 7:17,18).

As you pick up your cross daily and follow Him, try keeping a journal. There is something about writing our thoughts down that helps us crystallize our thinking. It is part of analyzing our fears and casting our anxiety onto Christ. A daily log of our struggles and victories is the best way to chart our progress and provide encouragement over the long haul. Many of the psalms can serve as examples. David modeled what it means to be painfully honest with God, "journaling" his relationship with God in song.

The Final Journey

At the turn of the century, a missionary couple had left their home in America in order to bring the gospel to Africa. For 50 years they labored on the mission field. In the process, they overcame their doubts and fears. God had proven Himself faithful time and time again. Now it was time to go back to the United States, and their physical strength and resources were nearly depleted.

After saying farewell to their beloved Africa and all their lifelong friends, they boarded a ship to England. From there they sailed to New York on one of the queen's ship. It just so happened that the Queen of England was also on board.

As they pulled into New York harbor, the ship was greeted by tugboats with their water cannons saluting the arrival of the queen. As they gently docked at the pier, the United States Marine Band was there to greet them. All the passengers were given paper streamers to throw off the side of the ship in honor of the queen. A red carpet was rolled up the walkway to the ship. The rest of the passengers waited while the queen and all her entourage departed.

The band put their instruments away and the red carpet was rolled up. The first class passengers were next to disembark, and then the second and finally the third class. While waiting their turn at the railing, this veteran missionary turned to his wife in a moment of sadness and said, "Look, honey, there is no one here to greet us. No one to welcome us home!"

She looked at her beloved husband of 50 years and said, "Honey, we're not home yet!"

But you, be sober in all things, endure hardship, do the work of an evangelist, fulfill your ministry. For I am already being poured out as a drink offering, and the time of my departure has come. I have fought the good fight, I have finished the course, I have kept the faith; in the future there is laid up for me the crown of righteousness, which the Lord, the righteous Judge, will award to me on that day; and not only to me, but also to all who have loved His appearing (2 Timothy 4:5-8).

This world is not your home.

Epilogue

What an exciting time to be alive. Not since Pentecost have we seen such phenomenal growth of the church worldwide. Africa was less than 5 percent Christian at the turn of the century. It is expected to be 50 percent by the end of this millennium. There were about 5 million believers in China when communism closed the door to the outside world. Now the estimates vary from 100 to as high as 150 million believers. Missiologists estimate that between 25,000 and 35,000 people are coming to Christ daily in China. Indonesia is the world's most populated Muslim nation, but the percentage of Christians has been progressing so rapidly that the government won't release accurate figures.[1]

Over 25,000 Christian radio and television stations broadcast the gospel daily to 4.6 billion people. I had the privilege to speak to the staff of HCJB, an international Christian shortwave radio station broadcasting from Quito, Ecuador, at their annual meeting. I was so impressed with their commitment and their technological expertise. The same holds true for Trans World Radio and Far Eastern Broadcasting Company, who are working together with HCJB to blanket this planet with the good news. They can now package a radio station in a suitcase and go anywhere in the world with it.

We are the first generation that can say without reservation, "We have the technology to actually fulfill the Great Commission in our generation." Billy Graham held a crusade via satellite that may have reached as many as 2.5 billion people. And we have only scratched the surface of what can and most certainly will be done with satellite communications and the Internet.

Ministries cooperating together is another significant sign that we are in for a great harvest. We may be driving different cars, but we are all driving them in the same kingdom and getting gas from the same station. There is a growing majority in the body of Christ who are sick and tired of Christians competing or defeating one another. It is beyond the time for the church to personally appropriate the truth of Ephesians 4:1-6:

> I, therefore, the prisoner of the Lord, entreat you to walk in a manner worthy of the calling with which you have been called, with all humility and gentleness, with patience, showing forbearance to one another in love, being diligent to preserve the unity of the Spirit in the bond of peace. There is one body and one Spirit, just as also you were called in one hope of your calling; one Lord, one faith, one baptism, one God and Father of all who is over all and through all and in all.

God is preparing His people and pulling His church together for the final harvest. In His high-priestly prayer, Jesus prays that we would all be one just as He and the Father are one (John 17:21). He is not praying for the old ecumenicalism that was deluded by liberalism. He is praying that the true, born-again, Bible-believing community known as the body of Christ would work together to stem the tide of liberalism, immorality, the rising threat of the New Age, and the secular movement of universalism.

Caution must be taken to not water down the movement. Unity in the Spirit is not universalism. Paul says, "Do not be bound together with unbelievers; for what partnership have righteousness and lawlessness, or what fellowship has light with darkness? Or what harmony has Christ with Belial, or what has a believer in common with an unbeliever?" (2 Corinthians 6:14,15). We must maintain an unshakable commitment to the authority of Scripture, and we must never compromise our characters in order to produce results. Most would agree that God is more concerned about Church purity than church growth because church purity is an essential prerequisite to bearing fruit.

Mission America has the goal of praying for and sharing Christ with every person in our nation by the end of the year 2000. That would be impossible unless the Holy Spirit draws the church together as partners in ministry. This united effort to reach our nation for Christ is being called "Celebrate Jesus." We don't have to throw away our denominational distinctives or doctrinal beliefs to preserve the unity of the Spirit. But we do have to believe in "a renewal in which there is no distinction between Greek and Jew, circumcised and uncircumcised, barbarian, Scythian, slave and freeman, but Christ is all, and in all" (Colossians 3:11).

Mission America will not end after the year 2000. This movement of God has over 70 denominations and 200 parachurch ministries working together. Their vision is to establish over 3 million lighthouses of prayer in the United States so that everybody in every community will be prayed for. This will require a great deal of cooperation. On what basis can we agree to work together?

The only legitimate basis for unity in the body of Christ is to realize that we (the true, born-again church) are all children of God. Partnering together will require forgiveness and reconciliation. It will necessitate tolerance of other people's perspectives without compromising personal convictions. We must respect the denominational distinctives of others and relate with integrity on all matters. The hardest part for some will be releasing personal goals and ambitions and working together to build the kingdom of God.

We want to encourage you to be a part of this great global harvest. The scope of this harvest is unprecedented in church history. We are praying that God's will be done on earth as it is in heaven. The time is short, the needs are great, the harvest is plentiful, the laborers are few. God has so much more for us than we have ever imagined!

Faith for the Future

Whenever the kingdom of God advances, the domain of darkness launches a counterattack. The clash between light and darkness will precipitate events that will cause many to fear. Cult leaders will arise and take advantage of a climate of fear, swaying many to their deceptions. Terrorist acts of violence will likely destabilize governments and tempt even believers to panic. These words from the book *Let Go of Fear* call for courage in troubled times:

> I say this to bring to the clearest possible light the fact that it is our fear that lays us open to manipulation. Fear is the handle we ourselves give to those

> who would turn us around at their will. Terrorism exists because we are afraid. There are international commissions that meet regularly to analyze the spread of terrorism and propose remedies. They are not likely to do away with the plague. The ultimate remedy lies in the human heart. Fearlessness alone can free us from the snares our own fears have built...[2]

As we move nearer and nearer to the time of our Lord's return, fear and anxiety will increase in intensity and pervasiveness. Jesus prophesied that it would be so in Luke 21:25,26: "And there will be signs in sun and moon and stars, and upon the earth dismay among nations, in perplexity at the roaring of the sea and the waves, men fainting from fear and the expectation of the things which are coming upon the world; for the powers of the heavens will be shaken." In days to come, the psalmist's words will become an anchor for troubled souls:

> God is our refuge and strength, a very present help in trouble. Therefore we will not fear, though the earth should change, and though the mountains slip into the heart of the sea.... "Cease striving and know that I am God; I will be exalted among the nations, I will be exalted in the earth." The Lord of hosts is with us; the God of Jacob is our stronghold (Psalm 46:1,2,10,11).

This is not the time to cower in fear and unbelief. It is the right time to trust God and encourage one another to stand strong and step out in faith. Psalm 112:1-8 says you will be blessed if you do:

> Praise the LORD! How blessed is the man who fears the LORD, who greatly delights in His commandments. His descendants will be mighty on earth; the generation of the upright will be blessed. Wealth and riches are in his house, and his righteousness endures forever. Light arises in the darkness for the upright; he is gracious and compassionate and righteous. It is well with the man who is gracious and lends; he will maintain his cause in judgment. For he will never be shaken; the righteous will be remembered forever.
>
> He will not fear evil tidings; his heart is steadfast, trusting in the LORD, His heart is upheld, he will not fear, until he looks with satisfaction on his adversaries.

The Key to This Treasure

There may be troubled days ahead, but Jesus said, "These things I have spoken to you, that in Me you may have peace. In the world you have tribulation, but take courage; I have overcome the world" (John 16:33). The peace of God is internal, not external. God is shaking the foundations of this world, but if our foundation is in Christ, we have nothing to fear. He will give us the grace, wisdom, and knowledge to endure. Let's exalt Him and discover the key to this treasure:

> The LORD is exalted, for he dwells on high; he will fill Zion with justice and righteousness. He will be the sure foundation for your times, a rich store of salvation and wisdom and knowledge; the fear of the LORD is the key to this treasure (Isaiah 33:5,6 NIV).

Steps to Freedom in Christ

"It was for freedom that Christ set us free; therefore keep standing firm and do not be subject again to a yoke of slavery" (Galatians 5:1). If you have received Christ as your Savior, He has already set you free through His victory over sin and death on the cross. The question is: Are you living victoriously in Christ's freedom or are you still living in slavery?

How can you tell if you are *living free in Christ?* Freedom in Christ is having the desire and power to know, love, worship, and obey God. It is the joyful liberty of knowing God's truth and walking according to that truth in the power of the Holy Spirit. It is not a perfect life, for that is impossible this side of heaven. But it is a *growing, abundant life* in Christ.

If you are not experiencing that kind of freedom, it may be because you have not stood firm in the faith or lived according to who you are *in Christ.* Somehow you have allowed a yoke of slavery to put you back in bondage. It is your responsibility, however, to do whatever is needed to walk in your freedom in Christ. If you are a Christian already, your eternal life is not at stake; you are safe and secure in Christ. But your daily victory is at stake if you choose not to walk according to the truth.

No matter how tough it might be for you spiritually right now, we've got great news for you! You are not a helpless victim caught in a tug-of-war match between two nearly equal but opposite heavenly superpowers—God and Satan. Only God is all-powerful, always present, and all-knowing. Satan was defeated by Christ the Victor at the cross, so don't believe the lie that your situation is hopeless or that you are helpless against the devil's attacks. Satan knows you have authority over him in Christ, but he doesn't want you to know it. He is a liar, and the only way he can have power over you is if you believe his lies.

The battle is for your mind. Do you experience nagging thoughts like "this isn't going to work" or "God doesn't love me"? Don't believe the devil's lies. If you believe Satan's deceptions, you will really struggle with making it through these "Steps to Freedom in Christ."

Remember, the only power Satan has over you is the power of the lie. Expose the lie by getting it out in the open, then choose the truth and the power of that lie is broken. In that way you will be able to maintain control. Don't pay any attention to accusing or threatening thoughts. If you are working through this with a trusted friend, pastor, or counselor (which we heartily encourage), then tell him or her any thoughts you are having that are in opposition to what you are trying to do. You must cooperate with the person who is trying to help you by sharing what is going on inside your mind. Also, if you experience any physical discomfort (such as headache, nausea, tightness in the throat), don't be alarmed. Just tell the person you are with so that he or she can pray for you. Don't let the devil set the agenda during this time; let the Holy Spirit call the shots.

As believers in Christ, we can pray with authority to stop any interference by Satan. Here is a prayer and declaration to get you going. Read them (and all the prayers and declarations in *italics*) out loud.

Opening Prayer

Dear heavenly Father, I know that You are right here in this room with me and that You are present in my life right now. You are the only all-knowing, all-powerful, and ever-present God. I am completely dependent upon You because without Jesus Christ I can do nothing. I choose to stand in the truth of Your Word, and I refuse to believe the devil's lies. Thank You that the risen Lord Jesus has all authority in heaven and on earth. Father, thank You that because I am in Christ I share His authority in order to make disciples and set captives free. I ask You to protect my mind and body during this time. Please fill me with the Holy Spirit so that He can guide me into all truth. I choose to submit to only His guidance during this time. Please reveal to my mind everything You want me to deal with today. I ask for and trust in Your wisdom. I pray all this in faith, in the name of Jesus. Amen.

Declaration

In the name and authority of the Lord Jesus Christ I command Satan and all evil spirits to release their hold on me in order that I can be free to know and choose to do the will of God. As a child of God, raised up and seated with Christ in the heavenly places, I know that every enemy of the Lord Jesus Christ can be bound. I say to

Satan and all his evil workers that you cannot inflict any pain or in any way prevent God's will from being done today in my life.

Before going through the "Steps to Freedom," review the events of your life to discern specific areas that might need to be addressed.

Family History

- ❏ Religious history of parents and grandparents
- ❏ Home life from childhood through high school
- ❏ History of physical or emotional illness in the family
- ❏ Adoption, foster care, guardians

Personal History

- ❏ Spiritual journey (salvation—when, how, assurance of)
- ❏ Eating habits (bulimia, bingeing and purging, anorexia, compulsive eating)
- ❏ Addictions (drugs, alcohol)
- ❏ Prescription medications (reason for use)
- ❏ Sleeping patterns and nightmares
- ❏ Rape or any sexual, physical, emotional abuse
- ❏ Thought life (obsessive, blasphemous, condemning, distracting, poor concentration, fantasy)
- ❏ Mental interference in church, prayer, or Bible study
- ❏ Emotional life (anger, anxiety, depression, bitterness, fears)

Now you are ready to start going through the "Steps to Freedom in Christ." The following are seven steps to help you experience freedom from your past. You will address the areas in which Satan commonly takes advantage of believers and where strongholds are often built.

Remember that the Lord Jesus Christ has already purchased your freedom over sin and Satan on the cross. Experiencing that freedom will be the result of what *you* choose to believe, confess, renounce, and forgive. No one can do that for you, not even God. The battle for your mind will only be won as you personally choose the truth.

During each step, it is very important that you submit to God inwardly while resisting the devil outwardly. Do this by praying each prayer and making each declaration *out loud*. The prayers and declarations are in *italics* to remind you to do that.

You will be taking a very thorough inventory of your life in order to make a rock-solid commitment to the truth. If your problems stem from another source not covered in these steps, you will have lost nothing by going through them. If you are open and honest during this time, you will greatly benefit by becoming right with God and drawing closer to Him.

May the Lord greatly touch your life during this time. He alone can and will give you the grace to make it through. Lean on His strength and wisdom, not on your own. It is crucial that you work through *all* seven steps during this session. Take short breaks as you need them, but don't allow yourself to become discouraged and give up.

Remember, the freedom that Christ purchased for all believers on the cross is meant for *you!*

Step 1: Counterfeit v. Real

The first step toward experiencing your freedom in Christ is to renounce (verbally reject) all past or present involvement with occult practices, cult teachings and rituals, as well as non-Christian religions.

You must renounce any activity or group which denies Jesus Christ or offers guidance through any source other than the absolute authority of the Bible. Any group that requires dark, secret initiations, ceremonies, promises or pacts should also be renounced. Begin this step by praying aloud:

> *Dear heavenly Father, I ask You to bring to my mind anything and everything that I have done knowingly or unknowingly that involves occult, cult, or non-Christian teachings or practices. I want to experience Your freedom by renouncing these things right now. In Jesus' name I pray, amen.*

Even if you took part in something and thought it was just a game or a joke, you need to renounce it. Satan will try to take advantage of anything he can in our lives, so it is always wise to be as thorough as possible. Even if you were just standing by and watching others do it, you need to renounce your passive involvement. You may not have even realized at the time that what was going on was evil. Still, go ahead and renounce it.

If something comes to your mind and you are not sure what to do about it, trust that the Spirit of God is answering the prayer you just prayed, and go ahead and renounce it.

Note the following "Non-Christian Spiritual Checklist." This inventory covers many of the more common occult, cult, and non-Christian religious groups and practices. It is not a complete list, however. Feel free to add others that you were personally involved with.

After that checklist, there are some additional questions designed to help you become aware of other things you may need to renounce. Below those questions is a short prayer of confession and renunciation. Pray it out loud, filling in the blanks with the groups, teachings, or practices that the Holy Spirit has prompted you to renounce during this time of personal evaluation.

Non-Christian Spiritual Checklist

(Check all those that you have participated in)

- ❑ Out of body experience (astral projection)
- ❑ Ouija board
- ❑ Bloody Mary
- ❑ Light as a feather (or other occult games)
- ❑ Table lifting
- ❑ Magic Eight Ball
- ❑ Spells or curses
- ❑ Mental telepathy or mental control of others
- ❑ Automatic writing
- ❑ Trances
- ❑ Spirit guides
- ❑ Fortune telling/divination (e.g., tea leaves)
- ❑ Tarot cards
- ❑ Levitation
- ❑ Magic—The Gathering
- ❑ Witchcraft/sorcery
- ❑ Satanism
- ❑ Palm reading
- ❑ Astrology/horoscopes
- ❑ Hypnosis (amateur or self-induced)
- ❑ Seances
- ❑ Black or white magic
- ❑ Dungeons & Dragons® (and similar games)
- ❑ Blood pacts or cutting yourself on purpose
- ❑ Objects of worship/crystals/good luck charms
- ❑ Sexual spirits
- ❑ Martial arts (mysticism/devotion to sensei)
- ❑ Superstitions
- ❑ Mormonism (Latter-day Saints)
- ❑ Jehovah Witness (Watchtower)
- ❑ New Age (books, objects, seminars, medicine)

- ❑ Masons
- ❑ Christian Science
- ❑ Mind Science cults
- ❑ The Way International
- ❑ Unification Church (Moonies)
- ❑ The Forum (est)
- ❑ Church of the Living Word
- ❑ Children of God (Children of Love)
- ❑ Church of Scientology
- ❑ Unitarianism/Universalism
- ❑ Roy Masters
- ❑ Silva Mind Control
- ❑ Transcendental meditation (TM)
- ❑ Yoga
- ❑ Hare Krishna
- ❑ Bahaism
- ❑ Native American spirit worship
- ❑ Islam
- ❑ Hinduism
- ❑ Buddhism (including Zen)
- ❑ Black Muslim
- ❑ Rosicrucianism
- ❑ Other non-Christian religions or cults
- ❑ Occult or violent video and computer games
- ❑ Movies, TV shows, music, books, magazines, or comics that the Lord is bringing to your mind (especially those that glorified Satan, caused fear or nightmares, were gruesomely violent, or stimulated the flesh). List them below:

Below are some additional questions designed to help you become aware of other things you may need to renounce.

1. Have you ever seen, heard, or felt a spiritual being in your room?
2. Do you have recurring nightmares? Specifically renounce any accompanying fear.
3. Do you now have, or have you ever had, an imaginary friend, spirit guide, or "angel" offering you guidance or companionship? (If it has a name, renounce it by name.)
4. Have you ever heard voices in your head or had repeating, nagging thoughts such as "I'm dumb," "I'm ugly," "Nobody loves me," "I can't do anything right"—as if there were a conversation going on inside your head? (List any specific nagging thoughts.)
5. Have you ever consulted a medium, spiritist, or channeler?
6. Have you ever seen or been contacted by beings you thought were aliens?
7. Have you ever made a secret vow or pact?
8. Have you ever been involved in a satanic ritual of any kind or attended a concert in which Satan was the focus?
9. What other spiritual experiences have you had that were evil, confusing, or frightening?

Once you have completed your checklist and the questions, confess and renounce *each* item you were involved in by praying the following prayer *out loud:*

Lord, I confess that I have participated in __________. I know it was evil and offensive in Your sight. Thank You for Your forgiveness. I renounce any and all involvement with __________, and I cancel out any and all ground that the enemy gained in my life through this activity. In Jesus' name, amen.

Renouncing Wrong Priorities

Who or what is most important to us becomes that which we worship. Our thoughts, love, devotion trust, adoration and obedience are directed to this object above all others. This object of worship is truly our God or god(s).

We were created to worship the true and living God. In fact, the Father seeks those who will worship Him in spirit and in truth (John 4:23). As children of God, "we know also that the Son of God has come and has given us understanding, so that we may know him who is true. And we are in him who is true—even in his Son, Jesus Christ. He is the true God and eternal life" (1 John 5:20 NIV).

The apostle John follows the above passage with a warning: "Little children, guard yourselves from idols" (1 John 5:21 NASB). An idol is a false god, any object of worship other than the true God. Though we may not bow down to statues, it is easy for people and things of this world to subtly become more important to us than the Lord. The following prayer expresses the commitment of a heart that chooses to "worship the Lord your God, and serve Him only" (Matthew 4:10).

Dear Lord God, I know how easy it is to allow other things and other people to become more important to me than You. I also know that this is terribly offensive to Your holy eyes as You have commanded that I "shall have no other gods before You."

I confess to You that I have not loved You with all my heart and soul and mind. As a result, I have sinned against

You, violating the first and greatest commandment. I repent of and turn away from this idolatry and now choose to return to You, Lord Jesus, as my first love. Please reveal to my mind now any and all idols in my life. I want to renounce each of them and, in so doing, cancel out any and all ground Satan may have gained in my life through my idolatry. In the name of Jesus, the true God, amen.

(See Exodus 20:3; Matthew 22:37; Revelation 2:4,5.)

The checklist below may help you recognize those areas where things or people have become more important to you than the true God, Jesus Christ. Notice that most (if not all) of the areas listed below are not evil in themselves; they become idols when they usurp God's rightful place as Lord of our lives.

- ❑ Ambition
- ❑ Food or any substance
- ❑ Money/possessions
- ❑ Computers/games/software
- ❑ Financial security
- ❑ Rock stars/media celebrities/athletes
- ❑ Church activities
- ❑ TV/movies/music/other media
- ❑ Sports or physical fitness
- ❑ Fun/pleasure
- ❑ Ministry
- ❑ Appearance/image
- ❑ Work
- ❑ Busyness/activity
- ❑ Friends
- ❑ Power/control
- ❑ Boyfriend/girlfriend

- ❑ Popularity/opinion of others
- ❑ Spouse
- ❑ Knowledge/being right
- ❑ Children
- ❑ Hobbies
- ❑ Parents

Use the following prayer to renounce any areas of idolatry or wrong priority the Holy Spirit brings to your mind.

> *In the name of the true and living God, Jesus Christ, I renounce my worship of the false god of (name the idol). I choose to worship only You, Lord. I ask You, Father, to enable me to keep this area of (name the idol) in its proper place in my life.*

If you have been involved in satanic rituals or heavy occult activity (or you suspect it because of blocked memories, severe and recurring nightmares, or sexual bondage or dysfunction), we strongly urge you to say out loud the "Special Renunciations for Satanic Ritual Involvement." Read across the page, renouncing the first item in the column under "Domain of Darkness" and then announcing the first truth in the column under "Kingdom of Light." Continue down the page in that manner.

In addition to the "Special Renunciations" list, all other satanic rituals, covenants (promises), and assignments must be specifically renounced as the Lord brings them to your mind.

Some people who have been subjected to Satanic Ritual Abuse (SRA) develop multiple or alter personalities in order to cope with their pain. If this is true in your case, you need someone who understands spiritual conflict to help you work through this problem. For now, walk through the rest of the

Special Renunciations for Satanic Ritual Involvement	
Domain of Darkness	**Kingdom of Light**
1. I renounce ever signing or having my name signed over to Satan.	1. I announce that my name is now written in the Lamb's book of life.
2. I renounce any ritual where I was wed to Satan.	2. I announce that I am the bride of Christ.
3. I renounce any and all covenants, agreements, or promises that I made to Satan.	3. I announce that I have made a new covenant with Jesus Christ alone that supersedes any previous agreements.
4. I renounce all satanic assignments for my life including duties, marriage, and children.	4. I announce and commit myself to know and do only the will of God, and I accept only His guidance for my life.
5. I renounce all spirit guides assigned to me.	5. I announce and accept only the leading of the Holy Spirit.
6. I renounce any giving of my blood in the service of Satan.	6. I trust only in the shed blood of my Lord, Jesus Christ.
7. I renounce ever eating flesh or drinking blood in satanic worship.	7. By faith, I take Holy Communion, the body and blood of the Lord Jesus.
8. I renounce all guardians and satanist parents that were assigned to me.	8. I announce that God is my heavenly Father and the Holy Spirit is my guardian by whom I am sealed.

9. I renounce any baptism whereby I am identified with Satan.	9. I announce that I have been baptized into Christ Jesus and my identity is now in Him alone.
10. I renounce any sacrifice made on my behalf by which Satan may claim ownership of me.	10. I announce that only the sacrifice of Christ has any claim on me. I belong to Him. I have been purchased by the blood of the Lamb.

"Steps to Freedom in Christ" as best you can. It is important that you remove any demonic strongholds in your life *before* trying to integrate the personalities. Eventually, *every* alter personality (if this is the case with you) must be identified and guided into resolving the issues that caused its formation. Then, all true personalities can agree to come together in Christ.

Step 2: Deception v. Truth

God's Word is true and we need to accept His truth in the innermost part of our being (Psalm 51:6). Whether or not we *feel* it is true, we need to *believe* it is true! Since Jesus is the truth, the Holy Spirit is the Spirit of truth, and the Word of God is truth, we ought to speak the truth in love. (See John 14:6; 16:13; 17:17; Ephesians 4:15.)

The believer in Christ has no business deceiving others by lying, telling "white" lies, exaggerating, stretching the truth, or anything relating to falsehoods. Satan is the father of lies, and he seeks to keep people in bondage through deception, but it is the truth in Jesus that sets us free. (See John 8:44; Revelation 12:9; 2 Timothy 2:26; John 8:32-36.) We will find real joy and freedom when we stop living a lie and walk openly in the truth. After confessing his sin, King David wrote, "How blessed [happy] is the man...in whose spirit there is no deceit!" (Psalm 32:2).

How can we find the strength to walk in the light (1 John 1:7)? When we are sure God loves and accepts us, we can be free to own up to our sins and face reality instead of running and hiding from painful circumstances.

Start this step by praying the following prayer out loud. Don't let any opposing thoughts, such as "This is a waste of time" or "I wish I could believe this stuff but I just can't," keep you from praying and choosing the truth. Even if this is difficult for you, work your way through this step. God will strengthen you as you rely on Him.

> *Dear heavenly Father, I know that You want me to know the truth, believe the truth, speak the truth, and live in accordance with the truth. Thank You that it is the truth that will set me free. In many ways I have been deceived by Satan, the father of lies, and I have deceived myself as well.*
>
> *Father, I pray in the name of the Lord Jesus Christ, by virtue of His shed blood and resurrection, asking You to rebuke all of Satan's demons that are deceiving me.*
>
> *I have trusted in Jesus alone to save me, and so I am Your forgiven child. Therefore, since You accept me just as I am in Christ, I can be free to face my sin and not try to hide. I ask for the Holy Spirit to guide me into all truth. I ask You to "search me, O God, and know my heart; try me and know my anxious thoughts; and see if there be any hurtful way in me, and lead me in the everlasting way." In the name of Jesus, who is the Truth, I pray. Amen.*
>
> (See Psalm 139:23,24.)

There are many ways in which Satan, "the god of this world," seeks to deceive us. Just as he did with Eve, the devil tries to convince us to rely on ourselves and to try to get our needs met through the world around us, rather than trusting in the provision of our Father in heaven.

The following exercise will help open your eyes to the ways you have been deceived by the world system. Check each area of deception that the Lord brings to your mind and confess it, using the prayer following the list.

Ways you can be deceived by the world

- ❑ Believing that acquiring money and things will bring lasting happiness (Matthew 13:22; 1 Timothy 6:10)
- ❑ Believing that consuming food and alcohol excessively will make me happy (Proverbs 20:1; 23:19-21)
- ❑ Believing that a great body and personality will get me what I want (Proverbs 31:10; 1 Peter 3:3,4)
- ❑ Believing that gratifying sexual lust will bring lasting satisfaction (Ephesians 4:22; 1 Peter 2:11)
- ❑ Believing that I can sin and get away with it and not have it affect my heart (Hebrews 3:12,13)
- ❑ Believing that I need more than what God has given me in Christ (2 Corinthians 11:2-4,13-15)
- ❑ Believing that I can do whatever I want and no one can touch me (Proverbs 16:18; Obadiah 3; 1 Peter 5:5)
- ❑ Believing that unrighteous people who refuse to accept Christ go to heaven anyway (1 Corinthians 6:9-11)
- ❑ Believing that I can hang around bad company and not become corrupted (1 Corinthians 15:33,34)
- ❑ Believing that there are no consequences on earth for my sin (Galatians 6:7,8)

- ❑ Believing that I must gain the approval of certain people in order to be happy (Galatians 1:10)
- ❑ Believing that I must measure up to certain standards in order to feel good about myself (Galatians 3:2,3; 5:1)

Lord, I confess that I have been deceived by ________. I thank You for Your forgiveness, and I commit myself to believing only Your truth. In Jesus' name, amen.

It is important to know that in addition to being deceived by the world, false teachers, and deceiving spirits, we can also deceive ourselves. In addition, now that you are alive in Christ, completely forgiven and totally accepted, you don't need to defend yourself the way you used to. Christ is now your defense. Confess the ways the Lord shows you that you have deceived yourself or defended yourself wrongly by using the following lists and prayers of confession:

Ways to deceive yourself

- ❑ Hearing God's Word but not doing what it says (James 1:22)
- ❑ Saying I have no sin (1 John 1:8)
- ❑ Thinking I am something I'm really not (Galatians 6:3)
- ❑ Thinking I am wise in this worldly age (1 Corinthians 3:18,19)
- ❑ Thinking I can be truly religious but not bridle my tongue (James 1:26)

Lord, I confess that I have deceived myself by ________. Thank You for Your forgiveness. I commit myself to believing only Your truth. In Jesus' name, amen.

Ways to wrongly defend yourself

- ❑ Denial of reality (conscious or unconscious)
- ❑ Fantasy (escaping reality by daydreaming, TV, movies, music, computer or video games, drugs, alcohol, etc.)
- ❑ Emotional insulation (withdrawing from people or keeping people at a distance to avoid rejection)
- ❑ Regression (reverting back to less threatening times)
- ❑ Displaced anger (taking out frustrations on innocent people)
- ❑ Projection (blaming others for my problems)
- ❑ Rationalization (making excuses for my own poor behavior)

Lord, I confess that I have defended myself wrongly by ______________. Thank You for Your forgiveness. I now commit myself to trusting in You to defend and protect me. In Jesus' name, amen.

Choosing the truth may be hard for you if you have been believing lies for many years. You may need some ongoing counseling to help weed out any defense mechanisms you have relied on to cope with life. Every Christian needs to learn that Christ is the only defense he or she needs. Realizing that you are already forgiven and accepted by God through Christ will help free you up to place all your dependence on Him.

Faith is the biblical response to the truth, and believing what God says is a choice we all can make. If you say, "I wish I could believe God, but I just can't," you are being deceived. Of course you can believe God because what God says is always true.

Sometimes we are greatly hindered from walking by faith in our Father God because of lies we have believed about Him.

We are to have a healthy fear of God (awe of His holiness, power, and presence), but we are not to be afraid of Him. Romans 8:15 says, "For you have not received a spirit of slavery leading to fear again, but you have received a spirit of adoption as sons by which we cry out, 'Abba! Father!'" The following exercise will help break the chains of those lies and enable you to begin to experience that intimate "Abba, Father" relationship with Him.

Work your way down the lists, one-by-one, left to right below. Begin each one with the statement in bold at the top of that list. Read through the lists *out loud*.

A central part of walking in the truth and rejecting deception is to deal with the fears that plague our lives. First Peter 5:8 says that our enemy, the devil, prowls around like a roaring lion, seeking people to devour. Just as a lion's roar strikes terror in the hearts of those who hear it, so Satan uses fear to try to paralyze Christians. His intimidation tactics are designed to rob us of faith in God and drive us to try to get our needs met through the world or the flesh.

I renounce the lie that my Father God is...	**I joyfully accept the truth that my Father God is...**
1. distant and disinterested	1. intimate and involved (Psalm 139:1-18)
2. insensitive and uncaring	2. kind and compassionate (Psalm 103:8-14)
3. stern and demanding	3. accepting and filled with joy and love (Romans 15:7; Zephaniah 3:17)
4. passive and cold	4. warm and affectionate (Isaiah 40:11; Hosea 11:3,4)

I renounce the lie that my Father God is...	I joyfully accept the truth that my Father God is...
5. absent or too busy for me	5. always with me and eager to be with me (Hebrews 13:5; Jeremiah 31:20; Ezekiel 34:11-16)
6. never satisfied with what I do, impatient, or angry	6. patient and slow to anger (Exodus 34:6; 2 Peter 3:9)
7. mean, cruel, or abusive	7. loving, gentle, and protective of me (Jeremiah 31:3; Isaiah 42:3; Psalm 18:2)
8. trying to take all the fun out of life	8. trustworthy and wants to give me a full life; His will is good, perfect, and acceptable (Lamentations 3:22,23; John 10:10; Romans 12:1,2)
9. controlling or manipulative	9. full of grace and mercy; He gives me freedom to fail (Hebrews 4:15,16; Luke 15:11-16)
10. condemning or unforgiving	10. tenderhearted and forgiving; His heart and arms are always open to me (Psalm 130:1-4; Luke 15:17-24)
11. nit-picking, exacting, or perfectionistic	11. committed to my growth and proud of me as His growing child (Romans 8:28,29; Hebrews 12:5-11; 2 Corinthians 7:4)
I am the apple of His eye! **(Deuteronomy 32:10 NIV)**	

Fear weakens us, causes us to be self-centered, and clouds our minds so that all we can think about is the thing that frightens us. But fear can only control us if we let it.

God, however, does not want us to be mastered by anything, including fear (1 Corinthians 6:12). Jesus Christ is to be our only Master (2 Timothy 2:21; John 13:13). In order to begin to experience freedom from the bondage of fear and the ability to walk by faith in God, pray the following prayer from your heart:

Dear Heavenly Father, I confess to You that I have listened to the devil's roar and have allowed fear to master me. I have not always walked by faith in You but instead have focused on my feelings and circumstances. Thank You for forgiving me for my unbelief. Right now I renounce the spirit of fear and affirm the truth that You have not given me a spirit of fear but of power, love, and a sound mind. Lord, please reveal to my mind now all the fears that have been controlling me so I can renounce them and be free to walk by faith in You.

I thank You for the freedom You give me to walk by faith and not by fear. In Jesus' powerful name, I pray. Amen.

(See 2 Corinthians 4:16-18; 5:7; 2 Timothy 1:7.)

The following list may help you recognize some of the fears the devil has used to keep you from walking by faith. Check the ones that apply to your life. Write down any others that the Spirit of God brings to your mind. Then, one-by-one, renounce those fears out loud, using the suggested renunciation after the list.

- ❑ Fear of death
- ❑ Fear of Satan
- ❑ Fear of failure
- ❑ Fear of rejection by people

- ❑ Fear of disapproval
- ❑ Fear of becoming/being homosexual
- ❑ Fear of financial problems
- ❑ Fear of never getting married
- ❑ Fear of the death of a loved one
- ❑ Fear of being a hopeless case
- ❑ Fear of losing salvation
- ❑ Fear of having committed the unpardonable sin
- ❑ Fear of not being loved by God
- ❑ Fear of never loving or being loved by others
- ❑ Fear of embarrassment
- ❑ Fear of being victimized by crime
- ❑ Fear of marriage
- ❑ Fear of divorce
- ❑ Fear of going crazy
- ❑ Fear of pain/illness
- ❑ Fear of the future
- ❑ Fear of confrontation
- ❑ Fear of specific individuals (list)
- ❑ Other specific fears that come to mind now:

I renounce the (name the fear) because God has not given me a spirit of fear. I choose to live by faith in the God who has promised to protect me and meet all my needs as I walk by faith in Him.

(See 2 Timothy 1:7; Psalm 27:1; Matthew 6:33,34.)

After you have finished renouncing all the specific fears you have allowed to control you, pray the following prayer:

Dear heavenly Father, I thank You that You are trustworthy. I choose to believe You, even when my feelings and circumstances tell me to fear. You have told me not to

fear, for You are with me; to not anxiously look about me, for You are my God. You will strengthen me, help me, and surely uphold me with Your righteous right hand. I pray this with faith in the name of Jesus my Master. Amen.
(See Isaiah 41:10.)

The New Age movement has twisted the concept of faith by saying that we make something true by believing it. No, we can't create reality with our minds; only God can do that. We can only *face* reality with our minds. Faith is choosing to believe and act upon what God says, regardless of feelings or circumstances Believing something, however, does not make it true. *It's true; therefore, we choose to believe it.*

Just "having faith" is not enough. The key question is whether the object of your faith is trustworthy. If the object of your faith is not reliable, then no amount of believing will change it. That is why our faith must be on the solid rock of God and His Word. That is the only way to live a responsible and fruitful life. On the other hand, if what you believe in is not true, then how you end up living will not be right.

For generations, Christians have known the importance of publicly declaring what they believe. Read aloud the following "Statement of Truth," thinking about what you are saying. You may find it very helpful to read it daily for several weeks to renew your mind with the truth and replace any lies you may be believing.

Statement of Truth

1. *I recognize that there is only one true and living God who exists as the Father, Son, and Holy Spirit. He is worthy of all honor, praise, and glory as the One who made all things and holds all things together.* (See Exodus 20:2,3; Colossians 1:16,17.)

2. *I recognize that Jesus Christ is the Messiah, the Word who became flesh and dwelt among us. I believe that He came to destroy the works of the devil, and that He disarmed the rulers and authorities and made a public display of them, having triumphed over them.* (See John 1:1,14; 1 John 3:8; Colossians 2:15.)

3. *I believe that God demonstrated His own love for me in that while I was still a sinner, Christ died for me. I believe that He has delivered me from the domain of darkness and transferred me to His kingdom, and in Him I have redemption, the forgiveness of sins.* (See Romans 5:8; Colossians 1:13,14.)

4. *I believe that I am now a child of God and that I am seated with Christ in the heavenlies. I believe that I was saved by the grace of God through faith, and that it was a gift and not a result of any works on my part.* (See 1 John 3:1-3; Ephesians 2:6; Ephesians 2:8,9.)

5. *I choose to be strong in the Lord and in the strength of His might. I put no confidence in the flesh, for the weapons of warfare are not of the flesh but are divinely powerful for the destruction of strongholds. I put on the full armor of God. I resolve to stand firm in my faith and resist the evil one.* (See Ephesians 6:10; Philippians 3:3; 2 Corinthians 10:4; Ephesians 6:10-20.)

6. *I believe that apart from Christ I can do nothing, so I declare my complete dependence on Him. I choose to abide in Christ in order to bear much fruit and*

glorify my Father. I announce to Satan that Jesus is my Lord. I reject any and all counterfeit gifts or works of Satan in my life. (See John 15:5,8; 1 Corinthians 12:3.)

7. *I believe that the truth will set me free and that Jesus is the truth. If He sets me free, I will be free indeed. I recognize that walking in the light is the only path of true fellowship with God and man. Therefore, I stand against all of Satan's deception by taking every thought captive in obedience to Christ. I declare that the Bible is the only authoritative standard for truth and life.* (See John 8:32; 14:6; 8:36; 1 John 1:3-7; 2 Corinthians 10:5; 2 Timothy 3:15-17.)

8. I *choose to present my body to God as a living and holy sacrifice and the members of my body as instruments of righteousness. I choose to renew my mind by the living Word of God in order that I may prove that the will of God is good, acceptable, and perfect. I put off the old self with its evil practices and put on the new self. I declare myself to be a new creation in Christ.* (See Romans 12:1; 6:13; 12:2; Colossians 3:9,10; 2 Corinthians 5:17 NIV.)

9. *By faith, I choose to be filled with the Spirit so that I can be guided into all truth. I choose to walk by the Spirit so that I will not carry out the desires of the flesh.* (See Ephesians 5:18; John 16:13; Galatians 5:16.)

10. *I renounce all selfish goals and choose the ultimate goal of love. I choose to obey the two greatest commandments: to love the Lord my God with all my*

heart, soul, mind, and strength and to love my neighbor as myself. (See 1 Timothy 1:5; Matthew 22:37-39.)

11. *I believe that the Lord Jesus has all authority in heaven and on earth, and He is the head over all rule and authority. I am complete in Him. I believe that Satan and his demons are subject to me in Christ since I am a member of Christ's body. Therefore, I obey the command to submit to God and resist the devil, and I command Satan in the name of Jesus Christ to leave my presence.* (See Matthew 28:18; Colossians 2:10; Ephesians 1:19-23; James 4:7.)

Step 3: Bitterness v. Forgiveness

We need to forgive others so Satan cannot take advantage of us (2 Corinthians 2:10,11). We are commanded to get rid of all bitterness in our lives and forgive others as we have been forgiven (Ephesians 4:31,32). Ask God to bring to your mind the people you need to forgive by praying the following prayer out loud:

Dear heavenly Father, I thank You for the riches of Your kindness, forbearance, and patience toward me, knowing that Your kindness has led me to repentance. I confess that I have not shown that same kindness and patience toward those who have hurt me. Instead, I have held on to my anger, bitterness, and resentment toward them. Please bring to my mind all the people I need to forgive in order that I may do so now. In Jesus' name, amen.

(See Romans 2:4.)

On a separate sheet of paper, list the names of people who come to your mind. At this point don't question whether you need to forgive them or not. If a name comes to mind, just write it down.

Often we hold things against ourselves as well, punishing ourselves for wrong choices we've made in the past. Write "myself" at the bottom of your list so you can forgive yourself. Forgiving yourself is accepting the truth that God has already forgiven you in Christ. If God forgives you, you can forgive yourself!

Also write down "thoughts against God" at the bottom of your list. Obviously, God has never done anything wrong so we don't have to forgive Him. Sometimes, however, we harbor angry thoughts against Him because He did not do what we wanted Him to do. Those feelings of anger or resentment against God can become a wall between us and Him so we must let them go.

Before you begin working through the process of forgiving those on your list, take a few minutes to review what forgiveness is and what it is not.

Forgiveness is not forgetting. People who want to forget all that was done to them will find they cannot do it. Don't put off forgiving those who have hurt you, hoping the pain will one day go away. Once you choose to forgive someone, *then* Christ can come and begin to heal you of your hurts. But the healing cannot begin until you first forgive.

Forgiveness is a choice, a decision of your will. Since God requires you to forgive, it is something you can do. Sometimes it is very hard to forgive someone because we naturally want revenge for the things we have suffered. Forgiveness seems to go against our sense of what is right and fair. So we hold on to our anger, punishing people over and over again in our minds for the pain they've caused us.

But we are told by God never to take our own revenge (Romans 12:19). Let God deal with the person. Let him or her off your hook because as long as you refuse to forgive someone, you are still hooked to that person. You are still chained to your past, bound up in your bitterness. By forgiving, you let the other person off your hook, but he or she is not off God's hook. You must trust that God will deal with the person justly and fairly, something you simply cannot do.

"But you don't know how much this person hurt me!" you say. You're right. We don't, but Jesus does, and He tells you to forgive. And don't you see? Until you let go of your anger and hatred, the person is still hurting you. You can't turn back the clock and change the past but you can be free from it. You can stop the pain, but there is only one way to do it—forgive.

Forgive others for your sake so you can be free. Forgiveness is mainly a matter of obedience to God. God wants you to be free; there is no other way.

Forgiveness is agreeing to live with the consequences of another person's sin. You are going to live with those consequences anyway whether you like it or not, so the only choice you have is whether you will do so in the *bondage of bitterness* or in the *freedom of forgiveness*. No one truly forgives without accepting and suffering the pain of another person's sin. That can seem unfair and you may wonder where the justice is in it, but justice is found at the cross, which makes forgiveness legally and morally right.

Jesus took the *eternal* consequences of sin upon Himself. God "made Him who knew no sin to be sin on our behalf, that we might become the righteousness of God in Him" (2 Corinthians 5:21). We, however, often suffer the temporary consequences of other people's sins. That is simply a harsh reality of life all of us have to face.

Do not wait for the other person to ask for your forgiveness. Remember, Jesus did not wait for those who were crucifying Him to apologize before He forgave them. Even while they mocked and jeered at Him, He prayed, "Father, forgive them; for they do not know what they are doing" (Luke 23:34).

Forgive from your heart. Allow God to bring to the surface the painful emotions you feel toward those who've hurt you. If your forgiveness doesn't touch the emotional core of your life, it will be incomplete. Too often we're afraid of the pain so we bury our emotions deep down inside us. Let God bring them to the surface so He can begin to heal those damaged emotions.

Forgiveness is choosing not to hold someone's sin against him or her any more. It is common for bitter people to bring up past issues with those who have hurt them. They want them to feel bad. But we must let go of the past and choose to reject any thought of revenge. This doesn't mean you continue to put up with the future sins of others. God does not tolerate sin and neither should you. Don't allow yourself to be continually abused by others. Take a stand against sin while continuing to exercise grace and forgiveness toward those who hurt you. If you need help setting wise limits and boundaries to protect yourself from further abuse, talk to a trusted friend, counselor, or pastor.

Don't wait until you feel like forgiving. You will never get there. Make the hard choice to forgive even if you don't feel like it. Once you choose to forgive, Satan will have lost his power over you in that area, and God's healing touch will be free to move. Freedom is what you will gain right now, not necessarily an immediate change in feelings.

Now you are ready to begin. Starting with the first person on your list, make the choice to forgive him or her for every painful memory that comes to your mind. Stay with that individual until you are sure you have dealt with all the remembered pain. Then work your way down the list in the same way.

As you begin forgiving people, God may bring to your mind painful memories you've totally forgotten. Let Him do this even if it hurts. God wants you to be free; forgiving those people is the only way. Don't try to excuse the offender's behavior, even if it is someone you are really close to.

Don't say, "Lord, please help me to forgive." He is already helping you and will be with you all the way through the process. Don't say, "Lord, I want to forgive..." because that bypasses the hard choice we have to make. Say, "Lord, I *choose* to forgive...."

For every painful memory you have for each person on your list, pray out loud:

> *Lord, I choose to forgive (name the person) for (what they did) even though it made me feel (share the painful feelings).*

After you have forgiven each person for all the offenses that came to your mind, and after you have honestly expressed how you felt, conclude your forgiveness of that person by praying out loud:

> *Lord, I choose not to hold any of these things against (name) any longer. I thank You for setting me free from the bondage of my bitterness toward (name). I now ask You to bless (name). In Jesus' name, I pray. Amen.*

(Feel free to revise the above prayer when praying in regard to someone who is deceased.)

Step 4: Rebellion v. Submission

We live in a rebellious age. Many people only obey laws and authorities when it is convenient for them. There is a general lack of respect for those in government, and Christians are often as guilty as the rest of society in fostering a critical, rebellious spirit. Certainly, we are not expected to agree with our leaders' policies that are in violation of Scripture, but we are to "honor all men; love the brotherhood, fear God, honor the king" (1 Peter 2:17).

It is easy to believe the lie that those in authority over us are only robbing us of the freedom to do what we want. The truth is that God has placed them there for our protection and liberty. Rebelling against God and the authorities He has set up is a very serious sin for it gives Satan a wide open avenue to attack. Submission is the only solution. God requires more, however, than just the outward appearance of submission; He wants us to sincerely submit from the heart to those in authority. When you stand under the authority of God and those He has placed over you, you cut off this dangerous opening for demonic attacks.

The Bible makes it clear that we have two main responsibilities toward those in authority over us: to pray for them and to submit to them (1 Timothy 2:1,2; Romans 13:1-7). To commit yourself to that godly lifestyle, pray the following prayer out loud from your heart:

> *Dear heavenly Father, You have said in the Bible that rebellion is the same thing as witchcraft and as bad as idolatry. I know I have not obeyed You in this area and have rebelled in my heart against You and against those You have placed in authority over me. Thank You for Your forgiveness of my rebellion. By the shed blood of the Lord Jesus Christ, I pray that all ground gained by evil spirits in my life due to my rebellion would be canceled. I pray that You would show me all the ways I have been rebellious. I choose now to adopt a submissive spirit and a servant's heart. In Jesus' precious name, I pray. Amen.*
>
> (See 1 Samuel 15:23.)

Being under authority is clearly an act of faith! By submitting, you are trusting God to work through His established lines of authority, even when they are harsh or unkind or tell you to do something you don't want to do. There may be times when those over you abuse their authority and break the laws that are ordained by God for the protection of innocent people. In those cases, you will need to seek help from a *higher authority* for your protection. The laws in your state may require that such abuse be reported to the police or other governmental agency. If there is continuing abuse (physical, mental, emotional, or sexual) where you live, you may need further counseling help to deal with that situation.

If authorities abuse their position by requiring you to break God's law or compromise your commitment to Him, then you need to obey God rather than man (Acts 4:19,20). Be careful though. Don't assume that an authority is violating God's Word just because they are telling you to do something you don't like. We all need to adopt a humble, submissive spirit to one another in the fear of Christ (Ephesians 5:21). In addition, however, God has set up specific lines of authority to protect us and to give order to our daily lives.

As you prayerfully look over the next list, allow the Lord to show you any *specific* ways in which you have been rebellious to authority. Then, using the prayer of confession that follows the list, specifically confess whatever the Lord brings to your mind.

- ❑ Civil Government (including traffic laws, tax laws, attitude toward government officials) (Romans 13:1-7; 1 Timothy 2:1-4; 1 Peter 2:13-17)
- ❑ Parents, stepparents, or legal guardians (Ephesians 6:1-3)
- ❑ Teachers, coaches, school officials (Romans 13:1-4)
- ❑ Employers (past and present) (1 Peter 2:18-23)
- ❑ Husband (1 Peter 3:1-4) [*Note to Husbands:* Take a moment and ask the Lord if your lack of love for

your wife could be fostering a rebellious spirit within her. If so, confess that now as a violation of Ephesians 5:22-33.]

- ❑ Church leaders (Hebrews 13:7)
- ❑ God (Daniel 9:5,9)

For each way in which the Spirit of God brings to your mind that you have been rebellious, use the following prayer to specifically confess that sin:

Lord, I confess that I have been rebellious toward *(name)* *by* *(say what you did specifically)*. *Thank You for forgiving my rebellion. I choose now to be submissive and obedient to Your Word. In Jesus' name, I pray. Amen.*

Step 5: Pride v. Humility

Pride kills. Pride says, "I don't need God or anyone else's help. I can handle it by myself." Oh no you can't! We absolutely need God, and we desperately need each other. The apostle Paul wisely wrote, "[we] worship in the Spirit of God and glory in Christ Jesus and put *no confidence in the flesh*" (Philippians 3:3, emphasis added). That is a good definition of humility: putting no confidence in the flesh, that is in ourselves; but, rather, being *"strong in the Lord, and in the strength of His might"* (Ephesians 6:10, emphasis added). Humility is confidence properly placed in God.

Proverbs 3:5-7 expresses a similar thought: "Trust in the LORD with all your heart, and do not lean on your own understanding. In all your ways acknowledge Him, and He will make your paths straight. Do not be wise in your own eyes; fear the LORD and turn away from evil." (James 4:6-10 and 1 Peter 5:1-10 also warn us that serious spiritual problems will result when we are proud.) Use the following prayer to express your commitment to living humbly before God:

Dear heavenly Father, You have said that pride goes before destruction and an arrogant spirit before stumbling. I confess that I have been thinking mainly of myself and not of others. I have not denied myself, picked up my cross daily, and followed You. As a result, I have given ground to the devil in my life. I have sinned by believing I could be happy and successful on my own. I confess that I have placed my will before Yours, and I have centered my life around myself instead of You.

I repent of my pride and selfishness and pray that all ground gained in my members by the enemies of the Lord Jesus Christ would be canceled. I choose to rely on the Holy Spirit's power and guidance so I will do nothing from selfishness or empty conceit. With humility of mind, I will regard others as more important than myself. And I choose to make You, Lord, the most important of all in my life.

Please show me now all the specific ways in which I have lived my life in pride. Enable me through love to serve others and in honor to prefer others. I ask all of this in the gentle and humble name of Jesus, my Lord. Amen.

(See Proverbs 16:18; Matthew 16:24; Philippians 2:3; Matthew 6:33; Romans 12:10.)

Having made that commitment to God in prayer, now allow Him to show you any specific ways in which you have lived in a proud manner. The following list may help you. As the Lord brings to your mind areas of pride, use the prayer on the next page to guide you in your confession.

- ❑ Having a stronger desire to do my will than God's will
- ❑ Leaning too much on my own understanding and experience rather than seeking God's guidance through prayer and His Word

- ❑ Relying on my own strengths and abilities instead of depending on the power of the Holy Spirit
- ❑ Being more concerned about controlling others than in developing self-control
- ❑ Being too busy doing "important" things to take time to do little things for others
- ❑ Having a tendency to think that I have no needs
- ❑ Finding it hard to admit when I am wrong
- ❑ Being more concerned about pleasing people than pleasing God
- ❑ Being concerned about getting the credit I feel I deserve
- ❑ Thinking I am more humble, spiritual, religious, or devoted than others
- ❑ Being driven to obtain recognition by attaining degrees, titles, or positions
- ❑ Often feeling that my needs are more important than another person's needs
- ❑ Considering myself better than others because of my academic, artistic, or athletic abilities and accomplishments
- ❑ Other ways I have thought more highly of myself than I should:

For each of the above areas that has been true in your life, pray out loud:

Lord, I agree I have been proud in <u>(name the area)</u>. *Thank You for forgiving me for my pride. I choose to humble myself before You and others. I choose to place all my confidence in You and none in my flesh. In Jesus' name, amen.*

Dealing with Prejudice and Bigotry

Pride is the original sin of Lucifer. It sets one person or group against another. Satan's strategy is always to divide and conquer, but God has given us a ministry of reconciliation (2 Corinthians 5:19). Consider for a moment the work of Christ in breaking down the long-standing barrier of racial prejudice between Jew and Gentile:

> For [Christ] is our peace, who has made the two one and has destroyed the barrier, the dividing wall of hostility, by abolishing in his flesh the law with its commandments and regulations. His purpose was to create in himself one new man out of the two, thus making peace, and in this one body to reconcile both of them to God through the cross, by which he put to death their hostility. He came and preached peace to you who were far away and peace to those who were near. For through him we both have access to the Father by one Spirit (Ephesians 2:14-18 NIV).

Many times we deny that there is prejudice or bigotry in our hearts, yet "nothing in all creation is hidden from God's sight. Everything is uncovered and laid bare before the eyes of him to whom we must give account" (Hebrews 4:13 NIV). The following is a prayer, asking God to shine His light upon your heart and reveal any area of proud prejudice:

Dear heavenly Father, I know that You love all people equally and that You do not show favoritism. You accept people from every nation who fear You and do what is right. You do not judge them based on skin color, race, economic standing, ethnic background, gender, denominational preference, or any other worldly matter. I confess that I have too often prejudged others or regarded myself superior because of these things. I have not always been a minister of reconciliation but have been a proud agent of division through my attitudes, words, and deeds. I repent of all hateful bigotry and proud prejudice, and I ask You, Lord, to now reveal to my mind all the specific ways in which this form of pride has corrupted my heart and mind. In Jesus' name, amen.

(See Acts 10:34; 2 Corinthians 5:16.)

For each area of prejudice, superiority or bigotry that the Lord brings to mind, pray the following prayer out loud from your heart:

I confess and renounce the prideful sin of prejudice against (name the group). I thank You for Your forgiveness, Lord, and ask now that You would change my heart and make me a loving agent of reconciliation with (name the group). In Jesus' name, amen.

Step 6: Bondage v. Freedom

Many times we feel trapped in a vicious cycle of "sin-confess-sin-confess" that never seems to end. We can become very discouraged and end up just giving up and giving in to the sins of our flesh. To find freedom we must follow James 4:7: "Submit therefore to God. Resist the devil and he will flee from you." We submit to God by confession of sin and repentance (turning away from sin). We resist the devil by rejecting his lies. Instead, we walk in the truth and put on the full armor of God (see Ephesians 6:10-20).

Sin that has become a habit often requires help from a trusted brother or sister in Christ. James 5:16 says, "Confess your sins to one another, and pray for one another, so that you may be healed. The effective prayer of a righteous man can accomplish much." Sometimes the assurance of 1 John 1:9 is enough: "If we confess our sins, He is faithful and righteous to forgive us our sins and to cleanse us from all unrighteousness."

Remember, confession is not saying, "I'm sorry"; it is openly admitting, "I did it." Whether you need help from other people or just the accountability of walking in the light before God, pray the following prayer out loud:

> *Dear heavenly Father, You have told me to put on the Lord Jesus Christ and make no provision for the flesh in regard to its lust. I confess that I have given in to fleshly lusts that wage war against my soul. I thank You that in Christ my sins are already forgiven, but I have broken Your holy law and given the devil a chance to wage war in my body. I come to You now to confess and renounce these sins of the flesh so that I might be cleansed and set free from the bondage of sin. Please reveal to my mind now all the sins of the flesh I have committed and the ways I have grieved the Holy Spirit. In Jesus' holy name, I pray. Amen.*
>
> (See Romans 13:14; 1 Peter 2:11; Romans 6:12,13; James 4:1; 1 Peter 5:8; Proverbs 28:13 NIV; 2 Corinthians 4:2.)

There are many sins of the flesh that can control us. The following list contains many of them, but a prayerful examination of Galatians 5:19-21, Ephesians 4:25-31, Mark 7:20-23, and other Scripture passages will help you to be even more thorough. Look over the list below and the Scriptures just listed and ask the Holy Spirit to bring to your mind the ones you need to confess. He may reveal to you others as well. For each one the Lord shows you, pray a prayer of confession from your heart. There is a sample prayer following the list. (*Note:* Sexual sins, divorce, eating disorders, substance abuse, abortion, suicidal tendencies, and perfectionism will be dealt with later in this step. Further counseling help may be necessary to find complete healing and freedom in these and other areas.)

- ❑ Stealing
- ❑ Quarreling/fighting
- ❑ Jealousy/envy
- ❑ Complaining/criticism
- ❑ Lustful actions
- ❑ Gossip/slander
- ❑ Swearing
- ❑ Apathy/laziness
- ❑ Lying
- ❑ Hatred
- ❑ Anger
- ❑ Lustful thoughts
- ❑ Drunkenness
- ❑ Cheating
- ❑ Procrastination
- ❑ Greed/materialism
- ❑ Others:

Lord, I confess that I have committed the sin of *(name the sin)*. *Thank You for Your forgiveness and cleansing. I now turn away from this sin and turn to You, Lord. Strengthen me by Your Holy Spirit to obey You. In Jesus' name, amen.*

It is our responsibility not to allow sin to have control over our bodies. We must not use our bodies or another person's body as an instrument of unrighteousness (see Romans 6:12,13). Sexual immorality is sin against your body, the temple of the Holy Spirit (1 Corinthians 6:18,19). To find freedom from sexual bondage, begin by praying the following prayer:

Lord, I ask You to bring to my mind every sexual use of my body as an instrument of unrighteousness so I can renounce these sins right now. In Jesus' name, I pray. Amen.

As the Lord brings to your mind every wrong sexual use of your body, whether it was done to you (rape, incest, sexual molestation) or willingly by you (pornography, masturbation, sexual immorality), renounce *every* occasion:

Lord, I renounce (name the specific use of your body) with (name any other person involved). I ask You to break that sinful bond with (name).

After you are finished, commit your body to the Lord by praying:

Lord, I renounce all these uses of my body as an instrument of unrighteousness, and I admit to any willful participation. I choose now to present my eyes, mouth, mind, heart, hands, feet, and sexual organs to You as instruments of righteousness. I present my whole body to You as a living sacrifice, holy and acceptable. I choose to reserve the sexual use of my body for marriage only.

I reject the devil's lie that my body is not clean or that it is dirty or in any way unacceptable to You as a result of my past sexual experiences. Lord, thank You that You have totally cleansed and forgiven me and that You love and accept me just the way I am. Therefore, I choose now to accept myself and my body as clean in Your eyes. Amen.

(See Hebrews 13:4.)

Special Prayers for Special Needs

Divorce

Lord, I confess to You any part that I played in my divorce (ask the Lord to show you specifics). Thank You for Your forgiveness, and I choose to forgive myself as well. I renounce the lie that my identity is now in "being divorced." I am a child of God, and I reject the lie that says I am a second-class Christian because of the divorce. I reject the lie that says I am worthless, unlovable, and that my life is empty and meaningless. I am complete in Christ who loves me and accepts me just as I am. Lord, I commit the healing of all hurts in my life to You as I have chosen to forgive those who have hurt me. I also place my future into Your hands and trust You to provide the human companionship You created me to need through Your church and, if it be Your will, through another spouse. I pray all this in the healing name of Jesus, my Savior, Lord, and closest friend. Amen.

Homosexuality

Lord, I renounce the lie that You have created me or anyone else to be homosexual, and I agree that in Your Word You clearly forbid homosexual behavior. I choose to accept myself as a child of God, and I thank You that You created me as a man (woman). I renounce all homosexual thoughts, urges, drives, and acts, and cancel out all ways that Satan has used these things to pervert my relationships. I announce that I am free in Christ to relate to the opposite sex and my own sex in the way that You intended. In Jesus' name, amen.

Abortion

Lord, I confess that I was not a proper guardian and keeper of the life You entrusted to me, and I admit that as sin. Thank You that because of Your forgiveness, I can forgive myself. I recognize the child is in Your caring hands for all eternity. In Jesus' name, amen.

Suicidal Tendencies

Lord, I renounce all suicidal thoughts and any attempts I've made to take my own life or in any way injure myself. I renounce the lie that life is hopeless and that I can find peace and freedom by taking my own life. Satan is a thief and comes to steal, kill, and destroy. I choose life in Christ who said He came to give me life and give it abundantly. Thank You for Your forgiveness that allows me to forgive myself. I choose to believe that there is always hope in Christ. In Jesus' name, I pray. Amen.

(See John 10:10.)

Drivenness and Perfectionism

Lord, I renounce the lie that my self-worth is dependent upon my ability to perform. I announce the truth that my identity and sense of worth is found in who I am as Your child. I renounce seeking the approval and acceptance of other people, and I choose to believe that I am already approved and accepted in Christ because of His death and resurrection for me. I choose to believe the truth that I have been saved, not by deeds done in righteousness, but according to Your mercy. I choose to believe that I am no longer under the curse of the law because Christ became a curse for me. I receive the free gift of life in Christ and choose to abide in Him. I renounce striving for perfection by living under the law. By Your grace, heavenly Father, I choose from this day forward to walk by faith in the power of Your Holy Spirit according to what You have said is true. In Jesus' name, amen.

Eating Disorders or Self-Mutilation

Lord, I renounce the lie that my value as a person is dependent upon my appearance or performance. I renounce cutting or abusing myself, vomiting, using laxatives or starving myself as a means of being in control, altering my appearance, or trying to cleanse myself of evil. I announce that only the blood of the Lord Jesus cleanses me from sin. I realize I have been bought with a price and my body, the temple of the Holy Spirit, belongs to God. Therefore, I choose to glorify God in my body. I renounce the lie that I am evil or that any part of my body is evil. Thank You that You accept me just the way I am in Christ. In Jesus' name, I pray. Amen.

Substance Abuse

Lord, I confess that I have misused substances (alcohol, tobacco, food, prescription or street drugs) for the purpose of pleasure, to escape reality, or to cope with difficult problems. I confess that I have abused my body and programmed my mind in a harmful way. I have quenched the Holy Spirit as well. Thank You for forgiving me. I renounce any satanic connection or influence in my life through my misuse of food or chemicals. I cast my anxieties on to Christ who loves me. I commit myself to yield no longer to substance abuse, but instead I choose to allow the Holy Spirit to direct and empower me. In Jesus' name, amen.

After you have confessed all known sin, pray:

Lord, I now confess these sins to You and claim through the blood of the Lord Jesus Christ my forgiveness and cleansing. I cancel out all ground that evil spirits have gained through my willful involvement in sin. I pray this in the wonderful name of my Lord and Savior, Jesus Christ. Amen.

Step 7: Curses v. Blessings

The next step to freedom is to renounce the sins of your ancestors as well as any curses which may have been placed on you by deceived and evil people or groups. In giving the Ten Commandments, God said, "You shall not make for yourself an idol, or any likeness of what is in heaven above or on the earth beneath or in the water under the earth. You shall not worship them or serve them; for I, the LORD your God, am a jealous God, visiting the iniquity of the fathers on the children, on the third and the fourth generations of those who hate Me, but showing lovingkindness to thousands, to those who love Me and keep My commandments" (Exodus 20:4-6).

Demonic or familiar spirits can be passed on from one generation to the next if you don't renounce the sins of your ancestors and claim your new spiritual heritage in Christ. You are not guilty for the sin of any ancestor, but because of their sin, Satan may have gained access to your family.

Some problems, of course, are hereditary or acquired from an immoral environment. But some problems are the result of generational sin. All three conditions can contribute toward causing someone to struggle with a particular sin. Ask the Lord to show you specifically what sins are characteristic of your family by praying the following prayer:

Dear heavenly Father, I ask You to reveal to my mind now all the sins of my ancestors that are being passed down through family lines. I want to be free from those influences and walk in my new identity as a child of God. In Jesus' name, amen.

As the Lord brings those areas of family sin to your mind, list them below. You will be specifically renouncing them later in this step.

In order to walk free from the sins of your ancestors and any curses and assignments targeted against you, read the following declaration and pray the following prayer out loud. Remember, you have all the authority and protection you need in Christ to take your stand against such activity.

Declaration

I here and now reject and disown all the sins of my ancestors. I specifically renounce the sins of (list here the areas of family sin the Lord revealed to you). As one who has now been delivered from the domain of darkness into the kingdom of God's Son, I cancel out all demonic working that has been passed down to me from my family. As one who has been crucified and raised with Jesus Christ and who sits with Him in heavenly places, I renounce all satanic assignments that are directed toward me and my ministry. I cancel out every curse that Satan and his workers have put on me. I announce to Satan and all his forces that Christ became a curse for me when He died for my sins on the cross. I reject any and every way in which Satan may claim ownership of me. I belong to the Lord Jesus Christ who purchased me with His own blood. I reject all blood sacrifices whereby Satan may claim ownership of me. I declare myself to be fully and eternally signed over and committed to the Lord Jesus Christ. By the authority I have in Christ, I now command every familiar spirit and every enemy of the Lord Jesus that is influencing me to leave my presence. I commit myself to my heavenly Father to do His will from this day forward.

(See Galatians 3:13.)

Prayer

Dear heavenly Father, I come to You as Your child, bought out of slavery to sin by the blood of the Lord Jesus Christ. You are the Lord of the universe and the Lord of my life. I submit my body to You as an instrument of righteousness, a living and holy sacrifice that I may glorify You in my body. I now ask You to fill me with the Holy Spirit. I commit myself to the renewing of my mind in order to prove that Your will is good, acceptable, and perfect for me. All this I pray in the name and authority of the risen Lord Jesus Christ. Amen.

Even after finding freedom in Christ by going through these seven steps, you may still be attacked by demonic influences trying to regain control of your mind, hours, days, or even weeks later. But you don't have to let them. As you continue to walk in humble submission to God, you can resist the devil and he *will* flee from you (James 4:7).

The devil is attracted to sin like flies are attracted to garbage. Get rid of the garbage and the flies will depart for smellier places. In the same way, walk in the truth, confessing all sin and forgiving those who hurt you, and the devil will have no place in your life to set up shop.

Realize that one victory does not mean the battles are over. Freedom must be maintained. After completing these steps to freedom, one happy lady asked, "Will I always be like this?" I told her she would stay free as long as she remained in right relationship with God. "Even if you slip and fall," I encouraged, "you know how to get right with God again."

One victim of horrible atrocities shared this illustration:

It's like being forced to play a game with an ugly stranger in my own home. I kept losing and wanting to quit but the ugly stranger wouldn't let me. Finally, I called the police (a higher authority) and they came and escorted the stranger out. He knocked on the door trying to regain entry but this time I recognized his voice and didn't let him in.

What a beautiful picture of gaining and keeping your freedom in Christ! We call upon Jesus, the ultimate authority, and He escorts the enemy of our souls out of our lives.

Maintaining Your Freedom

Your freedom must be maintained. We cannot emphasize that enough. You have won a very important battle in an ongoing war. Freedom will continue to be yours as long as you keep choosing the truth and standing firm in the strength of the Lord. If you become aware of lies you have believed, renounce them and choose the truth. If new, painful memories surface, forgive those who hurt you. If the Lord shows you other areas of sin in your life, confess those promptly. This tool can serve as a constant guide for you in dealing with the things God points out to you. Some people have found it helpful to walk through the "Steps to Freedom in Christ" again. As you do, read the instructions carefully.

For your encouragement and growth, we recommend these books: *Victory Over the Darkness* (or the youth version, *Stomping Out the Darkness*), *The Bondage Breaker* (adult or youth version), *Walking in Freedom* (a 21-day follow-up devotional), and *Living Free in Christ*. To maintain your freedom in Christ, we strongly suggest the following as well.

1. Be involved in a loving, caring church fellowship where you can be open and honest with others and where God's truth is taught with grace.
2. Read and meditate on the Bible daily. Memorize key verses from the "Steps to Freedom in Christ." You may want to read the "Statement of Truth" (see Step 2) out loud daily and study the verses mentioned.
3. Learn to take every thought captive to the obedience of Christ. Assume responsibility for your thought life. Don't let your mind become passive. Reject all lies, choose to focus on the truth, and

stand firm in your true identity as a child of God in Christ.

4. Don't drift back to old patterns of thinking, feeling, and acting. This can happen very easily if you become spiritually and mentally lazy. If you are struggling with walking in the truth, share your battles openly with a trusted friend who will pray for you and encourage you to stand firm.
5. Don't expect other people to fight your battles for you, however. They can help you, but they can't think, pray, read the Bible, or choose the truth for you.
6. Commit yourself to daily prayer. Prayer demonstrates a life of trusting in and depending on God. You can pray the following prayers often and with confidence. Let the words come from your heart as well as your lips and feel free to change them to make them *your* prayers.

Daily Prayer and Declaration

Dear heavenly Father, I praise You and honor You as my Lord. You are in control of all things. I thank You that You are always with me and will never leave me nor forsake me. You are the only all-powerful and only wise God. You are kind and loving in all Your ways. I love You and thank You that I am united with Christ and spiritually alive in Him. I choose not to love the world or the things in the world, and I crucify the flesh and all its passions.

Thank You for the life I now have in Christ. I ask You to fill me with the Holy Spirit so I may say no to sin and yes to You. I declare my total dependence upon You and I take my stand against Satan and all his lying ways. I choose to believe the truth of God's Word despite what my feelings may say. I refuse to be discouraged; You are the God of all hope. Nothing is too difficult for You. I am confident that You will supply all my needs as I seek to live according to Your Word. I thank You that I can be content and live a responsible life through Christ who strengthens me.

I now take my stand against Satan and command him and all his evil spirits to depart from me. I choose to put on the full armor of God so I may be able to stand firm against all the devil's schemes. I submit my body as a living and holy sacrifice to God, and I choose to renew my mind by the living Word of God. By so doing I will be able to prove that the will of God is good, acceptable, and perfect for me. In the name of my Lord and Savior, Jesus Christ. Amen.

Bedtime Prayer

Thank You, Lord, that You have brought me into Your family and have blessed me with every spiritual blessing in the heavenly places in Christ Jesus. Thank You for this time of renewal and refreshment through sleep. I accept it as one of Your blessings for Your children, and I trust You to guard my mind and my body during my sleep.

As I have thought about You and Your truth during the day, I choose to let those good thoughts continue in my mind while I am asleep. I commit myself to You for Your protection against every attempt of Satan and his demons to attack me during sleep. Guard my mind from nightmares. I renounce all fear and cast every anxiety upon You, Lord. I commit myself to You as my rock, my fortress, and my strong tower. May Your peace be upon this place of rest now. In the strong name of the Lord Jesus Christ, I pray. Amen.

Cleansing Home/Apartment/Room

After removing and destroying all objects of false worship, pray this prayer aloud in every room if necessary:

Heavenly Father, I acknowledge that You are the Lord of heaven and earth. In Your sovereign power and love, You have given me all things to enjoy. Thank You for this place to live. I claim my home as a place of spiritual safety for me and my family, and ask for Your protection from all the attacks of the enemy. As a child of God, raised up and seated with Christ in the heavenly places, I command every evil spirit claiming ground in this place, based on the activities of past or present occupants including me, to leave and never return. I renounce all curses and spells directed against this place. I ask You, heavenly Father, to post Your holy, warring angels around this place to guard it from any and all attempts of the enemy to enter and disturb Your purposes for me and my family. I thank You, Lord, for doing this in the name of the Lord Jesus Christ. Amen.

Living in a Non-Christian Environment

After removing and destroying all objects of false worship from your possession, pray this aloud in the place where you live:

Thank You, heavenly Father, for a place to live and to be renewed by sleep. I ask You to set aside my room (or portion of this room) as a place of spiritual safety for me. I renounce any allegiance given to false gods or spirits by other occupants. I renounce any claim to this room (space) by Satan based on the activities of past or present occupants, including me. On the basis of my position as a child of God and joint-heir with Christ, who has all authority in heaven and on earth, I command all evil spirits to leave this place and never return. I ask You, heavenly Father, to station Your holy, warring angels to protect me while I live here. In Jesus' mighty name, I pray. Amen.

Continue to walk in the truth that your identity and sense of worth comes through who you are in Christ. Renew your mind with the truth that your *acceptance, security,* and *significance* are in Christ alone.

We recommend that you meditate on the following truths daily, perhaps reading the entire list out loud, morning and evening, for the next few weeks. Think about what you are reading and let your heart rejoice in the truth.

In Christ

I renounce the lie that I am rejected, unloved, dirty, or shameful because in Christ *I am completely accepted. God says...*

I am God's child (John 1:12)
I am Christ's friend (John 15:5)
I have been justified (Romans 5:1)
I am united with the Lord and I am one spirit with Him (1 Corinthians 6:17)
I have been bought with a price. I belong to God (1 Corinthians 6:19, 20)
I am a member of Christ's body (1 Corinthians 12:27)
I am a saint, a holy one (Ephesians 1:1)
I have been adopted as God's child (Ephesians 1:5)
I have direct access to God through the Holy Spirit (Ephesians 2:18)
I have been redeemed and forgiven of all my sins (Colossians 1:14)
I am complete in Christ (Colossians 2:10)

I renounce the lie that I am guilty, unprotected, alone, or abandoned because in Christ *I am totally secure. God says...*

I am free forever from condemnation (Romans 8:1,2)
I am assured that all things work together for good (Romans 8:28)
I am free from any condemning charges against me (Romans 8:31-34)
I cannot be separated from the love of God (Romans 8:35-39)
I have been established, anointed, and sealed by God (2 Corinthians 1:21,22)
I am confident that the good work God has begun in me will be perfected (Philippians 1:6)
I am a citizen of heaven (Philippians 3:20)
I am hidden with Christ in God (Colossians 3:3)
I have not been given a spirit of fear, but of power, love, and a sound mind (2 Timothy 1:7)
I can find grace and mercy to help in time of need (Hebrews 4:16)
I am born of God and the evil one cannot touch me (1 John 5:18)

I renounce the lie that I am worthless, inadequate, helpless, or hopeless because in Christ *I am deeply significant. God says...*

I am the salt of the earth and the light of the world (Matthew 5:13,14)
I am a branch of the true vine, Jesus, a channel of His life (John 15:1,5)
I have been chosen and appointed by God to bear fruit (John 15:16)
I am a personal, Spirit-empowered witness of Christ's (Acts 1:8)

I am a temple of God (1 Corinthians 3:16)
I am a minister of reconciliation for God (2 Corinthians 5:17-21)
I am God's coworker (2 Corinthians 6:1)
I am seated with Christ in the heavenly realm (Ephesians 2:6)
I am God's workmanship, created for good works (Ephesians 2:10)
I may approach God with freedom and confidence (Ephesians 3:12)
I can do all things through Christ who strengthens me! (Philippians 4:13)

I am not the great "I Am," but by the grace of God I am what I am.
(See Exodus 3:14; John 8:24,28,58; 1 Corinthians 15:10.)

Seeking the Forgiveness of Others

> Therefore, if you are offering your gift on the altar, and there remember that your brother has something against you, leave your gift there in front of the altar. First go and be reconciled to your brother; then come and offer your gift. Agree with your adversary quickly, while you are on the way with him, lest your adversary deliver you to the judge, the judge hand you over to the officer, and you be thrown into prison. Assuredly, I say to you, you will by no means get out of there till you have paid the last penny (Matthew 5:23-26 NKJV).

The Motivation for Seeking Forgiveness

Matthew 5:23-26 is the key passage on seeking forgiveness. Several points in these verses bear emphasizing. The worshiper coming before God to offer a gift *remembers* that someone has something against him. The Holy Spirit is the One who brings to his or her mind the wrong that was done.

Only the actions which have hurt another person need to be confessed to them. If you have had jealous, lustful, or angry thoughts toward another, and they don't know about it, these are to be confessed to God alone.

An exception to this principle occurs when restitution needs to be made. If you stole or broke something, damaged someone's reputation, and so on, you need to go to that person and make it right, even if he or she is unaware of what you did.

The Process of Seeking Forgiveness

1. Write out what you did wrong and why you did it.

2. Make sure you have already forgiven them for whatever they may have done to you.

3. Think through exactly how you will ask them to forgive you. Be sure to:
   a. Label your action as "wrong."

   b. Be specific and admit what you did.

   c. Make no defenses or excuses.

   d. Do not blame the other people, and do not expect or demand that they ask for your forgiveness.

   e. Your confession should lead to the direct question: "Will you forgive me?"

4. Seek the right place and the right time to approach the offended person.

5. Ask for forgiveness in person with anyone with whom you can talk face-to-face with the following exception: *Do not go alone* when your safety is in danger.

6. Except where no other means of communication is possible, *do not write a letter* because: a letter can be very easily misread or misunderstood; a letter can be read by the wrong people (those having nothing to do with the offense or the confession); a letter can be kept when it should have been destroyed.

7. Once you sincerely seek forgiveness, you are free—whether the other person forgives you or not (Romans 12:18).

8. After forgiveness, fellowship with God in worship (Matthew 5:24).

Notes

Introduction

1. George Sweating, *Great Quotes & Illustrations* (Waco, TX: Word Books, 1985), p. 115.
2. Edmund J. Bourne, *The Anxiety and Phobia Workbook* rev. ed. (Oakland, CA: New Harbinger Publications, Inc., 1995).
3. Edmund J. Bourne, *Healing Fear* (Oakland, CA: New Harbinger Publications, Inc., 1998), p. 2.
4. Ibid., p. 3.
5. Ibid., p. 5.
6. Neil Anderson and Hal Baumchen, *Finding Hope Again* (Ventura, CA: Regal Books, 1999).
7. Sherwood Wirt and Kersten Beckstrom, *Living Quotations for Christians* (New York: Harper and Row, 1974), p. 76.

Chapter 1: A Fortress of Fear

1. "Anxiety Disorders Most Common U.S. Mental Illness," National Institute of Mental Health, October 1996, p. 1.
2. "Anxiety Disorders—In Brief," Anxiety Disorders Association of America.
3. "Anxiety Disorders Most Common U.S. Mental Illness," p. 1.
4. "Panic Disorder," National Anxiety Foundation, p. 4.
5. Erik Erikson *Childhood and Society*, 2d. ed. (New York: W.W. Norton & Company, Inc., 1963).
6. John Dacey & John Travers, *Human Development Across the Lifespan* (Dubuque, IA: Wm. C. Brown Publishers, 1995), p. 289.
7. Ibid.
8. Ibid., p. 317.
9. Ibid., p. 50.
10. Ibid., p. 51.
11. Ibid., p. 47.
12. "Anxiety Disorders," American Psychiatric Association, 1997, pp. 4, 5.

Chapter 2: Anxious Thinking

1. Demitri and Janice Papolos, *Overcoming Depression* (New York: Harper Perennial, 1992), pp. 88, 89.
2. See Neil's book *Finding Hope Again*, which he coauthored with Dr. Hal Baumchen, for a more detailed discussion on medication and depression.

Chapter 3: Casting All Your Anxiety on Christ

1. Adapted from Neil Anderson, *Living Free in Christ* (Ventura, CA: Regal Books, 1993).
2. For a detailed discussion on sanctification see Neil Anderson and Robert Saucy, *The Common Made Holy* (Eugene, OR: Harvest House Publishers, 1997).
3. Source unknown.

Chapter 4: The Fear of Man

1. Hannah Hurnard, *Hinds' Feet on High Places* (Wheaton, IL: Tyndale House Publishers, 1977), pp. 31, 32.
2. Ibid., pp. 32, 33.
3. Bill Bright, *Witnessing Without Fear* (San Bernadino, CA: Here's Life Publishers, Inc., 1987), p. 13.
4. Ibid., pp. 54-65.
5. Adapted from ibid., pp. 59-61.

Chapter 5: The Fear of Death

1. As quoted in *USA Weekend*, August 22-24, 1997, p. 6.
2. Ibid., p. 5.
3. Ibid.
4. Ibid.
5. Nickelodeon/Yankelovich *Youth Monitor* as quoted in *USA Today*, Oct. 6, 1998, p. D1.
6. Cheryl Wetzstein, "Preteens have great trust in parents," *The Washington Times*, May 16, 1995, p. A2.
7. Alison Bell, "The Fear Factor," *Teen*, April 1997, p. 6.
8. Ibid.
9. As quoted in *USA Weekend*, August 22–24, 1997, p. 6.
10. Ibid., p. 5.
11. Bell, "Fear Factor," pp. 66ff.
12. Ibid.
13. Ibid.
14. Ibid.

15. Ibid.
16. As quoted from Karen S. Peterson's book *Keeping Kids Safe or Scaring Them to Death?* in *USA Today*, Aug. 21, 1995, p. 4D.
17. Ibid.
18. Neil Anderson and Peter and Sue Vander Hook, *Spiritual Protection for Your Children* (Ventura, CA: Regal Books, 1996).
19. Bonnie Crandall, *Panic Buster* (Jamestown, NY: Hatch Creek Publishing, 1995), p. 14.
20. Ibid.

Chapter 6: The Fear of Failure

1. Adapted from John Pepper, *Detroit Daily News*, Sunday, August 17, 1997.
2. Susan Jeffers, *Feel the Fear and Do It Anyway* (New York: Fawcett Columbine, 1987), p. 4.
3. Ibid., pp. 22, 23.

Chapter 7: Panic Disorder

1. Bonnie Crandall, *Panic Buster* (Jamestown, NY: Hatch Creek Publishing, 1995), p. 9.
2. Ibid.
3. Ibid., p. 11.
4. David G. Benner, *Baker Encyclopedia of Psychology* (Grand Rapids, MI: Baker Book House, 1990), p. 786.
5. "Answers to Your Questions About Panic Disorder," American Psychological Association, p. 1.
6. Ibid.
7. "Panic Disorder," American Psychiatric Association, 1997, p. 2.
8. "Panic Disorder," National Anxiety Foundation, p. 2.
9. R. Reid Wilson, Ph.D., *Don't Panic* (New York: Harper Collins Publishers, 1996), p. 32.
10. Ibid., p. 34.
11. Ibid., pp. 13, 14.
12. Ibid., p. 15.
13. R. Reid Wilson, Ph.D., *Breaking the Panic Cycle*, Phobic Society of America, 1990, p. 20.
14. Ibid., p. 21.
15. Ibid.
16. Ibid.
17. Ibid., pp. 18, 19.

18. Lucinda Bassett, "Overcome Your Anxiety and Fear" (video), Midwest Center for Stress and Anxiety, Inc., 106 N. Church St., Oak Harbor, Ohio 43449.
19. See "Common Medications Used for Anxiety" on pp. 347-349.
20. Ibid.
21. Ibid.
22. Bill Hendrick, "Anxiety: New understanding and therapy may help those who cope every day," *The Atlantic Journal and Constitution*, Dec. 7, 1996.
23. Edmund J. Bourne, Ph.D., *The Anxiety and Phobia Workbook* (Oakland, CA: New Harbinger Publications, Inc., 1998), p. 175.
24. Ibid.
25. Ibid., p. 176.
26. Ibid.
27. Ibid., p. 177.

Chapter 8: Breaking Strongholds of Fear

1. Used by permission from C. Smith.
2. The "Phobic Finder" was originally contained in the book *Walking in the Light*, by Neil Anderson (Nashville, TN: Thomas Nelson, 1992), p. 68.
3. Edmund J. Bourne, *The Anxiety and Phobia Workbook* (Oakland, CA: New Harbinger Publications, Inc., 1998), pp. 152, 153.

Chapter 9: Building a Stronghold of Faith

1. We also recommend Nathan Stone, *Names of God* (Chicago: Moody Press, n.d.) for encouraging insights in your journey to draw nearer to God.

Chapter 10: The Fear that Dispels All Other Fears

1. *The New Bible Dictionary* (Grand Rapids, MI: Wm. B. Eerdmans Publishing Co., 1977), s.v.
2. Timothy Beougher and Lyle Dorsett, *Accounts of a Campus Revival* (Wheaton, IL: Harold Shaw Publishers, 1995), p. 129.
3. Ibid., pp. 67,68.

Chapter 11: Recovering the Fear of God

1. Caleb Rosado, "America the Brutal," *Christianity Today*, August 15, 1994, p. 24.

Epilogue

1. Adapted from *Rivers of Revival* by Neil Anderson and Elmer Towns (Ventura, CA: Regal Books, 1997).

2. Carlos G. Valles, *Let Go of Fear* (New York: Triumph Books, 1991), p. 88. Although there is much wisdom in this book, we do not agree with everything the author writes (for example, citing apocryphal books as authoritative Scripture).

Other Books by Neil Anderson and Dave Park

Bondage Breaker, Youth Edition

Bondage Breaker, Youth Edition Study Guide

Stomping Out the Darkness

Stomping Out the Darkness, Study Guide

Busting Free, Youth Curriculum

Freedom in Christ 4 Teens

Devotional Series

Awesome God
by Neil Anderson and Rich Miller

Extreme Faith
by Neil Anderson and Dave Park

Reality Check
by Neil Anderson and Rich Miller

Ultimate Love
by Neil Anderson and Dave Park

Other Student Resources from Freedom in Christ

Know Him, No Fear
by Rich Miller and Neil Anderson

Freedom in Christ Adult and Student Conferences

Stomping Out the Darkness
for high school and junior high students

Seduction of Our Teens
Parent seminar will help parents make a lasting
spiritual impact at home

Setting Your Youth Free
Equips adults to have a powerful freedom ministry in the church

Setting Your Youth Free
Equips adults to have a powerful freedom ministry in the church

Purity Under Pressure
Helps students overcome sexual pressures
and establish godly relationships

Total Abandon
This prayer conference will help you hear the voice of God
and follow His leading

Freedom in Christ Youth Ministries

A Resource Ministry to Youth and the Church
Leading Teens, Parents, and Youth Leaders
to the Message of Freedom in Christ

For more information about
Freedom in Christ Ministries in your area,
call, write or e-mail:

Freedom in Christ Youth Ministries
491 E. Lambert Road
La Habra, CA 90631
(562) 691-9128
www.freedominchrist.com

For student ministries information
and conferences contact:

Freedom in Christ Youth Ministries
16071 W. Sherman Street
Goodyear, AZ 85338
(602) 925-5555
www.ficyouth.com

Neil T. Anderson

is the president of Freedom in Christ Ministries and a much sought-after speaker on Christ-centered living. He is the author of the bestselling books *The Bondage Breaker* and *A Way of Escape.*

Rich Miller,

director of Prayer and Spiritual Renewal at Freedom in Christ ministries, is a popular conference speaker and author of *To My Dear Slimeball.* He has also coauthored six books with Neil Anderson, including: *Reality Check, Awesome God, Walking in Freedom,* and *Leading Teens to Freedom in Christ.* Rich and his wife, Shirley, and their children Michelle, Brian, and Emily currently reside in Georgia.